PROGRAMMI

FOR

BEGINNERS

THIS BOOK INCLUDES:

SQL COMPUTER PROGRAMMING FOR BEGINNERS,

PYTHON,

KALI LINUX,

HACKING WITH KALI LINUX.

LEARN CODING LANGUAGES 2020.

ANTHONY HACK

© Copyright 2020 – Author: Anthony Hack
All rights reserved.

The content contained within this book may not be reproduced, duplicated or transmitted without direct written permission from the author or the publisher. Under no circumstances will any blame or legal responsibility be held against the publisher, or author, for any damages, reparation, or monetary loss due to the information contained within this book. Either directly or indirectly.

Legal Notice:

This book is copyright protected. This book is only for personal use. You cannot amend, distribute, sell, use, quote or paraphrase any part, or the content within this book, without the consent of the author or publisher.

Disclaimer Notice:

Please note the information contained within this document is for educational and entertainment purposes only. All effort has been executed to present accurate, up to date, and reliable, complete information. No warranties of any kind are declared or implied. Readers acknowledge that the author is not engaging in the rendering of legal, financial, medical or professional advice. The content within this book has been derived from various sources. Please consult a licensed professional before attempting any techniques outlined in this book.

By reading this document, the reader agrees that under no circumstances is the author responsible for any losses, direct or indirect, which are incurred as a result of the use of information contained within this document, including, but not limited to, errors, omissions, or inaccuracies.

1. SQL COMPUTER PROGRAMMING FOR BEGINNERS

2. PYTHON FOR BEGINNERS

3. KALI LINUX

4. HACKING WITH KALI LINUX

SQL COMPUTER PROGRAMMING FOR BEGINNERS

THE ULTIMATE GUIDE TO LEARN SQL PROGRAMMING BASICS, SQL LANGUAGES, QUERIES AND PRACTICE PROBLEMS, SQL SERVER AND DATABASE, CODING LANGUAGES FOR BEGINNERS.

Introduction

Network programs are larger and more flexible. In many cases, the fundamental scheme of operations is mainly a mix of scripts that handle the command of a database.

Due to the variety of languages and pre-existing sources, the method to "talk" between one another may usually be challenging and complicated, fortunately for us, the presence of requirements that permit us to do the typical methods by way of a wide spread form can make this particular perplexing task even more simple.

That is what Structured Query Language (SQL) is based on, that typically is only a worldwide common language of interaction within databases. That is precisely why, the Structured Query Language (SQL) is really a standardized language which allows most people to apply some language e.g. PHP or ASP, in conjunction with any particular database e.g. MySQL, MS Access, SQL Server.

IBM made SQL throughout the1970's; in the novice, it had been named SEQUEL (Structure English Query Language). Years later, Oracle and Microsoft also began with the use of SEQUEL.

The global recognition grew after which the word SEQUEL was transformed. In 1986, the word SEQUEL was standardized by the American National Standards Institute (ANSI) to SQL. In other words, they ditched the earth "English" from the word.

Until this morning, there are plenty of owners that decline to reference it as SQL, to these individuals; SEQUEL definitely may be the proper rap because of this standardized data source language. SQL has also been revised in 1989 and 1992. Since then, SQL has undergone many revisions to improve their standardization.

SQL is certainly a worldwide-standardized vocabulary, but that doesn't imply that is very similar for every repository. Truth be told, many databases execute particular functions, which will not generally run in others.

That is the explanation why every business that gives database solutions, for example Oracle and Microsoft, have their own certification process ensuring that people who takes the certification examination are really well prepared and understand the differences in between the different types of SQL. Their knowledge is concentrating on their own distinctive certain variant of SQL.

SQL is not simply relevant due to the ability to standardize a usually confusing language; it offers two other special characteristics. On a single hand, it actually is tremendously adaptable and powerful. On the opposite hand, it is really accessible which makes it much easier to master.

There are lots of databases items that support SQL, nonetheless, two of the largest and most popular are Microsoft SQL server and Oracle website.

Each company that provides database product has their own path to be an "expert". For instance, Microsoft offers an assortment of accreditation to guarantee that each Microsoft SQL Certified meets their criteria. Oracle does exactly the same thing with their Certification process.

1. Basic SQL Commands

Listed in this chapter are all of the various commands that you can use in SQL. The more basic commands are at the beginning of the chapter whereas the more advanced commands will be found further on down the chapter. The command name will be listed along with how it can be used and how to properly use it with the syntax included. Operators and clauses along with keywords will be mentioned after the basic commands. Examples will be shown on how to properly use each command.

Commands

CREATE DATABASE
In order to create your own database, you would use the following syntax as shown below.

CREATE DATABASE database_name

CREATE TABLE

After you create your database, you want to start creating tables to be entered into the database as well.

The CREATE TABLE command can be used as shown below.

```
CREATE TABLE table_name

( column_name1 data_type,

column_name2 data_type,

column_name3 data_type,);
```

Here is an example:

```
CREATE TABLE Individuals

( Id number(20),

Last varchar (255)

First varchar (255)

Address varchar (255)

City varchar (255));
```

The result would give you a table of Individuals with their information sorted out by their first and last name, their address, and the city that they are located in. The Id at the top stands for their ID number that would be entered in as a number. The ID column is able to hold a number of up to 20 digits.

INSERT

After you have your database and your tables all set up, you may find yourself needing to add another row into an existing table. In order to do this without setting up a completely new table, you can use the

INSERT INTO command. The syntax is as shown below.

INSERT INTO table_name

VALUES (value1, value2, value3);

The following syntax will only be specific to the values of a column. It won't be able to specify any of the column names. In the instance that you want to specify the column values along with their names as well, you can use the following syntax as shown below.

INSERT INTO table_name

(column_1, column_2, column_3)

VALUES (value1, value2, value3)

If you wanted to be able to insert a new row into the table, it would be done using a similar syntax as shown below.

INSERT INTO table_name

VALUES ('insert various row information here') example: (3 such as 'row 3', 'Williams such as last name', 'Travis such as first name')

This will allow you to be able to insert multiple amounts of various data into different rows at the same time.

To be able to insert data into specific columns, you can use the following syntax shown below.

INSERT INTO Individuals

(Id, Last, First)

VALUES (5, 'Thompson', 'Jessica')

This would enter the information into row 5 and the column of the last name the name "Thompson" would be entered. Then the following name "Jessica" would be entered into the first name column.

Now that we have thoroughly covered the first few basic commands associated with the CREATE type commands of CRUD, it's now time to move on to the next type of commands of the acronym. The next step would be to query or read your data that you have created and inserted into your database. The next command will show you how to easily and specifically retrieve information from your database.

SELECT

In order to be able to query and read data in your database, you want to be able to select whatever data you want to be retrieved back to you. This is where the SELECT command comes into use. The command can be formed as shown in the syntax shown below.

SELECT columns

FROM tables

[JOIN joins]

WHERE search_condition]

[GROUP BY grouping_columns]

[HAVING search_condition]

[ORDER BY sort_columns];

This is a more complex syntax that can be used for a very specific search. The operators, clauses and keywords mentioned in the syntax will be introduced after the basic commands are presented. This is a syntax that you can come back to once you thoroughly understand how to use each part.

In order to retrieve a single column from a table, the following syntax can be used as shown below.

SELECT column

FROM table;

In order to retrieve multiple columns from a table, use the following syntax shown below.

SELECT columns

FROM table;

In order to retrieve all columns from a table, you are selecting the table as a whole since you are not wanting one or more columns over the others. In order to select a table, the keyword "FROM" comes into use. Use the following syntax as shown below.

SELECT * FROM table;

Just how we selected multiple columns from a table earlier, the same is applied as shown below. For instance, say you have a table named "Clients" and you want to search your clients by their first and last name. You would use the syntax as shown below.

SELECT Last, First

FROM Clients

Here is another example of how you would use the SELECT command to pull up a whole table instead of specified columns of a table. Let's say you just wanted to search your client list how it is in the database without searching clients by their first or last name. You would use the syntax shown below.

SELECT * FROM Clients

Now that we have covered the create and read type commands, the next commands will be update as a part of the CRUD commands. Now that you understand how to create and read the data that you enter into your database and tables, the next step that you will need to do is to be able to update the data that you've entered.

UPDATE

When you need to update data that exists in a table, you can use the UPDATE command in order to do so. It can be used as shown in the syntax below.

UPDATE table_name

SET column1=value, column2=value, column3=value

[WHERE search_condition];

Without properly placing the WHERE clause, all of the data or the improper data will be updated by the command. Listed below is another way to properly use the WHERE clause in the UPDATE command as an example of a specific table with specific data.

UPDATE Clients

(SET First= 'Jason'

City= 'Rochester'

WHERE Last= 'Knight');

This example would add in the first name and city that the client lives in by searching for his last name. Of course, you can be more specific with the WHERE clause as you might have plenty of clients in a chart with the same last name. You could use the WHERE clause to search for other conditions in a table to make sure your results will be specific and sure.

Now that you understand how to not only create and read data in a database but now you understand how to update it as well. The last step of "CRUD" is delete. There are several more ways to delete information in SQL than you would think. The following commands listed will be different ways that you can delete data to your own needs or preference.

DELETE

When you find yourself needing to delete rows in a table, the DELETE command can be used in order to do so. To properly use it, follow the syntax shown below.

DELETE FROM table_name

[WHERE search_condition];

Here, the search condition would be used to fill in the name or placement of the row. If the WHERE clause is improperly used with the DELETE command, all of the records will be deleted as a result.

When you want to be able to remove just one individual row from your table, you can use the following syntax example as shown below.

DELETE FROM Clients

WHERE Last= 'Johnson'

AND First= 'Sarah';

Here, the AND keyword is used as well as the WHERE clause. The AND keyword will be presented more in depth later on. Here, you can see that it is used to add a more specific search to aid the deletion process of an individual in the Clients table. The example would simply and only remove that one client with that first and last name. If you had other clients with the same name, this is where more specific identification can be used such as a unique ID number for your clients in your database.

In the case that you want to be able to delete all the rows in a table, you can use the following syntax as shown below.

DELETE * FROM table_name;

DROP

The DROP command can be used in order to delete an index that is contained in a table. The DROP command can also be used to delete a database or a table. Indexes can be created in order to speed up a search in your database by making your tables more defined. They won't be visible to those who view the table, only those who search for the table. Shown below is a syntax on how to properly use the DROP command when deleting an index. There are four variations for the syntax depending on what platform you are using SQL on.

Access:

DROP INDEX index_name

MS SQL Server:

DROP INDEX

table_name.index_name

Oracle:

DROP INDEX index_name

MySQL:

ALTER TABLE table_name

DROP INDEX index_name

When you want to be able to delete a table in your database, you can use the DROP TABLE command in order to do so. The syntax is properly shown below.

How to use the DROP TABLE command:

DROP TABLE table_name

When you want to be able to delete the whole database itself, you can use the DROP DATABASE command in order to do so. The proper syntax is shown below.

How to use the DROP DATABASE command:

DROP DATABASE database_name

TRUNCATE

The TRUNCATE command can be used whenever you want to delete data that is already contained in a table without removing the whole table itself. This can be useful for times when you want to start fresh without completely start over in your table. In order to properly use the TRUNCATE command, the syntax is shown below.

TRUNCATE TABLE table_name

That then completes the four categories of commands that "CRUD" stands for. The following syntaxes will be of operators, clauses and keywords that can be used in commands. Some of them have already been shown in the commands listed. These extras can add precise work to your commands and be quite useful.

Operators and Clauses

AND

When you want to look a client or anything in your table, you can use the AND operator to make the search more specific. If you were looking up a client, this could be used to look the individual up by their first AND last name. If you were looking for a Garrett Lee in your database, you would use the following syntax in order to use the AND operator to do so.

SELECT * FROM Clients

WHERE First= 'Garrett'

AND Last= 'Lee'

OR

This operator is similar to the AND operator. If you wanted to be able to find two different kinds of clients in your database by their first OR last name, you could use the following syntax as shown below.

SELECT * FROM Clients

WHERE First= 'John'

OR Last= 'Thomas'

This would be able to bring up any client in your database with either the first name of John or the last name of Thomas. Of course, you could use this operator in whatever way you wanted to in order to bring up more precise results.

AND/OR

This operator can be used in order to filter your records using more than one condition. The AND and OR operators can be quite useful by themselves but they become even more useful when combined together in order to refine your search. The AND operator will display two records due to the two specific conditions if the data search applies to both. When a record is adequate to either the first or second condition, the OR operator will display the more specific results. The syntax is example is shown below.

SELECT * FROM Clients

WHERE Last= 'Jones'

AND (First= 'Carl' OR First= 'Mark')

By combining these commands together, the results will select individuals that have the same last name that is specified. This will pick up on individuals that have the last name that is equal to the last name "Jones" and the first names of either "Carl" or "Mark".

NOT

This operator can be used in order to rule by one condition when searching your database. This operator is used as a clause with the SELECT command. The proper syntax is shown below.

SELECT * First, Last, State

FROM Clients

WHERE NOT (State = 'AK');

The results would bring up clients by their first and last name along with the state that they lived in. It would bring up all clients except for the ones that live in Alaska. Of course, you could add more states than just one for your search.

WHERE

The WHERE clause has been shown in previous commands in order to be specific to the use of the command. It is very important where you place the WHERE clause. In order to make sure you have a good idea of how to properly use it, included below are two syntaxes that are shown in correct and incorrect formats along with the initial syntax that should be used.

SELECT column_names

FROM table_name

WHERE test_column operator value;

Say you want to retrieve clients from a city:

SELECT * FROM Clients

WHERE City= 'Portland'

How to use WHERE clause with text and numeric values:

Correct:

SELECT * FROM Clients

[WHERE First='Amanda']

Incorrect:

SELECT * FROM Clients

(WHERE First=Amanda)

Correct:

SELECT * FROM Clients

WHERE Year=1985

Incorrect:

SELECT * FROM Clients

WHERE Year= '1985'

GROUP BY

This operator can be used with other commands in order to group the result of one or more columns of a table. The proper syntax use is shown below.

SELECT column_name

Aggregate_function (column_name)

FROM table_name

WHERE column_name operator value

GROUP BY column_name

This operator can also be used in order to find the total sum that a client has purchased from you in the case that you are a business owner that keeps your records in your database. A proper syntax in order to use this is shown below.

SELECT Clients, SUM (Orders Purchased)

FROM Products

GROUP BY Clients

This would bring up how much an individual had purchased from you by pulling up the orders that had been purchased from the products.

In order to bring up more than one column, you can use the syntax example below:

SELECT Clients, Date, SUM (Orders Purchased)

FROM Products

GROUP BY Clients, Date

This would bring up a column for each of the sums according to the clients and the date as well.

ORDER BY

Similar to the GROUP BY operator, the ORDER BY keyword is not much different. It will pull up your results in a specific order depending on what you decide to put in for your benefit. By default, your data that you retrieve will come back to you in ascending order. In the case that you wanted it to come back in a descending order, you would use the keyword 'DESC'. You can use this keyword in the following syntax example shown below.

SELECT column_names

FROM table_name

ORDER BY sort_columns [ASC | DESC];

In order to sort multiple columns, the following syntax example can be used:

SELECT column_names

FROM table_name

ORDER BY

sort_column1 [ASC | DESC],

sort_column2 [ASC | DESC],

sort_column3 [ASC | DESC];

In order to sort by column positions in relevance:

SELECT column_names

FROM table_name

ORDER BY

sort_number1 [ASC | DESC],

sort_number2 [ASC | DESC],

sort_number3 [ASC | DESC];

In order to sort by order in descending order:

SELECT * FROM Clients

ORDER BY Last name DESC

The results would bring up data of your clients by their last name from Z to A instead of alphabetical order. In the case of numbers, it would bring up the lowest numbers up to the highest numbers.

DISTINCT

In the event that you need to eliminate any duplicate rows, you can do this by using the DISTINCT keyword to do so. You can use this keyword in the following syntax shown below.

SELECT DISTINCT column_names

FROM table_name

You can also combine the SELECT command with the DISTINCT keyword. If you wanted to be able to find clients from a specific city, you could use the following syntax example shown below.

SELECT DISTINCT New York City

From Clients

This will bring up all the clients in your database that live specifically in New York City.

2. SQL Functions

SQL count function

The COUNT() function is used to return the number of rows that meets the given condition.

Here's the syntax:

In this statement, the expression can refer to an arithmetic operation or column name. You can also specify (*) if you want to calculate the total records stored in the table.

The examples in this section will use the data in SALES_REP table:

To perform a simple count operation like calculating how many rows are in the SALES_REP table, you will enter:

SELECT COUNT(EMP_NAME)

FROM SALES_REP;

Here's the result:

You can also use (*) instead of specifying a column name:

SELECT COUNT(EMP_NAME)

FROM SALES_REP;

This statement will produce the same result because the EMP_NAME field has no NULL value. Assuming, however, that one of the fields in the EMP_NAME contains a NULL value, this would not be included in the statement that specifies EMP_NAME but will be included in the COUNT() result if you use the * symbol as parameter.

You can also use the COUNT function with the GROUP by clause. For example, if you want to calculate the number of records for every branch, you can enter this statement:

SELECT BRANCH, COUNT(*) FROM SALES_REP

GROUP BY BRANCH;

This would be the output:

The COUNT() function can be used with DISTINCT to find the number of distinct entries. For instance, if you want to know how many distinct branches are saved in the SALES_REP table, you will enter this statement:

SELECT COUNT (DISTINCT BRANCH)

FROM SALES_REP;

It will produce this result:

SQL AVG Function

The AVG() function calculates the average value of columns with numeric data type.

Here is the syntax:

In the above statement, the expression can refer to an arithmetic operation or to a column name. Arithmetic operations can take single or multiple columns.

The examples in this section will use the SALES_REP table with this data:

In the first example, you will use the AVG() function to calculate the average sales amount. You can enter this statement:

SELECT AVG(Sales) FROM Sales_Rep;

Here's the result:

The figure 6245.500000 is the average of all sales data in the Sales_Rep table and it is computed by adding the Sales field and dividing the result by the number of records which, in this example, is 10 rows.

The AVG() function can be used in arithmetic operations. For example, assuming that sales tax is 6.6% of sales, you can use this statement to calculate the average sales tax figure:

SELECT AVG(Sales*.066) FROM Sales_Rep;

Here's the result:

To obtain the result, SQL had to calculate the result of the arithmetic operation 'Sales *.o66' before applying the AVG function.

You can combine the AVG() function with the GROUP BY clause to get the average figure for a specified grouping. For example, assume that you want to calculate the average sales for each branch, you can enter this statement:

SELECT Branch, AVG(Sales) FROM Sales_Rep

GROUP BY Branch;

Here's the result:

SQL ROUND Function

The ROUND() function is used to round a number to a given number of decimals or precision.

This is the syntax for SQL ROUND() function:

ROUND (expression, [decimal place])

In the above statement, the decimal place specifies the number of decimal points that will be returned. If you specify a negative number, it will round off the digit on the left of the decimal point. For instance, specifying -1 will round off the number to the nearest tens.

The examples on this section will use the Student_Grade table with the following data:

ID	Name	Grade
1	Jack Knight	87.6498
2	Daisy Poult	98.4359
3	James McDuff	97.7853
4	Alicia Stone	89.9753

Assuming that you want to round off the grades to the nearest tenths, you can enter this statement:

SELECT Name, ROUND (Grade, 1) Rounded_Grade FROM Student_Grade;

This would be the result:

Assuming that you want to round the grades to the nearest tens, you will use a negative parameter for the ROUND() function:

SELECT Name, ROUND (Grade, -1) Rounded_Grade FROM Student_Grade;

Here's the result:

SQL SUM Function

The SUM() function is used to return the total for an expression.

Here's the syntax for the SUM() function:

The expression parameter can refer to an arithmetic operation or a column name. Arithmetic operations may include one or more columns.

Likewise, there can be more than one column in the SELECT statement in addition to the column specified in the SUM() function. These columns should also form part of the GROUP BY clause. Here's the syntax:

For the examples in this section, you will use the SALES_REP table with the following data:

To calculate the total of all sales from the Sales_Rep, table, you will enter this statement:

SELECT SUM(Sales) FROM Sales_Rep;

This would be the result:

The figure 62455.00 represents the total of all entries in the Sales column.

To illustrate how you can use an arithmetic operation as an argument in the SUM() function, assume that you have to apply a sales tax of 6.6% on the sales figure. Here's the statement to obtain the total sales tax:

SELECT SUM(Sales*.066) FROM Sales_Rep;

You will get the following result:

In this example, you will combine the SUM() function and the GROUP BY clause to calculate the total sales for each branch. You can use this statement:

SELECT Branch, SUM(Sales) FROM Sales_Rep

GROUP BY Branch;

SQL MAX() Function

The MAX() function is used to obtain the largest value in a given expression.

Here's the syntax:

SELECT MAX (<expression>)

FROM table_name;

The expression parameter can be an arithmetic operation or a column name. Arithmetic operations can have multiple columns.

The SELECT statement can have one or more columns besides the column specified in the MAX() function. If this is the case, these columns will have to form part of the GROUP BY clause.

The syntax would be:

SELECT column1, column2, ... "columnN", MAX (<expression>)

FROM table_name;

GROUP BY column1, column2, ... "columnN";

To demonstrate, you will use the table Sales_Rep with this data:

To get the highest sales amount, you will enter this statement:

SELECT MAX(Sales) FROM Sales_Rep;

Here's the result:

To illustrate how the MAX() function is applied to an arithmetic operation, assume that you have to compute a sales tax of 6.6% on the sales figure. To get the highest sales tax figure, you will use this statement;

SELECT MAX(Sales*0.066) FROM Sales_Rep;

Here is the output:

You can combine the MAX() function with the GROUP BY clause to obtain the maximum sales value per branch. You will have to enter this statement:

SELECT Branch, MAX(Sales) FROM Sales_Rep GROUP BY Branch;

SQL MIN() Function

The MIN() function is used to obtain the lowest value in a given expression.

Here's the syntax:

SELECT MIN(<expression>)

FROM table_name;

The expression parameter can be an arithmetic operation or a column name. Arithmetic operations can also have several columns.

The SELECT statement can have one or several columns besides the column specified in the MIN() function. If this is the case, these columns will have to form part of the GROUP BY clause.

The syntax would be:

SELECT column1, column2, ... "columnN", MIN (<expression>)

FROM table_name;

GROUP BY column1, column2, ... "columnN";

To demonstrate how the MIN() function is used in SQL, you will use the Sales_Rep table with the following data:

To get the lowest sales amount, you can use this statement:

SELECT MIN(Sales) FROM Sales_Rep;

The output would be:

To demonstrate how the MIN() function is used on arithmetic operations, assume that you have to compute a sales tax of 6.6% on the sales figure. To get the lowest sales tax figure, you will use this statement;

SELECT MIN(Sales*0.066) FROM Sales_Rep;

Here's the output:

You can also use the MIN() function with the GROUP BY clause to calculate the minimum sales value per branch. You will have to enter this statement:

SELECT Branch, MIN(Sales) FROM Sales_Rep GROUP BY Branch.

3. Data Manipulation

DML (Data Manipulation Language) is the aspect of SQL that helps you to perform changes within a database. Through DML, you can fill tables with new information, update old tables, and remove unnecessary data from any table.

How to Populate a Table with New Information

You can complete this process in two ways: (1) enter the new data manually or (2) use computer programs to enter the data automatically. Manual data population refers to entering new data using a keyboard. Automated data population, on the other hand, refers to loading data from an outside source (e.g. a different database) and transferring it into the preferred database.

When entering new data, different factors can influence the type and quantity of data you can work with. Here are the main factors you have to consider: current constraints, the table's physical size, and the columns' length.

Important Note: You can run SQL statements without worrying about lowercase or uppercase characters. However, data is extremely case-sensitive. For instance, if you entered the data into a database using uppercase characters, you should use uppercase characters when referencing that data.

The examples given below use uppercase and lowercase characters just to prove that this factor cannot influence the result.

How to Insert Data

You should use INSERT command to insert data into an existing table. This command has several options; check the syntax below:

With this syntax, you should specify each column in the list named VALUES. As you can see, the values in this list are separated by commas. You should use quotation marks to enclose the values you want to insert, particularly if you are working with date/time and character data types. You don't have to use quotation marks for NULL values or numeric data. Each column within the table should contain a value.

In the example below, you will insert a record into a table named "PRODUCTS_TBL."

The table's current structure:

Use this INSERT statement:

For this example, you inserted three values into a table that has three columns. The values you inserted follow the arrangement of columns within the table. Two of the values are enclosed with quotation marks because their columns are of the character type. The final value (i.e. cost) is a number data type: quotation marks are optional.

How to Insert Data into Specific Columns

You may insert data into certain columns. For example, let's assume that you need to insert the values for your employee except his pager number. In this case, you should determine a VALUES list and a column list while running the INSERT statement. Here's a screenshot of the values you may use:

When inserting values into specific columns, here is the syntax you should use:

In the example below, you'll insert values into specific columns inside a table named ORDERS_TBL. This is the table's current structure:

Let's say you used this INSERT statement:

In this INSERT statement, you specified a list of columns by enclosing the columns' names in parentheses. Also, the column list must be entered after the table's name. You have specified the columns that you need. Basically, you excluded the column named ORD_DATE.

If you'll check the table definition, you'll see that ORD_DATE is an independent column: it doesn't need any data from the table. This column doesn't require information since you didn't specify NOT NULL in the definition for the table. The NOT NULL statement says that the column accepts NULL values. Moreover, the array of values should follow the arrangement of the columns.

How to Insert Data from a Different Table

You can accomplish this by combining two SQL statements: INSERT and SELECT. Here's the syntax you should follow:

This syntax has new keywords: FROM, WHERE, and SELECT. Let's discuss them one by one. FROM is a part of the database query that determines the location of the needed data. This part should contain the name of table/s. WHERE, another part of the database query, applies conditions to improve the search results. Here's a sample condition: WHERE PRODUCT = 'CAR.' Lastly, SELECT is the primary statement used to begin the SQL query.

Important Note: "Applying a condition" means adding criteria on the information influenced by an SQL command.

How to Insert NULL Values

Inserting NULL values into an existing table is easy and simple. Why would you add this kind of value into your tables or databases? Well, you need to insert NULL values into a column if you don't know the specific value that should be placed there. For example, not every individual owns a cellphone, so it is imprecise to insert a wrong cellphone number. You can use the word NULL to insert null values into your desired column. Here's the syntax:

How to Update Data

You can use the UPDATE statement to modify data. This SQL statement doesn't add or delete records – it simply updates the data inside the table/s you are working on. In general, UPDATE is used to modify tables one by one. You may update a single row or multiple rows, depending on your needs.

How to Update a Column

This is perhaps the simplest way of using the UPDATE command. If you'll update a column, you can update either a single row or multiple rows. Here is the syntax for this process:

How to Update Multiple Columns

As stated earlier, you may update many columns using the UPDATE statement. Check this syntax:

This syntax has one SET and three columns: the columns are separated by commas. In general, you should use a comma to segregate different kinds of arguments.

For this example, a comma separates the columns that must be updated.

How to Delete Data

You may use the DELETE statement to eliminate data rows from a table. This statement will remove a whole record (even columns). Thus, you shouldn't use it if you just want to remove some values from several columns. You must be extremely careful when using DELETE – it is an effective and efficient command. In this section, you'll learn about the different techniques in removing data.

To delete a record or multiple records, you should follow this syntax:

This syntax uses WHERE as a supporting clause. This clause is an important aspect of the DELETE command, particularly if you are trying to eliminate specific data rows. Actually, you'll use WHERE with DELETE most of the time. Without the WHERE clause, you'll get a result similar to this one:

Important Note: All data rows inside a table will be deleted if you'll omit WHERE.

Keep in mind that this SQL statement can inflict permanent damages on your database. In ideal situations, you can   undo erroneous deletions using a backup file. In some cases, however, it may be impossible to retrieve lost data. If you can no longer recover the deleted data, you have to re-enter it into your database. This is not a problem with a single data row, but this can make you pull your hair if you are dealing with hundreds (or thousands) of data rows.

How to Manage Database Transactions
Simply put, transactions are units or sets of work done on a database. You can accomplish database transactions manually (i.e. by typing) or automatically (i.e. using a database program). For relational databases that use SQL, you can use the DML statements to complete transactions. DML statements were discussed in the previous chapter.

A database transaction can either be a DML command or a sequence of commands. While conducting transactions, all of the transactions need to be successful. If at least one transaction fails, the remaining transactions will fail too.

Here are the characteristics of a database transaction:

- *Each transaction has a starting point and an endpoint.*

- *Each transaction can be undone or saved.*

- *If transactions fail to complete, none of them can be saved.*

Transactional Control

This is the capability to control different transactions that may happen inside a database management system. Whenever you talk about transactions, you will be referring to the DML commands (i.e. UPDATE, DELETE and INSERT).

Once a transaction is successfully completed, you won't see immediate changes in the affected data tables. Sometimes, you have to use transactional control statements to finalize your database transactions. These control statements can help you save or undo the changes you have made.

Here are the control statements that you can use:

- *ROLLBACK*

- *COMMIT*

- *SAVEPOINT*

When a database transaction is completed, the information about it is kept either in an assigned area or a short-term rollback area inside the database. These areas hold transactional information until a control statement is executed. As stated earlier, control statements may save or discard transactions. The rollback area will be emptied once the transaction is saved or discarded.

The image below shows how changes are performed on a database:

The ROLLBACK Statement

You must use this statement to reverse unsaved changes. ROLLBACK can only be applied to transactions made after the last ROLLBACK or COMMIT statement. Here's the syntax for the ROLLBACK statement:

Here, WORK is completely optional.

Important Note: Currently, MySQL doesn't support this statement.

The COMMIT Statement

You'll use this statement to save the changes caused by your transaction. This statement finalizes all transactions completed after the last ROLLBACK or COMMIT statement.

When using this command, you must follow this syntax:

This syntax has a mandatory part: COMMIT. This part comes with a character or statement used to finish the command. The keyword "WORK" is optional: use it to improve the command's user-friendliness.

The SAVEPOINT Statement

This is a part of a transaction where you can undo certain changes without affecting the whole transaction. This is the syntax for SAVEPOINT:

You can only use this statement when creating a SAVEPOINT in transactional commands. If you want to undo changes, you must use ROLLBACK. SAVEPOINT allows you to manage database transactions by dividing them into small groups.

Going Back to a Save Point

If you want to roll back to a certain SAVEPOINT, use the following syntax:

Removing a Save Point

You can use RELEASE SAVEPOINT to remove a save point you have made. After removing a save point this way, you won't be able to use that point in rolling back database changes. You can use the RELEASE SAVEPOINT statement to prevent unwanted reversals of database modifications. Here's the syntax that you should follow:

How to Get Excellent Results from Database Queries
This chapter will focus on database queries. Here, you'll learn how to use the SELECT command on the results of your queries. In general, you will use SELECT lots of times once your database has been established. This command helps you to search and view the information stored in your database.

The Query

Queries are inquiries into a database. These inquiries are submitted through the SELECT command. You must use queries to get data from a database. For example, if you have a product table, you may execute an SQL command to identify your best-selling product. This request for usable product information is normal for modern relational databases.

The Select Command

This command represents the DQL (i.e. Data Query Language) aspect of SQL. You can use the SELECT command to start and execute database queries. In general, this statement cannot stand alone: you have to use additional clauses to make queries possible. Aside from the mandatory clauses, optional clauses exist to help users in improving the effectiveness of database queries.

When using the SELECT command, there are four clauses (also called keywords) that you must consider. These clauses are:

1. SELECT – This command is combined with FROM to obtain data in a readable, organized format. You can use this to determine the data you need to get. Here's the syntax of a basic SELECT command:

The SELECT clause introduces the list of columns you like to see in the search results. FROM, on the other hand, introduces the tables you want to choose data from. You should use the asterisk to indicate that each column will be displayed in the query results. ALL allows you to view all of the values for any column, even redundant data. DISTINCT is an option that you can use to hide duplicate information. As you can see, commas are used to separate the columns for FROM and SELECT.

2. FROM – You should use this clause in combination with SELECT. It's a mandatory element of any database query. The purpose of this clause is to specify the tables that must be accessed during the search. When running a query, you should indicate at least one table in the FROM clause.

The syntax of this clause is:

3. WHERE – This clause can have multiple conditions (i.e. the element of a query that display selective data as selected by the database user). If you are using this feature, you should connect the conditions using the OR and AND operators. This is the syntax for WHERE:

4. ORDER BY – You can use this clause to arrange the output of a database query. This clause organizes the search results using your selected format. By default, this clause organizes query output in an

ascending order – the output will be displayed from A-Z if you are working with names. This statement's syntax is:

Case Sensitivity

You should understand this concept completely if you want to use SQL. Usually, SQL statements and clauses are not sensitive to uppercase and lower case characters. That means you can enter clauses and statements with the Caps Lock on: it won't affect your SQL commands in any way.

However, case sensitivity becomes extremely important when you are dealing with data objects. Most of the time, data is stored using uppercase letters. This method helps database users in maintaining the consistency of data.

For example, your database will be inconsistent if you'll enter data this way:

- *JOHN*

- *John*

- *John*

If the data was stored as JOHN and you executed a query for John, you won't get relevant output.

Categorize Information Using Database Operators

Operators – The Basics

Operators are reserved words or characters mainly used in the WHERE clause of SQL statements. As their name suggests, operators are used to perform operations (e.g. comparisons and mathematical operations). Operators can specify parameters for your SQL statements. Lastly, they can connect multiple parameters within the same SQL statement.

This chapter will use the following operators:

- *Logical Operators*
- *Comparison Operators*
- *Arithmetic Operators*
- *Operators for Negating Conditions*

Let's discuss each operator type in detail:

Logical Operators

These operators use keywords to perform comparisons. In this section, you'll learn about the following logical operators:

- *IN*
- *LIKE*
- *UNIQUE*
- *EXISTS*
- *BETWEEN*

- *IS NULL*

- *ANY and ALL*

IN

With this operator, you'll compare a value to a set of specified literal values. You will only get TRUE if at least one of the specified values is equal to the value being tested. Here's an example:

LIKE

Here, you'll use wildcard operators to compare a value against similar ones. You can combine LIKE with the following wildcard operators:

- "_" – (i.e. The underscore)

- "%" – (i.e. The percent sign)

You should use the underscore to represent a character or number. On the other hand, you must use "%" to represent one, zero, or several characters. You may combine these wildcard operators in your SQL statements. Here are some examples:

WHERE PRICE LIKE '100%' - This statement will find values that begin with 100.

WHERE PRICE LIKE '%100%' – This SQL statement will search for values the include 200.

WHERE PRICE LIKE '_11%' – This statement will search for any value that has "11" as its second and third digits.

WHERE PRICE LIKE '1_%_%_%' – This statement will find values that begin with 1 are at least four characters long.

WHERE PRICE LIKE '%1' – This will search for values that have 1 as their last character.

UNIQUE

With this operator, you can check the uniqueness of one or more data rows. Check this simple example:

EXISTS

You can use this operator to find data rows that meet your chosen criteria. Here's an example:

BETWEEN

You can use BETWEEN to find values within a specific range. Here, you'll assign the maximum value and the minimum value. You must include the maximum and minimum values in your conditional set. Check this example:

IS NULL

You can use IS NULL to compare your chosen value with a NULL one. For instance, you can identify the products that don't have wheels by checking for NULL values in the "WHEEL" column of your PRODUCTS_TBL table.

ANY and ALL

ANY is an operator that can compare a value against any legitimate value in a list. The list of values should have predetermined conditions. Here's an example:

ALL, however, compares your selected value against the values contained in a different value set.

Comparison Operators

These operators can test single values within SQL statements. This category is composed of <, >, <>, and =. You can use these operators to test:

- *Non-equality*

- *Equality*

- *Greater-than values*

- *Less-than values*

Non-equality

As an SQL user, you should use "<>" to test non-equality. The operation gives TRUE if the data is not equal; FALSE if the data is equal.

Important Note: You may also use the "!=" operator. Actually, many SQL implementations are using this operator to test inequality. Check the implementation you are using to find out more about this topic.

Equality

You can use this operator to test single values in your SQL statements. Obviously, "=" (i.e. the equal sign) represents equality. When checking for equality, you will only get data if the chosen values are identical. If the values are equal, you'll get TRUE as the result. If the values aren't equal, you'll get FALSE.

Greater-than, Less-than

In general, "<" and ">" can serve as stand-alone operators. However, you can improve the effectiveness of your operations if you'll combine them with other operators.

Comparison Operators – Simple Combos

You can combine "=" with "<" and ">." Check the examples below:

With "<= 20,000" (i.e. less-than or equal-to 20,000), you'll get 20,000 and all of the values below it. If a database object is within that range, you'll get TRUE from the operation. If the object's value is 20,001 or higher, on the other hand, you will get FALSE.

The second example follows the same principle. The only difference is that you'll get TRUE for objects whose value is 20,000 and above. You'll get FALSE for objects with the value of 19,999 and below.

Arithmetic Operators

These operators can help you perform mathematical operations in the SQL language. In this section, you'll learn about the typical operators used in relational databases: +. -, *, and /.

Let's discuss each operator in detail:

Addition

You can perform addition using "+" (i.e. the plus sign). Study the following SQL statements:

SELECT MATERIALS + OVERHEAD FROM PRODUCTION_COST_TBL – In this SQL statement, you'll add up the values in the MATERIALS column and the OVERHEAD column.

SELECT MATERIALS FROM PRODUCTION_COST_TBL WHERE MATERIALS + OVERHEAD < '500' – This operation will return values where the sum of MATERIALS and OVERHEAD is less than 500.

Subtraction

You can use "-" (i.e. the minus sign) to perform subtraction. To help you understand this process, two examples are given below:

SELECT SALES – COST FROM COMPANY_FINANCIALS_TBL – For this SQL statement, the COST column will be deducted from the SALES column.

SELECT SALES FROM COMPANY_FINANCIALS_TBL WHERE SALES – COST < '100000' – This statement will give you values where SALES minus COST is less than '100,000.'

Multiplication

You should use "*" (i.e. the asterisk) to perform multiplication. Check the examples below:

SELECT SALES * 10 FROM
COMPANY_FINANCIALS_TBL – The values in the
SALES column will be multiplied by ten.

SELECT SALES FROM COMPANY_FINANCIALS_TBL
WHERE SALES * 10 < '100000' – This statement will
return values where the product of (SALES * 10) is
less than 100,000.

Division

You must use "/" (i.e. the slash symbol) when
performing division. Here are two examples:

SELECT SALES / 5 FROM COMPANY_FINANCIALS_TBL
– The SALES column is divided by 5.

SELECT SALES FROM COMPANY_FINANCIALS_TBL
WHERE SALES / 5 < '100000' – This SQL statement
will return data rows where the result of (SALES / 5)
is less than 100,000.

Some Combinations of Arithmetic Operators

You may combine arithmetic operators to streamline
your database processes. Keep in mind that SQL
applies the principles of precedence in mathematics.
That means you'll perform multiplication and division
first. Then, you'll complete the process by performing
addition and subtraction. You can only control the

sequence of mathematical operations if you will use parentheses.

Important Note: Precedence is the sequence in which mathematical expressions are performed. Here are some basic examples:

EXPRESSION	RESULT
2 + 2 * 5	12
(2 + 2) * 5	20
20 − 8 / 4 + 2	20
(20 − 8) / (4 + 2)	2

When working with multiple arithmetic operators, always apply the principles of precedence. If you'll forget about precedence and the usage of parentheses, you will get inaccurate results from your arithmetic operations in SQL. Logical errors can still exist even if you have perfect syntaxes for your SQL statements.

For the next examples, the parentheses don't influence the result if only division and multiplication are performed. Keep in mind that precedence is not important in these situations. Study these examples:

EXPRESSION	RESULT
8 * 12 / 4	24
(8 * 12) / 4	24
8 * (12/4)	24

Operators for Negating Conditions

In this section, you'll learn how to negate the logical operators discussed above. Negating the effects of logical operators is necessary if you want to alter the viewpoint of a condition.

You should use NOT to cancel the operator it is used for. NOT is a logical operator in SQL that can be utilized with these techniques:

NOT EQUAL

Earlier, you learned how to check for inequality using "<" and ">." It is important to mention inequality here since if you are checking for it, you are already cancelling the "=" operator. Here's another technique that you can use to test inequality:

WHERE PRICE <> ''10000' – Price is not equal to 10,000

WHERE PRICE != '10000' – Price is not equal to 10,000

In the second statement, the "!" negates the comparison for equality. Some SQL implementations allow users to combine "!" with the typical inequality operators (i.e. "<" and ">").

NOT BETWEEN

You can negate BETWEEN using the NOT BETWEEN operator. Here's an example:

WHERE PRICE NOT BETWEEN '5000' AND '10000' – The value of PRICE can't fall within the 5,000 to 10,000 range.

NOT IN

You can use NOT IN to negate the IN operator. In the example below, all prices that are not included in the list will be returned.

WHERE PRICE NOT IN ('200', '300', '400') – Action will only be taken if PRICE is not equal to any value in the list.

NOT LIKE

NOT LIKE negates the wildcard operator LIKE. If you are using NOT LIKE, you will only get values different from the one you specified. Here are some examples:

WHERE PRICE NOT LIKE '100%' – This SQL statement will find values that begin with any number except "100."

WHERE PRICE NOT LIKE '%100%' - This statement will get values that don't have "200" in them.

WHERE PRICE NOT LIKE '_11%' – This SQL statement will give you values that don't have "11" in their second and third positions.

WHERE PRICE NOT LIKE '1_%_%' – This statement WILL NOT find values that begin with 1 and are three characters long.

IS NOT NULL

You can use IS NOT NULL operator to negate IS NULL. This procedure is usually done to check for data that isn't NULL. Here's an example:

WHERE PRICE IS NOT NULL – This operation will return price values that are not null.

NOT EXISTS

This operator can help you negate EXIST. Study the example below:

In this example, the maximum cost is shown in the output section. This is because the cost of all existing records is less than 100.

NOT UNIQUE

Use this operator to negate UNIQUE.

WHERE NOT UNIQUE PRICE (SELECT FROM PRODUCT_TBL) – This statement checks whether there are "non-UNIQUE" prices in the PRODUCT_TBL table.

Conjunctive Operators

Sometimes, you have to use multiple criteria. This is usually the case if you are getting confusing results from your database queries. You can combine different criteria in your SQL statements using the conjunctive operators. These are:

- *OR*

- *AND*

OR

You can use this operator to combine conditions in the WHERE clause of your SQL statement. Before an SQL statement can take any action, the criteria should be TRUE or separated by OR. Here's an example:

WHERE PRICE = '100' OR PRICE = '300' – This statement will find values in the PRICE column that match either 200 or 300.

AND

This operator allows you to include multiple criteria in your SQL statement's WHERE section. Your SQL statement will only take action if the criteria segregated by AND are all TRUE. Analyze the example below:

WHERE PRODUCT_ID = 'ABC' AND PRICE = '200' – This statement will look for data objects whose PRODUCT_ID value is ABC and PRICE value is 200.

Important Note: Keep in mind that you can always combine multiple operators and conditions in your SQL statements. You can also improve the readability of your statements by using parentheses.

4. Database Administration

Once you have your database up and running with tables and queries, it is up to you to keep the production database running smoothly. The database will need regular checks to ensure that it continues to perform as originally intended. If a database is poorly maintained, it can easily result in a connected website performing poorly, or it could result in down time or even data loss. There is usually a person, known as a Database Administrator or DBA, designated to look after the database. However, it is usually someone who is not a DBA who needs help with the database.

There are a number of different tasks that you can perform when carrying out maintenance, including the following:

- Database Integrity: When you check the integrity of the database, you are running checks on the data to make sure that both the physical and logical structure of the database is consistent and accurate.

- Index Reorganization: Once you start to insert and delete data on your database, there is going to be fragmentation (or a scattering) of indexes. Reorganizing the index will bring everything back together again and increase speed.

- Rebuild Index: You don't have to perform an index reorganization; you can drop an index and then recreate it.

- Database Backup: One of the most important tasks to perform. There are a number of different ways in which you can back up the database. These include: full - backs up the database entirely, differential - backs up the database since the last full backup, and transaction log - only backs up the transaction log.

- Check Database Statistics: You can check the statistics of the database that are kept on queries. If you update the statistics, which can get out of date, you can help aid the queries that are being run.

- Data and Log File: In general, make sure the data and log files are kept separate from each other. These files will grow when your database is being used, and it's best to allocate them an appropriate size going forward (and not just enable them to grow).

Depending on your database, some tasks may be more useful than others. Apart from database backup, which is probably mandatory if it's in production, you can pick through the other tasks depending on the state of the database.

For example, should the fragmentation of the database be below 30%, then you can choose to perform an index reorganization. However, if the database fragmentation is greater than 30%, then you should rebuild the index. You can rebuild the index on a weekly basis or more often, if possible.

You can run a maintenance plan on the SQL Server via its Server Agent depending on database requirements. It's important to set the times appropriately, not when your application is expected to be busy. You can choose a time, or you can run it when the server CPU is not busy. Choosing to run when the server is not busy is a preferred option for larger databases rather than selecting a particular time, as there may be no guaranteed time when the CPU will be idle. However, it is usually only a concern if your application is quite big and has a lot of requests.

When you do rebuild the indexes, it is important that you have the results sorted in tempdb. When using tempdb, the old indexes are kept until new ones are added. Normally, rebuilding the indexes uses the fixed space that was allocated to the database. Therefore, if you run out of disk space, then you would not be able to complete the index rebuilding. It's possible to use the tempdb and not have to increase the database disk size. The database maintenance can be run either synchronously (at the same time) or asynchronously (once task has been completed). However, you should ensure the tasks are running in the right order.

Setting up a Maintenance Plan in SQL Server

To set up a maintenance plan in SQL Server, you must first get the server to show advanced options. This is achieved through executing the following code in SQL Server as a new query:

```
sp_configure 'show advanced options', 1

GO

RECONFIGURE

GO

sp_configure 'Agent XPs', 1

GO

RECONFIGURE

GO
```

The SQL Server will now display the advanced options. Left-click the + icon to the left of Management, which is on the left-hand side of SQL Server Management Studio. Now, left-click Maintenance Plans and then right-click Maintenance Plans. Select New Maintenance Plan Wizard.

Enter an appropriate maintenance plan name and description. From here, you can either run one or all tasks in one plan and have as many plans as you want. After you have assigned a name, choose Single Schedule and click Next.

You will see a number of options that you can pick for your maintenance, including:

- Checking your Database Integrity

- Shrinking the Database

- Reorganizing Index

- Rebuilding the Index

- Updating the Statistics

- Clean up History

- Executing SQL Server Agent Job

- Back Up – full, differential or transaction log

- Maintenance Cleanup Task

Select which you want to perform (in this example, select all). This wizard will bring you through each of the items you have selected to fine-tune them.

Once you select the items you want in your plan, click Next. You can now rearrange them in the order that you want them to complete. It's best to have Database Backup first in case of power failure, so select it and move it to the top of the list. Click Next.

Define Backup Database (Full) Task

This screen will give you the freedom to pick which full database backup you wish to perform on. The best practice is to keep one plan per database; select one database and select Next.

Define Database Check Integrity Task

The integrity task is an SQL Server command that aims at inspecting the database's integrity to make sure that everything is stable. Select a database and click Next.

Define Shrink Database Task

You can now configure to shrink the database in order to free up space in the next screen. This will only shrink space if available, but should you need space in the future, you will have to allocate it again. However, this step will help backup speeds. Most developers don't use this feature that much. Click Next after selecting a database to shrink.

Define Reorganize Index Task

The next screen is the Define Reorganize Index Task screen. When you add, modify, and delete indexes you will, like tables, need to reorganize them. The process is the same as a hard disk, where you have fragmented files and space scattered across the disk. Perform this task once per week for a busy database. You can choose to compact large object, which compacts any index that has large binary object data. Click Next to proceed to the next screen.

Define Rebuild Index Task

This screen covers individual index rows and involves either reorganizing or reindexing. Doing both together in one plan is pointless. Depending on your fragmentation level, pick one or the other. In this example, select your database and sort results in tempdb. Click Next to proceed.

Define Update Statistics Task

The update statistics task helps the developer keep track of data retrieval as its created, modified, and deleted. You can keep the statistics up-to-date by performing this plan. Statistics for both indexes and individual columns are kept. Select your database and click Next to proceed.

Define History Cleanup Task
You should now see this screen, which specifies the historical data to delete. You can specify a shorter time frame to keep the backup and recovery, agent job history, and maintenance place on the drop down. Click Next to proceed.

Define Backup Database (Differential) Task
This screen allows you to back up every page in the database that has been altered since the previous or last full backup. Select a database you wish to use and click Next.

Define Backup Database (Transaction Log) Task
The transaction log backup backs up all the log records since the last backup. You can choose a folder to store it in. Performing this type of backup is the least resource-intensive backup. Select a database and storage location and click Next.

Define Execute SQL Server Agent Job Task
The SQL Server Agent Job Task deals with jobs that are outside the wizard. For example, it can check for nulls, check whether the database meets specified standards, and more. Any jobs that are specified in SQL Server Agent Job Task are listed here. Click Next to proceed.

Define Maintenance Cleanup Task

This screen defines the cleanup action of the maintenance task. This ensures that files are not taking up unnecessary space, and you can specify where to store them. You can also delete specific backup files. Click Next to proceed.

Report Options

The next screen covers where you want to store the report of the maintenance plan. Make a note of where you are going to store it. You need to have email setup on SQL Server in order to email it. Click Next to proceed.

Complete the Wizard

The final screen is a complete review of the wizard. You can review the summary of the plan and which options were selected. Clicking Finish ends the wizard and creates the plan. You should now see a success screen with the completed tasks.

Running the Maintenance Plan

Once you successfully complete the maintenance wizard, the next step is to run the plan you created. In order to get the plan to run, you need to have the SQL Server Agent running. It is visible two below

Management on SQL Server Management Studio. You can left-click SQL Server Agent, then right-click and select Start.

Alternatively, you can press the Windows key and press the letter R, then type services.msc and hit Enter. Once Services appears, scroll down and look for the SQL Server Agent (MSSQLEXPRESS). This book instructed you to install SQL Server Express, but you can select the other versions like (MSSQLSERVER) if you installed that. Left-click it, then right-click it and select Start.

You can go back to SSMS and right-click on the maintenance plan you created under maintenance plans, then select Execute. This will now run your plan. Upon successful completion of the plan, click OK and close the dialogue box. You can view the reports by right-clicking the maintenance plan you created and selecting View History. On the left-hand side are all the different plans in SQL Server, while the results of the specific plan are on the right.

Emailing the Reports
A lot of DBAs like to get their database reports via email. What you need to do is set up a database mail before you can fire off emails, and then set up a Server agent to send the emails.

Configuring the Database Mail

The first step is to right-click Database mail in SSMS and select Configure Database Mail. A wizard screen will appear; click Next. Now select, the first choice–Set Up Database Mail–and click Next. Enter a profile name and, if you want, an optional description of the profile. Now, click on the Add button to the right.

This will bring you to an add New Database Mail Account – SMTP. You need to enter the SMTP details for an email account. You may want to set up a new email account for this service. You can search online for SMTP details, and Gmail works quite well (server name: smtp.gmail.com, port number 587, SSL required, tick basic authentication, and confirm password). Click on OK. Click Next, and select Public; it is important to do this so it can be used by the rest of the database. Set it as Default Profile, click Next, and click Next again. You should now get a success screen. Click Close.

SQL Server Agent

To send off the database email, you need to set up a Server Agent. Start by right-clicking on SQL Server Agent → New → Operator. Give the operator a name like Maintenance Plan Operator, enter in the email address to which you want the report delivered, and click OK.

Now, right-click the maintenance plan that you have successfully executed and select Modify. The maintenance plan design screen will appear on the right-hand side, where you can see some graphics of the tasks completed in it. Now, click on Reporting and Logging; it is an icon situated on the menu bar of the design plan, to the left of Manage Connections.

The Reporting and Logging window will appear. Choose the option to Send Report to an Email Recipient, and select the maintenance plan operator you just created. The next time you run the plan, an email will be sent to the email address.

The running and maintenance of a database is an important job. Having the right plan for your database will ensure that it continues to work as originally designed, and you will be able to quickly identify and fix database errors or slowdowns early on.

Backup and Recovery

The most important task a DBA can perform is backing up the essential database in use. When you create a maintenance plan, it's important to have backup and recovery at the top of the maintenance list in case the job doesn't get fully completed. Firstly, it is important to understand the transaction log and why it is important.

The Transaction Log

Whenever a change is made to the database, be it a transaction or modification, it is stored in the transaction log. The transaction log is the most important file in an SQL Server database, and everything revolves around either saving it or using it.

Every transaction log can facilitate transaction recovery, recover all incomplete transactions, roll forward a restored file, filegroup, or page to a point of failure, replicate transactions, and facilitate disaster recovery.

Recovery

The first step in backing up a database is choosing a recovery option for the database. You can perform the three types of backups when the SQL Server is online, and even while users are making requests from the database at the same time.

When you perform the process of doing backup and restore in the SQL Server, you do so within the confines of the recovery model designed to control the maintenance of the transactional log. Such a recovery model is known to be a database property aimed at ensuring that all transactions are logged in a certain procedure.

There are three different recovery options: simple, full, and bulk-logged.

Simple Recovery

You cannot backup the transaction log when utilizing the simple recovery model. Usually, this model is used when updates are infrequent. Transactions are minimally logged and the log will be truncated.

Full Recovery

In the full recovery model, the transaction log backup must be taken. Only when the backup process begins will the transaction log be truncated. You can recover to any point in time. However, you also need the full chain of log files to restore the database to the nearest time possible.

Bulk-Logged Recovery

This model is designed to be utilized for short-term use when you use a bulk import operation. You use it along with the full recovery model whenever you don't need a recovery to a certain point in time. It has performance gains and doesn't fill up the transaction log.

Changing the Recovery Model

To change the recovery model, you can right-click on a database in SQL Server Management Studio and select Properties. Then, select Options and choose the recovery model from the drop-down box. Alternatively, you can use one of the following:

- ALTER DATABASE SQLEbook SET RECOVERY SIMPLE

GO

- ALTER DATABASE SQLEbook SET RECOVERY FULL

GO

- ALTER DATABASE SQLEbook SET RECOVERY BULK_LOGGED

GO

Backups

There are three types of backup: full, differential, and transaction log. When Database Administrators set up a backup plan, they base their plan on two measures: Recovery Time Objective (RTO) and Recovery Point Objective (RPO). The RTO records the period to recover after a notification of a disruption in the business process. RPO measures the timeframe that might pass during a disruption before the data size that has been lost exceeds the maximum limit of the business process.

If there was an RPO of only 60 minutes, you couldn't achieve this goal if your backup was set to every 24 hours. You need to set your backup plan based on these two measures.

Full Backup
When you create a full backup, the SQL Server creates a CHECKPOINT which ensures that any exiting dirty pages are written to disk. Then, the SQL Server backs up each and every page on the database. It then backs up the majority of the transaction log to ensure there is transactional consistency. What all of this means is that you are able to restore your database to the most recent point and recover all the transactions, including those right up to the very beginning of the backup.

Exercising this alone is the least flexible option. Essentially, you are only able to restore your database back to one point of time, which the is the last full backup. Thus, if the database went corrupt two hours from midnight (and your backup is at midnight) your RPO would be 22 hours. In addition, if a user truncated a table two hours from midnight, you would have the same 22-hour loss of business transactions.

Transaction Log Backup
With the transaction log backup, the SQL Server backs up the data in the transaction log only, in other words, only the transactions that were recently committed to the database. The transaction log is not as resource-hungry and is considered important because it can perform backups more often without having an impact on database performance.

If you select Full Recovery mode, you can run both a full backup and a transaction log backup. You can also run more frequent backups since running the transaction log backup takes less resources. This is a very good choice if your database is updated throughout the day.

In scheduling transaction log backups, it's best to follow the RPO. For example, if there is an RPO of 60 minutes, then set the log file backups to 60 minutes. However, you must check the RTO for such a backup. If you had an RPO of 60 minutes and are only performing a full backup once a week, you might not be able to restore all 330 backups in the allotted time.

Differential Backup

To get around the problem mentioned above, you can add differential backups to the plan. A differential backup is cumulative, which mean a serious reduction in the number of backups you would need to recover your database to the point just before failure.

The differential backup, as its name suggests, backs up every page in the database that has since been modified since the last backup. The SQL Server keeps track of all the different pages that have been modified via flags and DIFF pages.

Performing a Backup

To back up a database, right-click the database in SSMS, then select Tasks → Backup. You can select what kind of backup to perform (full, differential, or transaction log) and when to perform the backup. The copy-only backup allows you to perform a backup that doesn't affect the restore sequence.

Restoring a Database

When you want to restore a database in SSMS, right-click the database, then select Tasks → Restore → Database. You can choose the database contained in the drop-down menu and keep the rest of the tabs populated.

If you click on Timeline, you can see a graphical diagram of when the last backup was created, which shows how much data was lost. You may have the option of recovering up to the end of a log, or a specific date and time.

The Verify Backup Timeline media button enables you to verify the backup media before you actually restore it. If you want to change where you are going to store the backup, you can click on Files to select a different location. You can specify the restore options that you want to use on the Options page. Either overwrite the existing database or keep it. The recovery state either brings the database online or allows further backups to be applied.

Once you click OK, the database will be restored.

Attaching and Detaching Databases
The method of attaching and detaching databases is similar to that of backups and restores.

Essentially, here are the details of this method:

- Allows you to copy the .MDF file and .LDF file to a new disk or server.

- Performs like a backup and restore process, but can be faster at times, depending on the situation.

- The database is taken offline and cannot be accessed by any users or applications. It will remain offline until it's been reattached.

So, which one should you choose? Though a backup is the ideal option, there are cases where an attachment/detachment of the database may be your only choice.

Consider the following scenario:

Your database contains many filegroups. Attaching those can be quite cumbersome.

The appropriate solution is to back up the database and then restore it to the desired destination, as it will group all of the files together in the backup process.

Based on the size of the database, the backup/restore process takes a long time. However, the attaching/detaching of the database could be much quicker if it's needed as soon as possible.

In this scenario, you can take the database offline, detach it, and re-attach it to the new destination.

As mentioned above, there are two main file groups when following the method of attaching databases. These files are .MDF and .LDF. The .MDF file is the database's primary data file, which holds its structure and data. The .LDF file holds the transactional logging activity and history.

However, a .BAK file that's created when backing up a database, groups all of the files together and you restore different file versions from a single backup set.

Consider your situation before taking either option, but also consider a backup and restore first before looking into the attach/detach method as your next option. Also, be sure to test it before you move forward with live data!

Attaching/Detaching the AdventureWorks2012 Database

Since you already attached this database, we'll have you detach it from the server. After that, you'll attach it again using SQL syntax.

Detaching the Database

In SQL Server, there's a stored procedure that will detach the database for you. This particular stored procedure resides in the "master" database. Under the hood, you can see the complexity of the stored procedure by doing the following:

1. Click to expand the Databases folder

2. Click on System Databases, then the "master" database

3. Click on Programmability

4. Click on Stored Procedures, then System Stored Procedures

5. Find sys.sp_detach_db, right-click it and select 'Modify' in SSMS to see its syntax

For this, you'll just execute the stored procedure as is.

Below is the syntax:

USE master

GO

ALTER DATABASE DatabaseName SET SINGLE_USER WITH ROLLBACK IMMEDIATE
GO

EXEC master.dbo.sp_detach_db @dbname =
N'DatabaseName',
@skipchecks = 'false'
GO

We'll expand a little on what is happening. You want to use the "master" database to alter the database you'll be detaching and set it to single user instead of multi-user.

Last, the value after @dbname allows you to specify the name of the database to be detached, and the @skipchecks set to false means that the database engine will update the statistics information, identifying that the database has been detached. It's ideal to set this as @false whenever detaching a database so that the system holds current information about all databases.

Attaching Databases

Once you have detached your database, if you navigate to where your data directory is, you'll see that the AdventureWorks2012_Data.MDF file still exists – which it should since you only detached it and didn't delete it.

Next, take the file path of the .MDF file and copy and paste it in some place that you can easily access, like notepad. The location we use is C:\Program Files\Microsoft SQL Server\MSSQL13.MSSQLSERVER\MSSQL\DATA.

Now, go back into SSMS and click on the New Query button (if you're already connected). If you have not connected, then go ahead and connect to your instance.

Once you've connected to your instance and opened up a new query session, you'll just need to use the path of where the data file is stored. Once you have that, you can enter that value in the following SQL syntax examples in order to attach your database.

Below is the syntax for attaching database files and log files. Though in the following exercise, you'll be skipping attaching the log file completely, since you're not attaching this to a new server. Therefore, you may omit the statement to attach the log file.

CREATE DATABASE DatabaseName ON
(FILENAME = 'C:\SQL Data
Files\DatabaseName.mdf'),
(FILENAME = 'C:\SQL Data
Files\DatabaseName_log.ldf') FOR ATTACH
In the above example, we are calling out the statement to attach the log file if one is available. However, if you happen to not have the .LDF file and only the .MDF file, then that's fine, too. You can just attach the .MDF file and the database engine will create a new log file and start writing activity to that particular log.

5. Performing CRUD Operations

Now is time to perform CRUD operations on the database. CRUD is abbreviation of Create, Read, Update and Delete. These are the four most fundamental database operations. In this chapter we will see how to perform these operations.

Creating Data

To create data inside a table the INSERT query is used. The syntax for insert query is as follows:

INSERT INTO TABLE (Column1, Column2, Column3 …. Column N)

VALUES (Value1, Value2, Value3 …. Value N),
(Value1, Value2, Value3 …. Value N),

 (Value1, Value2, Value3 …. Value N)

The syntax for insert query is simple; you have to use keywords INSERT INTO TABLE followed by a pair of parenthesis. Inside the parenthesis you have to specify comma separated list of the columns where you want to insert the data. Next VALUES keyword is used followed by a pair of parenthesis that contain comma separated list of values that are to be stored in the columns. You can store multiple records at once.

Each set of columns should be separated by others via commas. It is important to mention that sequence of columns and values should be similar.

If you do not specify the columns within the parenthesis after the INSERT INTO TABLE keywords, the default table scheme is used.

Let's insert some data into our Hospital database. As with the table creation, first you should insert the records to the tables that do not have any foreign key. We will start with the Patients table. Take a look at the following query:

USE Hospital;

INSERT INTO Patients
VALUES ('Tom', 20, 'Male' ,'O+', 123589746),
('Kimer', 45,'Female', 'AB+', 45686412),
('James', 16,'Male', 'O-', 78452369),
('Matty', 43,'Female', 'B+', 15789634),
('Sal', 24,'Male', 'O+', 48963214),
('Julie', 26,'Female', 'A+', 12478963),
('Frank', 35,'Male', 'A-', 85473216),
('Alex', 21,'Male', 'AB-', 46971235),
('Hales', 54,'Male', 'B+', 74698125),

('Elice', 32,'Female', 'O+', 34169872)

In the above query we inserted records of 10 random patients in the Patients table. Here we did not specify the column names; therefore the default column sequence will be used. The values are inserted according to the default column sequence. By default, id is the first column of the Patients. However it has Identity constraint, therefore we do not need to add any value for the id. It will be automatically added. The second column is the name column. The first value will be inserted in this column. Be careful, the name column only accepts string type data. So you must insert string. To create string, enclose the value inside single quotes. Similar, age is the second column of the Patients table and it is of integer data type therefore we enter number as second value in our insert statement.

In the same way, let's insert data into Examinations and Doctors table. The following query inserts data in the Examinations table.

```
USE Hospital;

INSERT INTO Examinations
VALUES('XRay', 750),
('Ultrasound', 600),
('LFT', 800),
('RFT', 900),
('HIV', 500)
```

Similarly, let's insert some records in the Doctor's table.

USE Hospital;

```
INSERT INTO Doctors
VALUES('Orland', 'MS', 'Nephrology'),
('Mark', 'HOD', 'Pathology'),
('Evens', 'Professor', 'Cardiology'),
('John','Demonstrator', 'Pediatrician'),
```

('Fred', 'DMS', 'Neurology')

We have added data to all the independent tables, now let's some data to the Patient_Visits table. It has a foreign key columpatient_id. This column references the id column of the Patients table. This means that patient_id column of Patient_Visits table can only have values that exist in the id column of the Patients table. In Patients table, the id column has values between 1-10. We will randomly insert these values in the patient_id column. The following script inserts some random records in Patient_Visits table.

USE Hospital;

```
INSERT INTO Patient_Visits
VALUES(1, '19-Apr-2012'),
(2, '19-May-2012'),
(4, '25-Feb-2013'),
(6, '30-Nov-2014'),
(2, '21-Sep-2015'),
(3, '10-Oct-2011'),
(7, '01-Jan-2010'),
```

(9, '25-May-2012'),
(4, '17-Nov-2012'),
(8, '08-Sep-2016'),
(3, '19-Jan-2013'),
(10, '20-May-2011'),
(3, '17-Feb-2012'),
(7, '19-Mar-2014'),
(10, '05-May-2015'),
(8, '14-Feb-2011'),
(6, '29-Nov-2016'),
(10, '18-May-2010'),
(9, '09-Jun-2015'),

(8, '08-Sep-2014')

Now let's insert dummy records to the Treatments and Patient_Examinations table. Treatments table has two foreign key columns patient_id and doctor_id. The former references the id column of Patients table and while the latter references the id column of the Doctors table. So while inserting records for these foreign key columns we should insert only those values that exist in the corresponding referenced columns. The following script inserts record in the Treatment table.

USE Hospital;

INSERT INTO Treatment
VALUES (1,3, 'Fit'),
(1,3, 'Good condition'),
(2,5, 'Needs more treatment'),

(1,4, 'Referred for XRay'),
(8,1, 'Medicnes recommended'),
(5,2, 'Fit'),

 (9,3, 'Perfect')

 In the same way, execute the following script to add data to Patient_Examination table

USE Hospital

INSERT INTO Patient_Examination
VALUES (1,3, 'Positive'),
(1,3, 'Negative'),
(2,5, 'Positive'),
(1,4, 'Negative'),
(8,1, 'Positive'),
(5,2, 'Negative'),

 (9,3, 'Positive')

Selecting Data

We have inserted data in all of our tables. Now is the time to retrieve that data. To do in SQL, we use SELECT query. You can either select data from all the columns or data from individual columns. The syntax for both operations is as follows:

Selecting all columns

SELECT * FROM Table_Name

Selecting Individual Columns

SELECT column1, column2, column3 ... columnN
FROM Table_Name

Let's select all the records from the Patients table. Execute following query:

SELECT * FROM Patients

This query will retrieve all records with all column values from Patients table. The result of the above query will look like this:

id	name	age	gender	blood_group	phone
1	Tom	20	Male	O+	123589746
2	Kimer	45	Female	AB+	45686412
3	James	16	Male	O-	78452369
4	Matty	43	Female	B+	15789634
5	Sal	24	Male	O+	48963214

6	Julie	26	Female	A+	12478963
7	Frank	35	Male	A-	85473216
8	Alex	21	Male	AB-	46971235
9	Hales	54	Male	B+	74698125
10	Elice	32	Female	O+	34169872

For instance if you want to retrieve only the name, and blood_group columns for all the records in the Patients table, you can execute following query.

SELECT name, blood_group FROM Patients

The result set will look like this:

name	blood_group
Tom	O+
Kimer	AB+
James	O-
Matty	B+
Sal	O+
Julie	A+

Frank	A-
Alex	AB-
Hales	B+
Elice	O+

Updating Data

To update existing table data, the UPDATE query is used. The syntax of the update query looks like this:

UPDATE Table_Name

 SET Column_Name = Value

Let's increase the price of all the examinations by 10%. To do so we have to update the value of the price column of the Examinations table by multiplying it with 1.1. The following update query performs this operation.

UPDATE Examinations

 SET price = price * 1.1

Deleting Data

DELETE query is used to delete records from a table. The syntax of DELETE query is as follows:

DELETE FROM Table_Name

To delete all the records from Patient_Visits table, execute following query. (Do not forget to reinsert records in the Patient_Visits table. We will use this data to perform queries in the upcoming chapter)

DELETE FROM Patient_Visits

In this chapter we learned to create, insert, update and delete table records. However we saw that these operations are being performed on all the records. What if we want to delete only specific records? For instance what we will do if want to update records of only female patients?

6. The Hard Hitting Concept Of Nested Queries And Recursive

Just as the title suggests, in this chapter we are going to be dealing with two very distinct yet crucial aspects of SQL programming. Let's start by talking about Subqueries first which will basically be covering the Nested Queries part.

What Exactly Are Nested Queries!

We have already discussed in details about the WHERE clause, Nested queries are basically the enclosing statements within the WHERE clause that defines what function the WHERE clause is going to perform.

NESTED Queries For Returning Multiple Rows

We will be elaborating this whole concept through the usage of a simple example. Let us consider for a moment that you are working for a world renowned company which specializes in assembling various components and bringing them together for you to conveniently purchase them. The whole structure of your company might be comprised of many tables, but you are only concerned with COMPONENT, PRODUCT and COMP_USED tables as illustrated below.

Product

Column	Type	Constraints
Model	CHAR (6)	PRIMARY KEY
ProdName	CHAR (35)	
ProdDesc	CHAR (31)	
ListPrice	NUMERIC (9,2)	

Component

Column	Type	Constraints
CompID	CHAR (6)	PRIMARY KEY
CompType	CHAR (10)	
CompDesc	CHAR (31)	

COMP_USED

Column	Type	Constraints
Model	CHAR (6)	FOREIGN KEY (for PRODUCT)
CompID	CHAR (6)	FOREIGN KEY (for COMPONENT)

The skeleton which you will be using here to acquire the information you desire is the formation of Subqueries with the usage of IN keyword.

SELECT column_list

      FROM table

      HERE expression IN (subquery) ;

The above syntax implies that the "WHERE" clause is going to be bringing out the information that is present inside the list to which the expression is pointing towards.

From the above example, if we want to bring out all the monitors from our company, we can write a code similar to:

SELECT Model

     FROM COMP_USED

     WHERE CompID IN

          (SELECT CompID

               FROM COMPONENT

               WHERE CompType =
'Monitor');

What this code will do is to return all the CompID for every present row where the CompType matches with "Monitor"

The opposite of the IN syntax is the NOT IN syntax which will bring out the information that does not contain the specified field. Following through our given example, if we wanted to bring out a list of all the products that did not fall under as MONITOR, the following code would've been used

SELECT Model

     FROM COMP_USED

     WHERE CompID NOT IN

```
                    (SELECT CompID

                            FROM COMPONENT

                                    WHERE  CompType  =
'Monitor')) ;
```

Just as a head up, we would also like you to familiarize yourself with the DISTINCT keyword.

Using this keyword, you will be able to eliminate all the duplicate rows (if any) from your result with ease. The following example shows how that should be done:

```
SELECT DISTINC Model

            FROM COMP_USED

            WHERE CompID NOT IN

                    (SELECT CompID

                            FROM COMPONENT

                                    WHERE  CompType  =
'Monitor'));
```

Introducing The All, Any and Some Quantifiers

Here you will need to use a combination of ALL, SOME or ANY quantifier with comparison operators in order to make sure that the final result is single value form.

Let us consider the table below:

SELECT * FROM NATIONAL

First Name	Last Name	Complete Games
Sal	Maglie	11
Don	Newcombe	9
Sandy	Koufax	13
Don	Drysdale	12
Bob	Turley	8

SELECT * FROM AMERICAN

First Name	Last Name	Complete Games
Whitey	Ford	12
Don	Larson	10
Bob	Turley	8

Allie	Reynolds	14

Here we are going to making an assumption that we need all the information of pitchers who have completed the most game and are from American League. The code for the said example would be:

SELECT *

    FROM AMERICAN

    WHERE CompleteGames > ALL

        (SELECT CompleteGames FROM NATIONAL) ;

This should bear the result similar to:

FirstName	LastName	CompleteGames
----------	---------	---------
Allie	Reynolds	14

The Insertion Of Subqueries With UPDATE, INSERT and DELETE Statements

As you may already notice, subqueries are very versatile when it comes to being able to combine with different statements in order to manipulate multiple data. Combining the WHERE clause (with Subqueries) alongside any of the UPDATE, INSERT or DELETE statement you will also be able to obtain some pretty interesting results.

Continuing from the example of our hypothetical company, if at one point, we want to increase our credit for all last month purchases by 10%, would update our data as follows:

UPDATE TRANSMASTER

SET NetAmount = NetAmount * 0.9

WHERE SaleDate > (CurrentDate – 30) DAY AND CustID =

(SELECT CustID

FROM CUSTOMER

WHERE Company =

'Olympic Sales') ;

Dealing With The Concept Of Recursion

Now that we are done with the first part of this chapter, let us talk about Recursion. So, this is primarily a feature which has been around for quiet sometime in other languages. But it took an unfortunate delay to be integrated with the SQL framework. To understand recursion, you will need to understand a simple mechanism.

In any programming language such as LISP, Logo, C++ or SQL, whenever you are defining a function which will perform a specific action, the program automatically imitates that function by creating a command called "function call". A simplest example of recursion taking place would be a scenario where, alongside while performing a function, the function starts by calling itself!

To make things more clear, let us show you an example of recursion through a program written in C++ that has been designed to draw a spiral on your monitor. Keep in mind that it has been assumed that the drawing tool is initially pointing towards the top of the screen.

The code for the program is

```
void spiral(int segment)

        line(segment)

        left_turn(90)

        spiral(segment + 1)

};
```

When you are going to start the program by calling spiral (1) the following actions are going to take place

- Spiral(1) draws just a one unit line alongside the top of the screen
- Spiral(1) takes a 90 degree turn to the left
- Spiral(1) calls upon spiral(2)
- Spiral(2) draws just a one unit line alongside the top of the screen
- Spiral(2) takes a 90 degree turn to the left

And so on the cycle continues, until eventually you will end up with this.

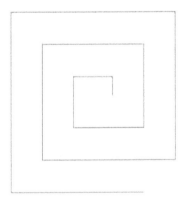

Notice how the program is calling upon itself over and over again? That is recursion. You can relate them to simple loops as found in Java.

```
call spiral2(1)
    └── call spiral2(2)
            └── call spiral2(3)
                    └── call spiral2(4)
                            └── call spiral2(5)
                                    └── call spiral2(6)
                                            └── call spiral2(7)
                                                    └── call spiral2(8)
                                                            └── call spiral2(9)
                                                                    └── call spiral2(10)
                                                                            └── call spiral2(11)
```

The Introduction To Recursive Query

Now that you know what recursion is, it should not be difficult for you to grasp the concept of a recursive query. This is simply a query which is functionally dependent upon itself. So, for example if we have an expression embodied within query 1, running that very expression would invoke itself in the body of the query expression.

Sounds weird? Don't worry! Let us clear things up with a real life example.

Let's consider in a scenario that a hypothetical Airlines called "The Secretive International" has decided to give you a completely free air travel opportunity. The obvious question that will pop up in your mind then is "Where can I go for free?"

Below is a table which contains the flight number, source and destination of the available flights

Using the data above, you will want to create a complete table which will act as your vacation planner using the code below.

CREATE TABLE LIGHT (

FlightNo INTEGER

NOT NULL,

 Source CHAR (30),

 Destination CHAR (30));

Once you have chosen a starting destination, you are going to want to decide which cities you will be able to reach. If say for example, you are starting from Portland or from Montgomery! Finding a solution to such a query can be outright cumbersome if you tackle each of the following queries one by one. This is a perfect example where recursive query should be utilized through the code below:

WITH RECURSIVE

            REACHABLEFROM (Source, Destination)

                    AS (SELECT Source, Destination

                            FROM FLIGHT

                    UNION

SELECT in.Source, out.Destination

FROM REACHABLEFROM in, FLIGHT out

WHERE in.Destination = out.Source

)

SELECT * FROM REACHABLEFROM

WHERE Source = 'Portland';

The result will be something similar to the table below which shows you through recursion, the possible reachable cities when starting from each of the source cities.

7. Making Your Database Secure

Being a system administrator for large scale databases is not easy as you may think. Not only are you going to deal with the demands of the clients, but you will also have to maintain and provide a much secured environment so that your clients can feel safe knowing that their data is in safe hands. SQL provides a diverse array of functions which can be combined to create very sophisticated and seamless security systems that will give you control over granting or revoking access rights to individual users.

The 9 Functions of Control

The following functions contribute to the way you can re-enforce your security system.

- INSERT
- DELETE
- UPDATE
- SELECT
- REFRENCE
- USAGE
- UNDER
- TRIGGER
- EXECUTE

The Hierarchy Of Database System

When it comes to establishing a secured system, it is crucial that you understand the hierarchy of the database system. The hierarchy gives you an idea of how the whole system is working. At its very core, the parts of the SQL security system have been classified as follows:

- *The DBA (Database Administrator):* The database administrator is generally the person who holds the supreme authority over all the actions occurring within a database. All the powers of modification are at the disposal of DBA and he can very well destroy everything with just a single mistake.
- *Database Object Owners:* This is another set of user with high privileges. In general, the people who create any data objects such as tables, views etc. are referred to as being the owners of those objects and they have privileges within them associated with the manipulations and protection of those objects.
- *The Public:* Once the DBA and Database Owners have been taken out, the remaining people working with the database with no special privilege are called the PUBLIC. The access rights of the public largely relies on

the rights granted to them from the privileged users.

-

Setting the Privileges

As the DBA of a database, you will have the power to allow certain users access specific parts of your database and prevent them from accessing the rest. This is done using the GRANT statement.

GRANT privilege-list

ON object

TO user-list

[WITH HIERARCHY OPTION]

[WITH GRANT OPTION]

[GRANTED BY grantor] ;

A Privilege here is defined as

SELECT

| DELETE

| INSERT [(column-name [, column-name]...)]

| UPDATE [(column-name [, column-name]...)]

| REFERENCES [(column-name [, column-name]...)]

| USAGE

| UNDER

| TRIGGER

| EXECUTE

While an object is defined as

[TABLE] <table name>

| DOMAIN <domain name>

| COLLATION <collation name>

| CHARACTER SET <character set name>

| TRANSLATION <transliteration name>

| TYPE <schema-resolved user-defined type name>

| SEQUENCE <sequence generator name>

| <specific routine designator>

And finally the user list is as follows

login-ID [, login-ID]...

| PUBLIC

The Significance Of Role Assignment

Roles are nothing but an alternative to user name which can be used as an authorization identifier. You can set a role using a syntax such as

CREATE ROLE SalesClerk ;

After which, you can assign people to the created role using GRANT

GRANT SalesClerk to Becky ;

This essentially will help you create a group of people with similar privileges with ease.

A role can be allowed to INSERT data by:

GRANT INSERT

ON CUSTOMER

TO SalesClerk ;

A role can be allowed to view the data:

GRANT SELECT

ON PRODUCT

TO PUBLIC ;

A role can be allowed to modify data by:

GRANT UPDATE

ON BONUSRATE

TO VPSales ;

Granting The Power To Grant Privileges

This concept somewhat works like granting other users whom you trust with a little bit of your power to control the database access privileges. This actually makes a lot of sense especially if you are attempting to work with a large group. You can't always be around, sometimes you may fall sick and at that point you are going to need someone to temporarily take over!

This can be done using the grant option, the below is the example of the sales manager that has been given the power to provide the UPDATE privilege to others.

GRANT UPDATE (BonusPct)

ON BONUSRATE

TO SalesMgr

WITH GRANT OPTION ;

GRANT UPDATE (BonusPct)

ON BONUSRATE

TO AsstSalesMgr ;

Take Away Privileges

As painful as the title suggests, sometimes you might be required to take crucial and serious steps in order to revoke a user from his/her privileges. And this is done by the REVOKE statement as follows:

REVOKE [GRANT OPTION FOR] privilege-list

ON object

FROM user-list [RESTRICT|CASCADE] ;

Understanding The Threats To Data Integrity

Now that you know how to control your structure, you should have a clear grasp of the most common threats which you might face that may hamper with your data stability.

- *Platform Instability:* Unexpected problems such as unseen bugs or problems in a new DBMS or operating system release falls under this category.
- *Equipment Failure:* This is, as the name implies, unforeseen events where your highly reliable state of the art equipment might fail sending your data to the afterlife.

Keeping a redundancy backup which constantly copies everything will allow to protect against such an event.

- *The Problem Of Concurrent Access:* Even if you are completely sure that you program is free of bugs and hardware errors, problem might still arise if multiple users are trying to access your database at the same time. In situations like this the system struggles to decide who gets to enter first (Contention). A good method to tackle against this is to invoke a serialization system where the first user is given access first, then the second and so on...

-

Techniques To Reduce Possibility Of Data Corruption

While there are several steps that you can take in order to make sure that your data are safe. Here are some of the more common ones that you should be familiar with:

- *The Usage Of SQL Transaction:* This is one of the prime method through which SQL maintains the database integrity. We have already discussed about this earlier. It simply encapsulates all of the SQL statement which may affect the database and are only carried out using the COMMIT or ROLLBACK option.

Start of the application

Various SQL statements (SQL transaction-1)

COMMIT or ROLLBACK

Various SQL statements (SQL transaction-2)

COMMIT or ROLLBACK

Various SQL statements (SQL transaction-3)

COMMIT or ROLLBACK

End of the application

- *Isolation:* Another method is to isolate the individual transaction so that they are not conflicting with one another, even if multiple users are working at the same time. Using the SET TRANSACTION command, Isolation can very well lock up objects in the database if they are being fringed with in the wrong way.

SET TRANSACTION

READ ONLY,

ISOLATION LEVEL READ UNCOMMITTED,

DIAGNOSTICS SIZE 4 ;

SET TRANSACTION

READ WRITE,

ISOLATION LEVEL SERIALIZABLE,

DIAGNOSTICS SIZE 8 ;

- *Usage Of Savepoints:* Combining the ROLLBACK and SAVEPOINT statements, the flow of a transaction can be controlled. The SAVEPOINT is set up essentially to terminate a transaction. This gives you the opportunity to roll back to the last save point should any problem occur right after the former transaction has been made.

SAVEPOINT savepoint_name ;

To Rollback

ROLLBACK TO SAVEPOINT savepoint_name ;

8. Tables Modifying And Controlling

Altering table

The ALTER TABLE command is used to modify existing database tables. This is a powerful command that will let you change a table's name, add new fields, remove columns, edit field definitions, modify the table's storage values, and include or exclude constraints.

Here's the basic syntax for altering a table:

Changing a Table's Name

The ALTER TABLE command can be used with the RENAME function to change a table's name.

To demonstrate the use of this statement, you will use the EMPLOYEES table with the following records:

Assuming that you want to change the EMPLOYEES table name to INVESTORS, you can easily do so with this statement:

Your table is now named INVESTORS.

Modifying Column Attributes

A column's attributes refer to the properties and behaviors of data entered in a column. You will normally set the column attributes at the time you create the table. However, you may still change one or more attributes using the ALTER TABLE command.

You may modify the following:

- Column name
- Column Data type assigned to a column
- The scale, length, or precision of a column
- Use or non-use of NULL values in a column

Renaming Columns

You may want to modify a column's name to reflect the data that they contain. For instance, since you renamed the EMPLOYEES database to INVESTORS, the column name SALARY will no longer be appropriate. You can change the column name to something like CAPITAL. Likewise, you may want to change its data type from DECIMAL to an INTEGER TYPE with a maximum of ten digits.

Deleting a Column

The column Position is no longer applicable at this point. You can drop the column using this statement:

ALTER TABLE INVESTORS

DROP COLUMN Position;

Here's the updated INVESTORS table:

Adding a New Column

Since you're now working on a different set of data, you may decide to add another column to make the data on the INVESTORS table more relevant. You can add a column that will store the number of stocks owned by each investor. You may name the new column as STOCKS. This column will accept integers up to 9 digits.

You can use this statement to add the STOCKS column:

ALTER TABLE INVESTORS ADD STOCKS INT(9);

Here's the updated INVESTOR'S table:

Modifying an Existing Column without Changing its Name

You may also combine the ALTER TABLE command with the MODIFY keyword to change the data type and specifications of a table. To demonstrate, you can use the following statement to modify the data type of the column CAPITAL from an INT type to a DECIMAL type with up to 9 digits and two decimal numbers.

By this time, you may be curious to see the column names and attributes of the INVESTORS table. You can use the 'SHOW COLUMNS' statement to display the table's structure. Enter the following statement:

SHOW COLUMNS FROM INVESTORS;

Here's a screenshot of the result:

You will also get the same results with this statement:

DESC INVESTORS;

Rules to Remember when Using ALTER TABLE
 • Adding Columns to a Database Table
When adding a new column, bear in mind that you can't add a column with a NOT NULL attribute to a table with existing data. You will generally specify a column to be NOT NULL to indicate that it will hold a value. Adding a NOT NULL column with contradict the constraint if the existing data don't have values for a new column.

 • Modifying Fields/Columns
You should pay close attention to the following rules when modifying current database column:

1. You can easily modify the data type of a column.
2. You can always increase the length of a column but you may only decrease the length of a column if it is equal to or shorter than the desired column length.
    3. You can increase the number of digits that numeric data types will hold but you will only be able to decrease it if the largest number of digits stored by a table is

equal to or lower than the desired number of digits.

4. You can increase or decrease the decimal places of numeric data types as long as they don't exceed the maximum allowable decimal places.

Deleting and modifying tables can result to loss of valuable information if not handled properly. Hence, be extremely careful when you're executing the ALTER TABLE and DROP TABLE statements.

Deleting Tables

The DROP TABLE command is used to remove a table and its definitions from a database. Dropping a table will also remove its data, associated index, triggers, constraints, and permission data. You should be careful when using this statement.

Here's the syntax::

For example, if you want to delete the INVESTORS TABLE from the xyzcompany database, you may use this statement:

DROP TABLE INVESTORS;

The DROP TABLE command effectively removed the INVESTORS table from the current database.

If you try to access the INVESTORS table with this command:

SELECT* FROM INVESTORS;

SQL will return an error like this;

Combining and joining tables

You can combine data from several tables if a common field exists between them. The JOIN statement is used to perform this action.

SQL supports several types of JOIN operations:

INNER JOIN

The INNER JOIN, or simply JOIN, is the most commonly used type of JOIN. It displays the rows when the tables to be joined have a matching field.

Here's the syntax:

In this variation, the JOIN clause is used instead of INNER JOIN.

LEFT JOIN

The LEFT JOIN operation returns all left table rows with the matching right table rows. If no match is found, the right side returns NULL.

Here's the syntax for LEFT JOIN:

In some database systems, the keyword LEFT OUTER JOIN is used instead of LEFT JOIN. Here's the syntax for this variation:

RIGHT JOIN

This JOIN operation returns all right table rows with the matching left table rows. If no match is found, the left side returns NULL.

Here's the syntax for this operation:

In some database systems, the RIGHT OUTER JOIN is used instead of LEFT JOIN. Here's the syntax for this variation:

FULL OUTER JOIN
This JOIN operation will display all rows when at least one table meets the condition. It combines the results from both RIGHT and LEFT join operations.

Here's the syntax:

To demonstrate the JOIN operation in SQL, you will use the tables Branch_Sales and Branch_Location:

Branch_Sales Table

Branch	Product_ID	Sales
New York	101	7500.00
Los Angeles	102	6450.00
Chicago	101	1560.00
Philadelphia	101	1980.00

Denver	102	3500.00
Seattle	101	2500.00
Detroit	102	1450.00

Location Table

Region	Branch
East	New York City
East	Chicago
East	Philadelphia
East	Detroit
West	Los Angeles
West	Denver
West	Seattle

The objective is to fetch the sales by region. The Location table contains the data on regions and branches while the Branch_Sales table holds the sales data for each branch. To find the sales per region, you will need to combine the data from the Location and Branch_Sales tables. Notice that these tables have a common field, the Branch. This field links the two tables.

The following statement will demonstrate how you can link these two tables by using table aliases:

SELECT A1.Region Region, SUM(A2.Sales) Sales

FROM Location A1, Branch_Sales A2

WHERE A1.Branch = A2.Branch

GROUP BY A1.Region;

This would be the result:

In the first two lines, the statement tells SQL to select the fields 'Region' from the Location table and the total of the 'Sales' field from the Branch_Sales table. The statement uses table aliases. The 'Region' field was aliased as Region while the sum of the SALES field was aliased as SALES.

Table aliasing is the practice of using a temporary name for a table or a table column. Using aliases helps make statements more readable and concise. For example, if you opt not to use a table alias for the first line, you would have used the following statement to achieve the same result:

SELECT Location.Region Region,

SUM(Branch_Sales.Sales) SALES

Alternatively, you can specify a join between two tables by using the JOIN and ON keywords. For instance, using these keywords, the query would be:

SELECT A1.Region REGION, SUM(A2.Sales) SALES

FROM Location A1

JOIN Branch_Sales A2

ON A1.Branch = A2.Branch

GROUP BY A1.Region;

The query would produce an identical result:

Using Inner Join
An inner join displays rows when there is one or more matches on two tables. To demonstrate, you will use the following tables:

Branch_Sales table

Branch	Product_ID	Sales
New York	101	7500.00

Philadelphia	101	1980.00
Denver	102	3500.00
Seattle	101	2500.00
Detroit	102	1450.00

Location_table

Region	Branch
East	New York
East	Chicago
East	Philadelphia
East	Detroit
West	Los Angeles
West	Denver

West	Seattle

The objective of the query is to fetch the sales data per branch and only for branches that are listed in the Branch_Sales table. You can achieve this by using the INNER JOIN statement.

You can enter the following:

SELECT A1.Branch BRANCH, SUM(A2.Sales) SALES

FROM Location A1

INNER JOIN Branch_Sales A2

ON A1.Branch = A2.Branch

GROUP BY A1.Branch;

This would be the result:

Take note that by using the INNER JOIN, only the branches with records in the Branch_Sales report were included in the results even though you are actually applying the SELECT statement on the Location table. The 'Chicago' and 'Los Angeles' branches were excluded because there are no records for these branches in the Branch_Sales table.

Using Outer Join

In the previous example, you have used the Inner Join to combine tables with common rows. In some cases, you may need to select all elements of a table whether or not they have a matching record in the second table. The OUTER JOIN command is used for this purpose.

The example for the OUTER JOIN will use the same tables used for INNER JOIN: the Branch_Sales table and Location_table.

This time, you want a list of sales figures for all stores. A regular join would have excluded Chicago and Los Angeles because these branches were not part of the Branch_Sales table. You will want, therefore, to do an OUTER JOIN.

Here's the statement:

SELECT A1.Branch, SUM(A2.Sales) SALES

FROM Location A1, Branch_Sales A2

WHERE A1.Branch = A2.Branch (+)

GROUP BY A1.Branch;

Take note that the Outer Join syntax is database-dependent. The above statement uses the Oracle syntax.

Here's the result:

When combining tables, be aware that some JOIN syntax will have different results across database systems. To maximize this powerful database

feature, it is imporant to read the RDBMS
documentation.

9. Aggregate Functions, Delete, & Update

Up till now, we have been dealing with individual records. We saw how to insert individual records in a database, how to retrieve records from the database based on criteria, and how to apply different types of filters to fetch a desired output. What if we want to retrieve the maximum age of the patients from the PatientAge column? SQL Aggregate functions help us perform this task. We shall see some of the most commonly used aggregate functions in SQL. We shall also see how we can delete records from a table and how we can update existing records.

Contents

- **Aggregate Functions**
1. Count()
2. Avg()
3. Sum()
4. Max()
5. Min()
6. First/Top()
7. Ucase/Upper()
8. Lcase/Lower()
- **Delete Statement**
- **Update Statement**

   1-   Aggregate Functions

The following are some of the most commonly used functions.

1. Count()

The Count() function counts the number of rows which satisfy a particular criteria. For instance, if you want to count the number of patients who have Heart disease, you can use Count() function as follows:

Query 1
SELECT   COUNT(PatientID)   as
PatientsWithHeartDisease

From Patient
WHERE DiseaseDescription LIKE ('%heart%')
The above query counts the patient with heart disease and displays the result in the "PatientsWithHeartDisease" column.

2. Avg()

The Avg() function returns the average of values in a particular table column based on some criteria. For instance, if you want to retrieve the average age of all patients with heart disease, you can employ the Avg() function as follows:

Query 2
SELECT   AVG(PatientAge)   as
AverageAgeofHeartDisease

From Patient

WHERE DiseaseDescription LIKE ('%heart%')

3. Sum()

The Sum() function returns the sum of the values in a particular table column based on some criteria. For instance, if you want to retrieve the sum of the ages of all patients, you can employ the Sum() function as follows:

Query 3

SELECT Sum(PatientAge) as SumOfAges

From Patient

4. Max()

The Max() function returns the maximum of all of the values in a particular table column. For instance, if you want to retrieve the maximum age of all the patients, you can use the Max() function as follows:

Query 4

SELECT Max(PatientAge) as MaximumAge

From Patient

5. Min()

Similarly, to retrieve the minimum patient age, the following query can be executed:

Query 5

SELECT Min(PatientAge) as MaximumAge

From Patient

6. Top/First()

The Top() or First() functions return the top 'n' of all of the values in a particular table column, where "n" is any integer. For instance, if you want to retrieve the age of the first three patients in the "Patient" table, you can use the Top() function as follows:

Query 6

SELECT Top 3 PatientAge as First3Ages

From Patient
The above query will retrieve the ages of the first three patients. The output will look like this:

First3Ages
10
26
15

To retrieve the ages of the last three patients in the "Patient" table, you can use the Top() query in conjunction with the "Order By" clause as follows:

Query 7

SELECT Top 3 PatientAge as Last3Ages

From Patient Order by PatientAge desc
The output of Query 7 is as follows:

Last3Ages
47
42
31

7. Upper()/Ucase

The Upper() or Ucase() function converts all the values in the selected column to uppercase. This function applies only to columns with string or character values.

Query 8

SELECT Upper(PatientName) as PatientNameUpper

From Patient

The output of Query 8 is as follows:

PatientNameUpper
JAMES
JOSEPH
SARAH
JULIAN
ISAAC
MARGRET
MIKE
RUSS
MARIA
CANDICE

8. Lcase()/Lower()

Similarly, to convert column values to lower case, the Lcase() or Lower() function is used. Since I am using MS SQL Server for demonstration purposes, I will use Lower() in my Query.

Query 9

SELECT Lower(PatientName) as PatientNameLower

From Patient

The output will contain all the PatientName values in lower case as follows:

PatientNameLower
james
joseph
sarah
julian
isaac
margret
mike
russ
maria
candice

Delete Statement

We know how to insert records into a database; we also know how to retrieve records using a SELECT statement and how to filter records using a "where" clause with various SQL operators. Now we will learn how to delete records from the table.

To delete records, the SQL DELETE statement is used. Like the SELECT statement, the DELETE statement can also be used in conjunction with a SELECT statement to delete filtered records. Let's look at how we can delete all the records from the table. To do so, the following query can be executed:

Query 10

DELETE From Patient

This query will delete all the records from the patient table. However, in some scenarios, we want only records that satisfy particular criteria to be deleted. For instance, you can delete the records of all patients with heart disease using the following query:

Query 11

Delete From Patient

where DiseaseDescription like('%heart%')
The above query will delete all the patient records which have heart disease in the DiseaseDescription column.

3- Update Statement

We know how to insert, retrieve, and delete records; in this section, we shall learn how to update an existing record. To update a record, the UPDATE statement is used in SQL, followed by the SET keyword, which is used to update an existing value.

If you want to replace the string "Heart Disease" in the DiseaseDescription column with the string "Cardiac Disease", you can use an UPDATE statement as follows:

Query 12

UPDATE Patient

SET DiseaseDescription = 'Cardiac Disease'
where DiseaseDescription like('%heart%')

Exercise 7

Task:

Delete the records of all patients aged greater than 30 who have ear diseases. Set the age of all patients with lung disease to 40.

Solution

Deleting Records

Delete From Patient

where PatientAge > 30 AND DiseaseDescription LIKE ('%ear%')

Updating Records

```
UPDATE Patient
set PatientAge = 40
    where DiseaseDescription LIKE ('%lung%')
```

10. Relationships & Join Queries

Up to this point, we have been executing all our queries on a single table. However, real life databases contain hundreds, or even thousands, of tables. These tables are associated with each other via relationships. We saw how the "Student" table was associated with the "Department" table via a column, DID, which stored the ID of the department to which student belonged. This is one type of database relationship. In this chapter, we shall study different types of database relationships and Join queries.

Contents

- **Table Relationships**
1. **One-to-One Relationship**
2. **One-to-Many Relationship**
3. **Many-to-Many Relationship**

- **Join Statements**
1. **Inner Join**
2. **Left Join**
3. **Right Join**
4. **Outer Join**

- **Group By**

- **Having**

1-   Table Relationships

Database tables can be linked with each other via one of the three types of relationships.

• One-to-One Relationship

In a "one-to-one" relationship between two tables, for every record in the first table, there is exactly one record in the second table. The Primary key of the first table exists as the Foreign key in the second table and vice versa. For example, there is a "one-to-one" relationship between the "Employee" table and the "Pension" table, since one Pension record belongs to one Employee and one Employee can have only one Pension record. In most scenarios, "one-to-one" relationships are removed by merging the data into a single column.

Note:

A Foreign key is basically a column in the table which stores the primary key of the table with which it is linked. In we saw that the Student table had a column labeled DID, which stored the ID of the department to which a student belonged.

• One-to-Many Relationship

In a "one-to-many" relationship, against one record in the first table, there can be multiple records in the second table. In a "one-to-many" relationship, the table on the "many" side of the relationship is stored as a Foreign key and the Primary key of the table is on the "one" side of the relationship. The relationship between the "Department" and "Student" tables is the perfect example of a "one-to-many" relationship, since one department can have multiple students. In the "Student" table, many records can have one department.

- **Many-to-Many Relationships**

In "many-to-many" relationships, for one record in the first table, there can be multiple records in the second table; for one record in the second table, there can be multiple records in the first table. The relationship between the "Author" and "Book" tables is a good example of "many-to-many" relationships. A book can be written by multiple authors while an author can write multiple books. In most cases, "many-to-many" relationships are broken down into "one-to-many" relationships by creating an intermediate table that has "one-to-many" relationships with both the actual tables.

2-   Join Statements

Join statements are used to select column values from two or more tables which are linked with each other. For instance, take a scenario where you have to display the names of students along with the names of the departments to which they belong. However, there is no department name column in the "Student" table; it only contains the department ID, which serves as a Foreign key to Department. Therefore, we need some mechanism to select column values from multiple tables which are linked together. JOIN queries help us perform this function.

Before executing JOIN queries, run the following script in your query window.

Script 1
Create Database School

Use School
Go
CREATE TABLE Student
  (StudID int PRIMARY KEY NOT NULL,
   StudName varchar(50) NOT NULL,
   StudentAge int NULL,
   StudentGender varchar(10) NOT NULL,
        DepID int NULL)
CREATE TABLE Department
  (DepID int PRIMARY KEY NOT NULL,
   DepName varchar(50) NOT NULL,
        DepCapacity int NULL)
ALTER TABLE Student ADD CONSTRAINT StudDepRel
FOREIGN   KEY   (DepID)   references
Department(DepID)
INSERT INTO Department Values

(1, 'English', 100),
(2, 'Math', 80),
(3, 'History', 70),
(4, 'French', 90),
(5, 'Geography', 100),
(6, 'Drawing', 150),
(7, 'Architecture', 120)
INSERT INTO Student Values
(1, 'Alice', 21, 'Male', 2),
(2, 'Alfred', 20, 'Male', 3),
(3, 'Henry', 19, 'Male', 3),
(4, 'Jacobs', 22, 'Male', 5),
(5, 'Bob', 20, 'Male', 4),
(6, 'Shane', 22, 'Male', 4),
(7, 'Linda', 24, 'Female', 4),
(8, 'Stacy', 20, 'Female', 1),
(9, 'Wolfred', 21, 'Male', 2),
(10, 'Sandy', 25, 'Female', 1),
(11, 'Colin', 18, 'Male', 1),
(12, 'Maria', 19, 'Female', 3),
(13, 'Ziva', 20, 'Female', 5),
(14, 'Mark', 23, 'Male', 5),
(15, 'Fred', 25, 'Male', 2),
(16, 'Vic', 25, 'Male',null),
(17, 'Nick', 25, 'Male',null)

The above script will create a new database, School, with two tables, "Department" and "Student". A "one-to-many" relationship has been defined between the "Department" and

"Student" tables using following query:

ALTER TABLE Student ADD CONSTRAINT StudDepRel FOREIGN KEY (DepID) references Department(DepID)

The above query states that, in the Student column, a Foreign key constraint named "StudDepRel" (you can use any name) will be added, which sets the DepID column of the Student table as a Foreign key which references the DepID column of the Department table.

After you run Script 1, you should have "Department" and "Student" tables containing following data:

Department Table

DepID	DepName	DepCapacity
1	English	100
2	Math	80
3	History	70
4	French	90
5	Geography	100
6	Drawing	150
7	Architecture	120

Student Table

StudID	StudName	StudAge	StudGender	DepID
1	Alice	21	Male	2
2	Alfred	20	Male	3
3	Henry	19	Male	3
4	Jacobs	22	Male	5
5	Bob	20	Male	4
6	Shane	22	Male	4
7	Linda	24	Female	4
8	Stacy	20	Female	1
9	Wolfred	21	Male	2
10	Sandy	25	Female	1
11	Colin	18	Male	1
12	Maria	19	Female	3
13	Ziva	20	Female	5
14	Mark	23	Male	5
15	Fred	25	Male	2
16	Vic	25	Male	NULL
17	Nick	25	Male	NULL

- INNER JOIN

INNER JOIN (also called JOIN) retrieves data from the selected column from both tables if, and only if, there exists a common value in both tables in the column specified by the JOIN condition. For instance, to retrieve the names of students from the student column along with their department names from the department column, the following INNER JOIN query is used:

Query 1
SELECT Student.StudName, Department.DepName

From Student
Join Department
On Student.DepID = Department.DepID
The output of the above query is as follows:

StudName	DepName
Alice	Math
Alfred	History
Henry	History
Jacobs	Geography
Bob	French
Shane	French
Linda	French
Stacy	English
Wolfred	Math
Sandy	English
Colin	English
Maria	History
Ziva	Geography
Mark	Geography
Fred	Math

You can see only those records from the "Student" and "Department" tables have been retrieved where there was a common value in the DepID of the "Student" table and the DepID of the "Department" table. The last two records from the "Student" table have not been retrieved, since there is no corresponding DepID. Similarly, the last two records from the "Department" table have also not been retrieved, since they are not referenced by any of the records in the "Student" table.

- **LEFT JOIN**

LEFT JOIN retrieves all the records from the first table and only those records from the second table where a common value exists in both tables, as specified by the JOIN condition. For instance, the following query retrieves all the records from the "Student" table and only those records from the "Department" table where there is a corresponding DepID value in the "Student" table.

Query 2
SELECT Student.StudName, Department.DepName

From Student
Left Join Department
On Student.DepID = Department.DepID
The output of Query 2 is as follows:

StudName	DepName
Alice	Math
Alfred	History
Henry	History
Jacobs	Geography
Bob	French
Shane	French
Linda	French
Stacy	English
Wolfred	Math
Sandy	English
Colin	English
Maria	History
Ziva	Geography

Mark	Geography
Fred	Math
Vic	NULL
Nick	NULL

You can see that the last two students don't have any corresponding DepID, yet they have been retrieved.

- **RIGHT JOIN**

RIGHT JOIN retrieves all the records from the second table and only those records from the first table where a common value exists in both tables, as specified by the JOIN condition. For instance, the following query retrieves all the records from the "Department" table and only those records from the "Student" table where there is a corresponding DepID value in the "Department" table.

Query 3
SELECT Student.StudName, Department.DepName

From Student
Right Join Department
On Student.DepID = Department.DepID

StudName	DepName
Stacy	English
Sandy	English
Colin	English
Alice	Math
Wolfred	Math
Fred	Math
Alfred	History
Henry	History
Maria	History
Bob	French
Shane	French
Linda	French
Jacobs	Geography
Ziva	Geography
Mark	Geography
NULL	Drawing

NULL	Architecture

- **FULL JOIN**

FULL JOIN is the union of RIGHT JOIN and LEFT JOIN. FULL JOIN retrieves all records from both tables, whether or not a match is found between the Foreign key and Primary key of the linked table. Have a look at the following query:

Query 4
SELECT Student.StudName, Department.DepName

From Student
Full Join Department
On Student.DepID = Department.DepID
The output of the code in Query 4 is as follows:

StudName	DepName
Alice	Math
Alfred	History
Henry	History
Jacobs	Geography
Bob	French
Shane	French
Linda	French
Stacy	English
Wolfred	Math

Sandy	English
Colin	English
Maria	History
Ziva	Geography
Mark	Geography
Fred	Math
Vic	NULL
Nick	NULL
NULL	Drawing
NULL	Architecture

3-   Group By

The "Group By" statement allows us to group data based on results from some aggregate functions. For instance, if you want to display the name of each department along with the average age of the student from that department, you can use a "Group By" statement as follows:

Query 5
SELECT   Department.DepName,
AVG(Student.StudentAge) as AverageStudentAge

From Student
Right Join Department
On Student.DepID = Department.DepID
Group by DepName

The above query will calculate the average age of students belonging to each department and will display them against each department's name.

DepName	AverageStudentAge
Architecture	NULL
Drawing	NULL
English	21
French	22
Geography	21
History	19
Math	22

4-   HAVING

Since a "Where" clause cannot be used to filter data grouped by aggregate functions, the "Having" statement was introduced in the SQL. For instance, if you want to retrieve the names of only those departments where the average age of students is greater than 20, you can use a "Having" statement as follows:

Query 6
SELECT   Department.DepName, AVG(Student.StudentAge) as AverageStudentAge

 From Student
Right Join Department

On Student.DepID = Department.DepID
Group by DepName
Having AVG(Student.StudentAge) > 20
The result of Query 6 is as follows:

DepName	AverageStudentAge
English	21
French	22
Geography	21
Math	22

Exercise 8

Task:

For each department, display the department name and maximum age of students in that department if the age is between 21 and 24.

Solution

SELECT Department.DepName,
Max(Student.StudentAge) as Age
 From Student
Right Join Department
 On Student.DepID = Department.DepID
 Group by DepName
 Having Max(Student.StudentAge) Between 21 AND
24

11. Expressions

When operators, functions and values are used together in such a manner that the same can be evaluated to compute a value, this combination is referred to as an expression. You can visualize SQL expression as a mathematical formula that is written using the SQL syntax. In order to help you understand how a typical SQL expression looks like, let us take an example.

SELECT col1, col2, colN FROM t_name WHERE [exp];
In the given example, the expression is performing a SELECT operation and requests selection of columns 1 to N from the table 't_name'. The results corresponding to rows for which the given expression evaluates to true must be outputted. SQL supports three types of expressions, each of which has been discussed below.

Boolean Expressions

In case of boolean expressions, fetching of data is done after a single value is matched. The syntax for such expressions is as follows –

SELECT col1, col2, colN FROM t_name WHERE exp_matching_single_value;
This statement selects columns 1 to N from the table 't_name' and outputs the rows that satisfy the

condition specified by exp_matching_single_value. In order to gain better understanding of boolean expressions, let us take an example. Consider a table named CUSTOMERS. The SQL statement given below shall print all the records available in the CUSTOMERS table.

SELECT * FROM CUSTOMERS;
The output will typically look like –

ID	Name	Age	Salary
98701	Rohan	45	50000.00
98675	Amit	32	37000.00
98706	Shayla	22	12000.00
98718	Mathews	37	41000.00

The following SQL statement is the simplest example of a boolean expression.

SELECT * FROM CUSTOMERS WHERE Salary=37000;
The execution of this query will return the following.

ID	Name	Age	Salary
98675	Amit	32	37000.00

Numeric Expression

Expressions that are of the numeric type are typically used to perform mathematical operations in a SQL statement. Syntax for numeric expressions is as follows –

SELECT formula_arith as Op_Name [FROM t_name WHERE cond];
Here formula_arith is any mathematical formula that can be specified to perform an arithmetic operation in the SQL query. Besides this, t_name is the name of the table and cond is the condition of the WHERE clause. A simple example to demonstrate the working of numeric expressions is given below –

SELECT (100+76) AS ADD;
Execution of this query shall give the result 176. Many other SQL functions like sum(), avg() and count, in addition to many others, may be used as formula_arith to perform data calculations against the values selected from the columns of the table concerned. For example, the SQL statement given below shall count the number of entries in the CUSTOMERS table.

SELECT count(*) FROM CUSTOMERS;
Execution of this query will return the value 4.

Date Expressions

Such expressions are typically used to get information about the current date or time on the system. Functions like GETDATE() or CURRENT_TIMESTAMP may be used in the SQL query to get the desired results. Sample statements for their usage have been given below –

SELECT CURRENT_TIMESTAMP;
SELECT GETDATE();

12. Sequences & Injection

Make sure you've understood the rest of this book before moving onto this chapter. In it we will be discussing some of the most complex elements of SQL, such as increments, and injections. If you're having trouble with this chapter, don't worry too much, it's the most difficult, and effort-intensive part of the book. Without further ado, let's dive in!

Increments

Increments are possible in SQL. For the uninitiated, to increment a value means to increase it by a given number. Usually, this number is one, and usually, the value is an integer.

SQL's AUTO-INCREMENT function allows you to automatically increase a number by one every time it is invoked. Now, this may seem a bit foreign at first. That's why we'll give you a general example of how the SQL AUTO INCREMENT function is generally used.

CREATE TABLE Table1

(

ID int NOT NULL AUTO_INCREMENT,

Name varchar(200) NOT NULL,

Title varchar(200),

Location varchar(200),

Country varchar(255),

PRIMARY KEY (ID)

)

This is an excellent example of how SQL performs increments. When it comes to dialects like MySQL, replacements like AUTO_INCREMENT also exist. According to default, the starting value, if left undeclared, will be presumed to be 1, and will be incremented by 1 every time the loop is run.

If 1 is not the desired value you want to start with, use the following syntax:

ALTER TABLE Table1 AUTO_INCREMENT=X

Where X is the number you want to increment by. If you're trying to start a new data point in say, table 1, then you won't need to specify for every value.

For example, let's suppose Table 1 contains some sort of people, with a name and the title. Take a gander at this SQL snippet:

INSERT INTO Students (Name,Title)

VALUES ('Ilija','Mr')

This statement will make a brand new data point in the table table1, and will insert a person named Ilija with the prefix Mr. Naturally, these columns will be changed to reflect this.

Renumbering and Starting At A Value

Now, this was addressed in a minor way previously, however, there are multiple ways to start the numbering at a certain value, and increment by a larger, or lower number as you see fit.

This can be quite useful, for example, when you're grading students, you only need different scores in increments of say 10 points, so you could easily write a program that auto-fills every student into a grade by their scores.

In general, this is one of the easier features of SQL to learn. This is the syntax for incrementing at a larger starting value, and with a number N:

CREATE TABLE Table1

(

ID int 10 AUTO_INCREMENT,

Name varchar(200) NOT NULL,

Title varchar(200),

Location varchar(200),

Country varchar(255),

PRIMARY KEY (ID)

)

ALTER TABLE Table1 AUTO_INCREMENT=N

Easy isn't it? Great! Now move on and give your own attempts a try, let your imagination run wild on it.

Stopping SQL Injection

Now, SQL injection is one of the most common mistakes beginner SQL developers make. We'll try to teach you how to prevent this security issue from happening to you in this section, although these are the basics and you could easily write another whole book purely on this subject.

Generally, injection will happen when you take user input through a webpage. After this is inserted into the SQL database, there is a variety of things that can happen. Heck, you might accidentally get an SQL statement that will straight-up run through your database.

This means it's extremely easy to insert a virus through your webpage, as they might give you an SQL command instead of say, their name, or their order. When this happens, it can have disastrous consequences. This is generally restricted by limiting what your users can input. For example, the following script limits the number of characters that can be used for ordering to being between 6 and 40.

```
if (found_match("/^\w{4,40}$/", $_GET['order'],
$matches)) {

   $result = mysql_query("SELECT * FROM BUYS

      WHERE name = $matches[false]");
} else {

   echo " You have entered an invalid order";

}
```

If you're wondering how exactly people can do this, let's presume a user gives this input:

```
$name= "A"; DELETE FROM BUYS;
```

```
mysql_query( "SELECT FROM BUYS WHERE
order='{$order}')
```

Now this, when processed, will run the query that was inserted in the 'order' field. This query, as you can see, will straight-up delete every order you have. Imagine a business having to recover from all of their orders being entirely lost? That's right, they don't like that very much, and their SQL dev is probably getting fired.

With that being said, most modern SQL derivatives like MySQL don't allow you to stack SQL functions. This is good because it leads to failure if the user tries to do something like that.

One of the few saving graces of MySQL, is that it will ban every myql_query() call that is stacked within another one. This helps save you from SQL injections.

Other PHP-based database extensions aren't quite so kind. SQLite for example, will happily let your users stack their queries, and execute everything told to them. This is part of the reason why they are generally not used by large companies.

13. Creating Databases and Definition Table Relationships

In this book we will follow a step by step approach to explain different SQL concepts. We shall start with Entity Relationship Diagram (ERD) which serves as blue print for the database. ERD defines database scheme. We will then create our database according to that scheme. The next step will be to add some data in the database. Once we have a database with some data in it we are good to experiment with it. So let's start with ERD.

Entity Relationship Diagram (ERD)

ERD is the graphical representation of database scheme. ERD contains tables in the database, the columns within those tables and relationships between the tables.

The database that we are going to develop in this book is a Hospital database. It will contain six tables: Patients, Treatment, Doctors Examinations, Patient_Examination and Patient_Visits. Figure 2.1 contains ERD for the hospital database.

The Hospital database ERD contains all the tables in the hospital database along with their relationship.

These relationships will be explained later in this chapter.

Creating a Database

We have an ERD, now we must actually create our database as defined by ERD. Let's execute our first query of the book. This query will create database on the database server.

CREATE DATABASE Hospital;

The syntax of CREATE database query is very simple, you have to use the keyword CREATE DATABASE followed by the name of the database. You can give any name to your database.

Note:

It is also important to mention here that SQL is case insensitive. It is also worth mentioning that we are using MS SQL Server 2017 as our DBMS in this book. You can use any other relational database system such as MySQL, SQL Lite etc. The core SQL is similar for all the databases with only slight variations.

You could write the above query as follows:

Create database Hospital;

There will be no difference.

Deleting a Database

To delete existing database we use DROP DATABASE query. For instance if you want to delete Hospital database that we created, execute the following query:

DROP DATABASE Hospital;

Before moving forward, recreate the Hospital database if you have deleted it, since in the next section we are going to create tables within the Hospital database.

Creating a Table

We have created Hospital database but it is empty at the moment. There is no data in the database. Databases store data in tables. Therefore the first step after creating database is to create tables.

As a rule of thumb, create all the independent tables first and then the dependent tables. A table is independent if does not contain any foreign key and vice versa. The relationships between the tables define dependency and independency of tables.

If we look at the ERD Patients, Doctors and Examinations tables are independent table because they do not contain any foreign key. Therefore we will create these tables first. The syntax for creating a table is as follows:

CREATE TABLE table_name

(

Colum1_name data_type constraints,
Colum2_name data_type constraints,
)
Now let's create Patients table using this syntax. Execute the following query on your database server to create Patient table.

USE Hospital;

CREATE Table Patients

(

Id int IDENTITY (1,1) PRIMARY KEY NOT NULL,
name VARCHAR (50) NOT NULL,
age int NOT NULL,
gender VARCHAR (50) NOT NULL,
blood_group VARCHAR (50),
phone BIGINT
);
The first line in the above query is USE Hospital. The USE command is used to specify the database in which you are creating your database. We are creating Patients table inside the Hospital database, therefore mentioned it via USE command.

Look how we defined columns inside the Patients table. To define a column we start with the column name, followed by the type of the data stored by the column and the constraints upon the key column. For instance the first column inside the Patients is the 'id' column. The third part of the column definition is the constraint specifications. A constraint implements certain rules on table columns. The id column has three constraints:

- IDENTITY: THAT DATA WILL BE AUTOMATICALLY ADDED TO THIS COLUMN STARTING FROM ONE AND IT WILL BE INCREMENTED BY 1 FOR EACH NEW RECORD.
- PRIMARY KEY: SPECIFIES THAT THIS COLUMN IS THE PRIMARY KEY COLUMN?

- NOT NULL: Column cannot hold null values

Notice that the columns in the Patients table corresponds to those defined for the Patient table in the ERD.

Similarly create Doctors and Examinations tables using following queries:

USE Hospital

CREATE Table Doctors

(

```
Id int IDENTITY (1,1) PRIMARY KEY NOT NULL,
name VARCHAR (50) NOT NULL,
designition VARCHAR (50),
specialization VARCHAR (50),


);
USE Hospital
CREATE Table Examinations


(

id int IDENTITY (1,1) PRIMARY KEY NOT NULL,
name VARCHAR (50) NOT NULL,
price int NOT NULL,
);
```

We have created all the three independent tables. The next step is to create dependent tables i.e. Patient_Examination, Treatments and Patient_Visits table. These tables are bound in a relationship to the Patients table. Before creating these tables, let us first study the type of relationships that database tables can have.

Table Relationships

There are three major types of relationships between tables in a relational database:

- One to One Relation

- One to Many Relation
- Many to Many Relation

One to One Relation

In a one to one relation, for a record in the first table, there can be one and only one record in the related or dependent table. A simple example of one to relation is the relation between patient and his contact info. A patient can have one contact info, while particular contact info belongs to one patient. One to one relations are avoided in most of the cases and the tables participating in one to one relation are merged together. For instance you can have patient info e.g. name, last name, date of birth and contact info e.g. phone, address, email in a single table.

One to Many Relation

In one to many relation, each record in the first table can be referenced by multiple records in the second table. For instance in our Hospital database, Patients and Patient_Visits tables have one to many relationships with each other. For each record in the Patients table, there can be multiple records in the Patient_Visits table. In simple terms, a patient can have multiple visits to a hospital; however one visit belongs to only belongs to one Person.

To implement one to many relation in the database, we have to add a foreign key in the table that is on the "many" side of the relationship. This foreign key references the primary key of the table that is on the "one" side of the relationship. In the case of Patients and Patient_Visits tables, the latter will have a foreign key column that references the primary key of the former table. Let's implement it using a query.

USE Hospital

```
CREATE Table Patient_Visits (
id int IDENTITY(1,1) PRIMARY KEY NOT NULL,
patient_id int FOREIGN KEY REFERENCES
Patients(id),
visit_time DATETIME NOT NULL
);
```

The above script creates Patient_Visits table in the Hospital database. It also implements one to many relation between Patient and Patient_Visits table. Take a look at the following line of code from the above script:

```
patient_id int FOREIGN KEY REFERENCES
Patients(id),
```

This creates a foreign key column patient_id in the Patient_Visits table. This column references the id column of the Patients table. This is how we actually implement one to many relationships in the database.

Many to Many Relation

In many to many relation, each record in the first table can be referenced by multiple records in the second table. Similarly each record in the second table can be referenced by multiple records in the first table. For instance one patient can have multiple examinations; similarly one examination can be undertaken by multiple patients. In other words, for each record in the Patients table, there can be multiple records in the Patient_Examination table and vice versa.

Many to many relations are usually broken down into two one to many relations using a junction table. Both the tables involved in the many to many relation have one to many relation with the junction table. Junction table has foreign keys from all the tables involved in many to many relation. In the ERD for Hospital table we have defined Patient_Examination table as junction table to implement one to many relation between Patients and Examinations table. This Patient_Examination table will have two foreign keys: One that references the primary key column of the Patients table and the other that references the primary key column of the Examinations table. The following script creates Patient_Examination table in the hospital database.

CREATE Table Patient_Examination(

id int IDENTITY(1,1) PRIMARY KEY NOT NULL,
patient_id int FOREIGN KEY REFERENCES
Patients(id),
examination_id int FOREIGN KEY REFERENCES
Examinations(id),
result VARCHAR(50)

);

Similarly Patients and Doctors also have one to many relation between them since a patient can be treated by many doctors and one doctor can treat many doctors. Here Treatments table is the junction table that implements the relation between Patient and Doctors table. The script for creating Treatments table is as follows:

CREATE Table Treatment(

id int IDENTITY(1,1) PRIMARY KEY NOT NULL,
patient_id int FOREIGN KEY REFERENCES
Patients(id),
doctor_id int FOREIGN KEY REFERENCES Doctors(id),
remarks VARCHAR(50)
);

14. Filtering with Operators, Sorting with ORDER BY

In this chapter we are going to see, how we can filter data using different types of SQL operators in conjunction with the WHERE clause.

SQL Operators

There are four major types of operators in SQL:

- Comparison Operators
- Conjunctive Operators
- Logical Operators
- Negation Operators

The WHERE Clause

Before studying SQL operators in detail, first we need to understand WHERE clause. The WHERE clause filters records based on the operator used in the query. The syntax of WHERE clause is simple. Let's see a simple example of WHERE clause. This query filters all those patient records where id is greater than 5.

SELECT * FROM Patients

 WHERE id > 5

The output of the above query is as follows:

name	age	gender	blood_group	phone
Julie	26	Female	A+	12478963
Frank	35	Male	A-	85473216
Alex	21	Male	AB-	46971235
Hales	54	Male	B+	74698125
Elice	32	Female	O+	34169872

Now, let's study each SQL Operator in detail.

Comparison Operators

SQL comparison operators can be further divided into six types. These operators filter records by comparing values of the operands.

- EQUALITY (=)
- NON-EQUALITY (<>)
- LESS THAN VALUES (<)
- GREATER THAN VALUES (>)
- LESS THAN EQUAL TO (<=)

- Greater than equal to(>=)

The working principle of each of these operators has been demonstrated by examples. Take a look at them.

Equality Operator (=)

SELECT * FROM Patients

 WHERE name = 'Frank'

The above query returns record of the patient named 'Frank'.

Non-Equality (!=)

SELECT * FROM Patients

WHERE name != 'Frank'

The above query returns records of all the patients except the one named 'Frank'.

Less Than (<)

UPDATE Examinations

*SET price = price * 1.1*

 WHERE price < 250

The above query updates the price column of those records in the Examinations table where price is less than 250.

Greater Than (>)

SELECT * FROM Patients

 WHERE id > 5

Less than Equal To (<=)

SELECT * FROM Patients

 WHERE age <= 30

The above query selects all the records from Patients table where age is less than or equal to 30. The output of the above query will look like this:

id	name	age	gender	blood_group	phone
1	Tom	20	Male	O+	123589746
3	James	16	Male	O-	78452369
5	Sal	24	Male	O+	48963214
6	Julie	26	Female	A+	12478963
8	Alex	21	Male	AB-	46971235

Greater than Equal To (>=)

SELECT * FROM Patients

 WHERE age >= 30

The above query selects all the records from Patients table where age is greater than or equal to 30. The output of the above query will look like this:

id	name	age	gender	blood_group	phone
2	Kimer	45	Female	AB+	45686412

4	Matty	43	Female	B+	15789634
7	Frank	35	Male	A-	85473216
9	Hales	54	Male	B+	74698125
10	Elice	32	Female	O+	34169872

Conjunctive Operators

In the previous examples we used only one operator to filter data. If we want to filter records that satisfy multiple conditions, we can use Conjunctive operators. There are two commonly used conjunctive operators in SQL.

- AND

- OR

Let's see both of them in action:

AND

SELECT * FROM Patients

 WHERE age > 30 AND gender = 'Female'

The above query will retrieve records of all the patients with age greater than 30 and gender Female. The output of the above query will look like this:

id	name	age	gender	blood_group	phone

2	Kimer	45	Female	AB+	45686412
4	Matty	43	Female	B+	15789634
10	Elice	32	Female	O+	34169872

OR

SELECT * FROM Patients

 WHERE age > 30 OR gender = 'Female'
This query will select records of all patients with either age greater than 30 or gender Female. The output of the above query will be:

id	name	age	gender	blood_group	phone
2	Kimer	45	Female	AB+	45686412
4	Matty	43	Female	B+	15789634
6	Julie	26	Female	A+	12478963
7	Frank	35	Male	A-	85473216
9	Hales	54	Male	B+	74698125
10	Elice	32	Female	O+	34169872

Logical Operators

Following are the most commonly used logical operators in SQL:

- IN
- BETWEEN
- LIKE
- DISTINCT

- IS NULL

IN

The IN operator is used to filter records based on the values specified in the IN operator. The IN operator takes comma separated values inside parenthesis as input. For instance if you want to retrieve records of all the patients whose blood group is O+ or O-, you can use IN operator as follows:

SELECT * FROM Patients

 WHERE blood_groupIN('O+','O-')

The output of the above query will be records of all the patients with blood group O+ or O- as shown below:

id	name	age	gender	blood_group	phone
1	Tom	20	Male	O+	123589746
3	James	16	Male	O-	78452369
5	Sal	24	Male	O+	48963214
10	Elice	32	Female	O+	34169872

BETWEEN

BETWEEN operators filter records that falls between specified ranges. The range is specified using AND operator. For instance if you want to retrieve records of all the patients with id between 3 and 7, you can use BETWEEN operator as follows:

SELECT * FROM Patients

 WHERE id BETWEEN 3 AND 7
The output of the above query will look be:

id	name	age	gender	blood_group	phone
3	James	16	Male	O-	78452369
4	Matty	43	Female	B+	15789634

5	Sal	24	Male	O+	48963214
6	Julie	26	Female	A+	12478963
7	Frank	35	Male	A-	85473216

LIKE

Like operator fetches records based on string matching. For instance if you want to select records of all patients whose name starts with 'J', you can use LIKE operator. The LIKE operator uses two wild cards for string matching. They are denoted by a percentage sign (%) and underscore sign (_). The % wild card specifies any number of characters whereas _ specifies only one character. So, if you want to fetch records of all the patients where name starts with J, you can use like operator as follows:

SELECT * FROM Patients

 WHERE name LIKE('J%')

Here you can see we use % wild card. Here 'J%' means that the name should start with J and after that there can be any number of characters. The output of this query will be:

id	name	age	gender	blood_group	phone
3	James	16	Male	O-	78452369
6	Julie	26	Female	A+	12478963

Similarly, if you want to select all the records where 'a' is the second character in the name, you can use '_' wildcard as follows:

SELECT * FROM Patients

 WHERE name LIKE('_a%')

Here '_a%' specifies that there can be one and only one character before character 'a' and after that there can be any number of characters. The output of this query will look like this:

id	name	age	gender	blood_group	phone
3	James	16	Male	O-	78452369
4	Matty	43	Female	B+	15789634
5	Sal	24	Male	O+	48963214
9	Hales	54	Male	B+	74698125

You can see, all the names have character 'a' in the second place.

DISTINCT

The DISTINCT selects only the distinct values from the specified column. For instance if you want to retrieve distinct patient ids from Patient_Examination table, you use DISTINCT operator as follows:

SELECT DISTINCT patient_id from Patient_Examination

IS NULL

IS NULL operator is used to retrieve those records where value for a particular column is NULL. A NULL value is used when we don't specify any value for the column. For instance if we want to retrieve records of all the patients where phone number is NULL, we can use following query:

SELECT * FROM Patients

 WHERE phone IS NULL
The above query will not retrieve any record, since there is no record in the Patients table where phone is NULL.

NEGATION Operators

Negation operators reverse the value of the operators used in conjunction with it. Following are the most commonly used negation operators in SQL.

- NOT NULL
- NOT IN
- NOT BETWEEN
- NOT LIKE

Let's see each of these negation operators in action.

NOT NULL

The NOT NULL operator fetches records where the column specified in the WHERE clause has no NULL values. The following query retrieves records of those patients whose phone is not NULL.

SELECT * FROM Patients

 WHERE phone IS NOT NULL
You will see all the records from the Patients table in the output since no record has NULL value in its phone column.

NOT IN

The NOT IN operator reverses the output of the IN operator. For instance if you want to retrieve records of all the patients except those with blood group O+ and O-, you can use NOT IN operator as follows:

SELECT * FROM Patients

 WHERE blood_group NOT IN('O+', 'O-')
The output will look like this:

id	name	age	gender	blood_group	phone
2	Kimer	45	Female	AB+	45686412
4	Matty	43	Female	B+	15789634
6	Julie	26	Female	A+	12478963
7	Frank	35	Male	A-	85473216
8	Alex	21	Male	AB-	46971235
9	Hales	54	Male	B+	74698125

NOT BETWEEN

Similarly NOT BETWEEN operators retrieverecords that do not fall between specified ranges. To retrieve records from the Patients table where id is not between 3 and 7, you can use NOT BETWEEN operator as follows:

SELECT * FROM Patients

WHERE id NOT BETWEEN 3 and 7
The output of the above query will be:

id	name	age	gender	blood_group	phone
1	Tom	20	Male	O+	123589746
2	Kimer	45	Female	AB+	45686412
8	Alex	21	Male	AB-	46971235
9	Hales	54	Male	B+	74698125
10	Elice	32	Female	O+	34169872

NOT LIKE

Finally, the NOT LIKE operator retrieves those records that do not satisfy the criteria set by the LIKE operator. For example, the following query retrieves records of all the patients who do not have 'a' as second character in their names.

SELECT * FROM Patients

WHERE name NOT LIKE('_a%')
The above query will retrieve following records.

id	name	age	gender	blood_group	phone
1	Tom	20	Male	O+	123589746
2	Kimer	45	Female	AB+	45686412
6	Julie	26	Female	A+	12478963
7	Frank	35	Male	A-	85473216
8	Alex	21	Male	AB-	46971235
10	Elice	32	Female	O+	34169872

ORDER BY Clause

By default the data is retrieved in the order in which it was inserted. However you can sort the data according to some order. For instance you can sort the data by age, or alphabetically and so on. The ORDER BY clause is used for ordering data. Let's take a simple example of ORDER BY clause where data is sorted by age.

SELECT * FROM Patients

ORDER BY age

In the output you will see that the records will be arranged by the ascending order of age. The output will look like this:

id	name	age	gender	blood_group	phone
3	James	16	Male	O-	78452369
1	Tom	20	Male	O+	123589746
8	Alex	21	Male	AB-	46971235
5	Sal	24	Male	O+	48963214
6	Julie	26	Female	A+	12478963
10	Elice	32	Female	O+	34169872
7	Frank	35	Male	A-	85473216
4	Matty	43	Female	B+	15789634
2	Kimer	45	Female	AB+	45686412
9	Hales	54	Male	B+	74698125

By default the data is arranged in the ascending order if the sorted column is integer and in alphabetical order if the sorting is implemented via string column. However, you can reverse the output of default sorting by adding DESC after the ORDER BY clause.

The following query retrieves records from the Patients table in reverse alphabetical order.

SELECT * FROM Patients

ORDER BY name ASC

id	name	age	gender	blood_ group	phone
8	Alex	21	Male	AB-	46971235
10	Elice	32	Female	O+	34169872
7	Frank	35	Male	A-	85473216
9	Hales	54	Male	B+	74698125
3	James	16	Male	O-	78452369
6	Julie	26	Female	A+	12478963

2	Kimer	45	Female	AB+	45686412
4	Matty	43	Female	B+	15789634
5	Sal	24	Male	O+	48963214
1	Tom	20	Male	O+	123589746

In this chapter we studied how we can filter records based on conditions. We also studied how to implement these conditions using operators and WHERE clause. Finally we covered how we can sort data in ascending and descending order using ORDER BY clause.

Conclusion

Well, we've come to the end. I hope you started this book as a somewhat intermediate-advanced user of SQL, and left, if not a better SQL developer, a better programmer.

If there was one takeaway I want you to have from this book, that is "SQL is a declarative language." It's been repeated throughout this book countless times, and yet still not enough.

Besides that, remember the importance of practice. It won't matter if you're an SQL prodigy if you don't put in the hours. Becoming a master at anything will take a huge amount of time, be it sewing or becoming an advanced web developer. Pour in the hours, and SQL's vast depths will reward you.

It's important to put in the necessary reps into theory before moving on to more complex practices.

In this book, we've also looked over the various prospects of SQL as a career path. Remember that if you find yourself not wanting to completely dedicate your life to becoming a web dev, that is not the end, nor have you wasted your time.

Your time learning SQL will have taught you a valuable skill which can be put to practice in a variety of jobs and positions, and most importantly, it taught you how to think. It's easy to underestimate the amount of impact that learning something complex like SQL can have on someone's thought process.

It's also very important to remember to exercise your brain properly. This is because not sleeping enough lets your brain cells deteriorate.

A balanced, healthy diet is also very important. Eating a lot of fish and seafood has proven benefits for the brain.

In the end, the most important thing to remember here is that almost everything is connected. The ability to exercise is as intimately connected to SQL as learning what a JOIN is.

If some parts of this book have been confusing, don't fret. That's a part of every programmer's learning curve. You can't just get out of bed one day and be a professional programmer working at Microsoft.

Try using the internet to help you out; online portals like Stack Overflow and similar have much more information than a single book ever could. Keep in mind not to use too many solutions from there, as it's quite a lazy practice and can mess you up professionally later. This is because the skill you'll be learning is not "Coding in SQL" it is "coding in Stack Overflow" and well, let's just say this book isn't about the latter.

Remember that these portals are resources, not all of your knowledge. This is another reason why you should learn the theoretical foundations behind SQL. The answers you find elsewhere won't mean much to you unless you have the necessary theoretical foundations to understand them fully.

For a second, I want to turn your eyes towards debugging. Yes, the most annoying part of coding, and yet so vital.

Debugging is actually one of the most marketable parts of coding, because to your boss, you'll seem like the guy that got what he asked for done, even if someone else wrote the code.

When it comes to debugging, look for common rookie mistakes. Missed calls, missed semicolons, improper joins and similar issues riddle the code of even seasoned professionals.

It's far too common for even seasoned developers to forget their reason for learning to code. Keeping that reason in mind is vital for pretty much every programmer's success. Similar to bodybuilders, if you lose sight of your reason, you might as well have lost sight of everything that made you an SQL developer.

When it comes to learning advanced programming techniques, this is doubly so. You will fail routinely. Chances are, you've failed multiple examples in this book, and yet you got up. It is that endurance, that drive to get up after failure that separates the mediocre developers from the cream of the crop.

If you simply want bragging rights, put that bragging in front of yourself and tunnel to it. Don't let anyone tell you that you can't, don't let them stop you.

If what you want is money, chase that cash. The worst thing that can happen to a developer is not forgetting all of their programming language know-how, but falling into decadence and forgetting why they're doing it in the first place.

It's natural to write buggy code, it's natural to want to fight the computer every time you try running your script. Instead of getting hung up on it, learn to improve.

Soon, you'll be running error-free, smooth scripts at your dream job. There's no limit to the vertical mobility a good developer can have. Even when the frustration and hopelessness feel almost unbearable, remind yourself of the feeling you get when your code finally runs. There are few better feelings in this world than your code working right the first time you run it.

With that said, it's always important to keep in mind the career prospects of SQL development. You will never have the risk of unemployment for long. With most other jobs, their employment rate grows at sub 10%, but in the US, programming jobs easily eclipse that by twice or more. This means that there'll always be companies looking for you, and that is an excellent feeling.

Heck, you can even go freelance! Rid yourself of the shackles presented to you by the corporate world and become your own boss. Find your own clients, run your own SQL-automated marketing campaigns. Don't let anything stop you until you're a true star developer.

If you need some encouragement, simply look at some freelancing sites like UpWork, look at who's making the most money there? Marketers and web developers. An excellent web developer can easily charge $100 an hour and always be booked out. And I don't mean "making ends meet". I mean, if they wanted to, they could work at 20 grand a month. Yes, 200,000 USD a year, or even more, is achievable from being a freelance developer.

This is not even counting the possibility of being employed at one of the best companies in the world. Google and Microsoft are always looking for competent, seasoned developers to join their ranks.

Because of all this professional viability, many people are electing to enter the world of web development. You, as an advanced reader, are a step in front of the rest, but if you want to stay competitive, you can't let them catch up.

You need to be constantly improving yourself, constantly working on your knowledge, expanding the areas you're an expert on.

While it may seem odd to recommend in a book about SQL, do learn some other languages. Pure SQL can be powerful, but it is a true beast when coupled with a good object-oriented language, in the hands of a competent programmer.

Don't shy away from markup languages like HTML and CSS either, they're really easy to learn and can boost your employability significantly.

Even if you don't end up going into programming, your knowledge of SQL will come in handy. For example, if you become a writer, you can make your own website, or as an artist, your own online portfolio. If you end up as a manager, you'll know how to speak to the web development team much better than anyone else there, ensuring you an easy promotion.

Learning advanced SQL is merely step one; you'll have to keep up with this pace for the rest of your professional career if you want to stay at the top.

Most importantly, remember to take breaks and relax. Don't tire yourself too much and end up burning out. This is what happens to many promising developers.

Keep working on what you enjoy, you should always have at least one passion project besides your job. It will help keep your love for programming and SQL alive.

So, to recoup everything said:

- Practice a lot, there's never enough hours put in.

- Keep yourself healthy, it helps your brain stay sharp.

- Always have a passion project to keep your interest high.

- Never stop improving.

- Learn a few other languages to complement your SQL knowledge.

- You can always switch careers easily, and freelancing is a very promising avenue if you're good enough.

And above all else, *make sure you love what you're doing* and don't burn out!

PYTHON FOR BEGINNERS

THE ULTIMATE GUIDE TO LEARN PYTHON, THE SECRETS OF MACHINE LANGUAGE LEARNING, DATA SCIENCE ANALYSIS AND DATA ANALYTICS, CODING LANGUAGE FOR BEGINNERS.

Introduction

Python - a language named after Monty Python. A programming language that has taken the world by storm. The applications we have seen so far, the examples we have discovered, and the future prospects of the language, when combined, point out one thing for sure. If you are a programmer, Python is your ticket to the future.

When learning a new language, there will always be challenges. There will be times where you might even be frustrated and call it a day. The thing to remember here is this: many others have gone through this road just like you. Some have gone on to become successful while others have remained within the shadow of someone else. It is up to you to grab the opportunity and become a programmer that is unique and different, and learning Python is just a part of the journey. Through Python, you will be able to do so much more than just design 2D snake games.

Python has paved the way for many success stories and has certainly become the most popular language. Now you know why! It is time for you to add Python to your resume and deliver results in the most effective and efficient manner possible. Good luck and have a great programming journey ahead!

Before we look into Python, let's talk about the alternatives we can use for programming.

The C Family

UNIX is arguably the first operating system that was widely used across different computer systems. AT&T Bell Laboratories developed the operating system for minicomputers in the late 1960s based upon a language that we now call the C language. AT&T forced companies using Bell systems to use UNIX which meant UNIX was ported to various different computer systems along with the C language. Because the C language became so common, many languages that were developed later provided a similar coding environment to make it easier for C language programmers to use them.

The list of C-family programming languages is a long one, but some became more famous than others. C, C++ and C# are the three most popular, closely followed by Objective C.

Advantages

• As of October 2019, C is the most widely used language family after Java and Python. Embedded systems and operating systems still depend heavily on C language

- Every programmer should learn at least one of the C, C++ or C# languages to understand what happens in the background during program execution

Disadvantages

- It is difficult to learn as it forces programmer to focus on things that modern programming languages take care of automatically

- The syntax, although it inspired a lot of other languages, is very ugly.

- A lot of extraneous lines of codes are required to even perform the most basic tasks.

Java Platform

Thanks to the millions of web applications developed using the language, Java is possibly the most widely used programming language in the world. Released as a core component of the Java platform in 1995 by Sun Microsystems, it enabled applications built using Java to run on any computer system that has Java Virtual Machine (JVM). Although it has a syntax similar to C and C++ languages, it doesn't demand low-level considerations from the programmers. Oracle has acquired Sun Microsystems and now manages Java platform.

For years, Microsoft's C# and Sun's Java remained in a cold war, each trying to outdo the other programming language. Both languages were heavily criticized for adding new features just to win a competition instead of following a standard direction. It was not until 2004 that both languages took to separate ways and developed into the unique languages as we know them today.

Even then, Java remains the top programming language in the world and Java platform runs on almost every laptop, game console, data center, and even supercomputers.

Advantages

• Java frees the programmer from computer dependencies and offers a vast degree of freedom

• Java is compatible with almost all computer systems. It means almost every program created using Java language will run on all those systems without any issues.

Disadvantages

• There have been serious security issues with Java over the years. Severe security vulnerabilities were found in the last Java version and Oracle advised every Java user to update to the latest version.

- Java programs are known to be slower than the competition even though there have been huge performance improvements in recent versions.

- For a long time Java remained a proprietary platform. Even after Sun previously declared it open-source, a long copyright battle ensued between Oracle and Google over the use of Java in Google's Android.

Python is Different

We have briefly discussed the best options we have if we don't want to use Python. They are great options but before you jump ship, let me tell you why I chose Python over others.

- Python is one of the easiest high-level programming languages to learn. It means the time it takes from setup to coding programs is very short.

- Code written in Python is easier to understand. It enables programmers to consult codes written by other programmers to adapt for their project.

- Python is an interpreter language. Code is executed one line at a time which makes debugging easier for beginners.

- Python code can run on any computer no matter if it's Windows, Linux, UNIS, or a macOS based system.

- Python has a vast standard library that provides methods for unique project requirements.

- Python supports various coding paradigms including Object Oriented Programming (OOP) and functional programming.

- Python programming language is free and open source. This has helped create an active programmer community and detailed tutorials are available for free on the Internet.

- The open source nature of the language has also enabled many programmers to extend Python capabilities by writing special libraries. These libraries are available on the Internet free of charge for everyone's use.

- It's very easy to create Graphical User Interface (GUI) through Python.

- One of the biggest advantages of Python is its ability to integrate with different programming languages. You can import a specific library and start coding in a completely different language and Python will understand the codes. Python supports extended integration with C++ and Java. Not only that, Python code can be placed inside a code written with another programming language.

These are the general advantages of Python over other programming languages. Depending upon your project, Python might be able to provide even more benefits. We are going to see how Python makes data analysis easy.

Advantages of Using Python in Data Analysis

Strong with Strings

Python has a special place for strings. There are multiple string related operations supported by Python. These operations are a big help in data analysis stages of parsing and processing if you are dealing with string data.

Dedicated Libraries

There are dedicated libraries in Python that help make data analysis projects easier to handle. The libraries are regularly updated which means they are compatible with the latest analysis algorithms.

Some of the popular data analysis libraries available on Python are:

1. NumPy: Collection of mathematical functions for fast calculations

2. SciPy: Offers advanced scientific tools

3. Pandas: Offers robust handling of mathematical components using data structures

4. Matplotlib: Offers data visualization methods including line plots, bar charts, and scatter plots.

Highly Scalable

Python is very efficient in handling large and complex datasets. This quality has made this programming language invaluable to companies like YouTube, Facebook, and Amazon that deal with huge data on a consistent basis.

Fast Deployment

With a simple coding syntax and straightforward development process, it's definitely faster to create and deploy applications using Python as compared to other languages.

If you look at the larger picture, Python provides the easiest yet most robust coding environment. It's faster to learn and deploy applications. It integrates well with other programming languages and technologies. There are tons of free tutorials and documentations available online for help if you are not able to resolve an issue.

All of the above qualities make Python the best package when it comes to programming languages. Yes, you might find that another programming language suits your needs better for a specific application, for example, for web applications JavaScript is more popular, and for database, SQL is used more. But, as a whole, Python offers you everything you need for 90% of the programming tasks.

Knowing all this, do you still think I made a mistake sticking with Python? Personally, I think it was a great decision. I told my friend all these points and he was amazed by how versatile Python is. Whenever I meet someone who asks me where they should start with programming, I recommend they start with Python.

Data analysis is a multistage process. Python supports exceptional methods and procedures in every stage of the data analysis process. There are external libraries that further extend the capabilities of Python for a specific application. It makes Python well-suited for data analysis as well as many other general applications.

1. Python Variables

If you plan to write complex code, then you must include data that will change the execution of the program.

That is what you are going to learn in this chapter. At the end of the chapter, you will learn how the abstract object term can explain each section of data in Python and you will learn how to change objects with the help of variables.

Variables in Python programming are the data types in Python as the name implies. In the programming world, variables are memory location where you store a value. The value that you store might change in the future depending on the descriptions.

In Python, a variable is created once a value is assigned to it. It doesn't need any extra commands to declare a variable in Python. There are specific rules and guidelines to adhere while writing a variable.

Assignment of Variable

Look at variables as a name linked to a specific object. In Python programming, you don't need to declare variables before you use like it is in other programming languages. Instead, you assign a value to a variable and begin to use it immediately. The assignment occurs using a single equals sign (=):

Y= 100

The same way a literal value can be shown from the interpreter using a REPL session, so it is to a variable:

Later if you assign a new value to Y and use it again, the new value is replaced.

Still, Python has room for chained assignment. In other words, you can assign the same value to different variables at the same time.

Example:

This chained assignment allocates 300 to the three variables simultaneously. Most variables in other programming languages are statically typed. This means that a variable is always declared to hold a given data type. Now any value that is assigned to this variable should be similar to the data type of the variable.

However, variables in Python don't follow this pattern. In fact, a variable can hold a value featuring a different data type and later re-assigned to hold another type.

Object References

What really happens when you assign a variable?

This is a vital question in Python programming because it is different from what goes on in other languages.

First, Python is an object-oriented language. In fact, each data item in Python is an object of a given type.

Consider the following example:

When the interpreter comes across the statement print (300), the following takes place:

- Assigns it the value 300.

- Builds an integer object.

- Outputs it to the console.

Python variables are the symbolic name that can act as a pointer to an object. When an object is allocated a variable, a reference to the object can be done using a name. However, the data itself is contained within the object.

The life of an object starts once it is created; at this point, the object may have one reference. In the lifetime of an object, other references to the object can be created. An object will remain active as long as it has one reference.

But when the number of references to the object drops to zero, it cannot be accessed again. The lifetime of the object is then said to be over. Python will finally realize that it is inaccessible and take the allocated space so that it can be used for something different. This process is called garbage collection.

Object Identity

Every object created in Python is assigned a number to identify it. In other words, there is no point where two objects will share the same identifier during a time when the lifetimes of the object overlap. When the count of an object reference drops to zero and it is garbage collected, then the identifying number of the object is reclaimed to be used again.

```
>>> n = 300
>>> m = n
>>> id(n)
60127840
>>> id(m)
60127840

>>> m = 400
>>> id(m)
60127872
```

Cache Small Integer Values

From your knowledge of the variable assignment and referencing of variables in Python, you will not be surprised by:

In this code, Python defines the object of integer type using the value 300 and allows m to refer to it. Similarly, n is allocated to an integer object using the value 300 but not with a different object. Let us consider the following:

In this example, both m and n have been separately allocated to integer objects holding the value 30. But in this instance, id (m) and id (n) are similar.

The interpreter will develop objects between [-5, 256] at the start, and later reuse it. Therefore, if you assign unique variables to an integer value, it will point to the same object.

Variable Names

The previous examples have used short variables like m and n. But still, you can create variable names with long words. This really helps to explain the use of the variable when a user sees the variable.

In general, Python variable names can be of any length and can have upper case and lowercase letters. Also, the variable names can include digits from 0-9 and the underscore character. Another restriction is that the first character of a variable cannot be an integer.

For instance, all these are important variable names:

Since a variable cannot start with a digit, this program will show the following result:

Keep in mind too that lowercase letters and uppercase letters are different. Using the underscore character is important as well:

Nothing will prevent you from defining two variables in the same program that have names like number and Number. However, this is not advised at all. It would definitely confuse anyone going through your code, and even yourself, after you have stayed for a while without looking at the code.

It is important to assign descriptive variable names to make it clear on what it is being used for. For instance, say you are determining the number of people who have graduated from college. You may choose any of the following:

All are great choices than n , or any other variable. At least you can understand from the name the value of the variable.

Reserved Keywords

There is one limit on identifiers names. The Python language has a unique set of keyword that defines specific language functionality. No object can use the same name as a reserved keyword.

Python Keywords

You can see reserved words in python by typing help ("keywords") on the Python interpreter. Reserved keywords are case-sensitive. So you should never change them but use them exactly as they appear. All of them are in lowercase, except for the following:

True, False, and None.

If you attempt to create a variable using a reserved word, it will result in an error.

2. Python Oops Concepts

Python OOPs Concepts

Python object-oriented programming concepts play a vital role in the software industry. It has all the concepts of object-oriented programming. There are many other languages of the same core programming family, but Python is based on OOP concepts from the very beginning. Here, a software expert has the liberty to call functions, objects, and classes to perform any programming task. This language is highly recommended for data science concepts.

- Let's discuss some important parts of OOPs Python:
- Object framework- Quality and methods in Python

- Class- Collection of Objects

- Method- Capacity of an object

- Inheritance- Inherits the qualities of parent object

- Polymorphism- Multiple structures

- Data Abstraction- Central quality of a program

- Encapsulation- Code and data wrapping together

Object framework

This framework has a similar concept in programming as in real world. Any existing substance with some quality is an object. In Python, there is an everywhere object-oriented approach, and all these objects have some specific qualities and functions. Having some defined capacity, objects contain all the important information that is being used to make a comprehensive result-oriented information out of it.

Class- Group of Objects

Class is about the group of objects. These classes have elements with specific attributes. Like in real life, we define classes in programming world as well. For example, we can have a class of students, workers, officers, etc. All classes have some kind of similar traits within the class.

Syntax for Class

class Name of Class:

<statement-1>

<statement-2>

<statement-N>

Method- Capacity of an Object

Method is about the capacity of an object defined in a program. It is based on how many methods an object can have. It is frequently used in Python programming.

Inheritance- Inheriting the quality of parent Object

It is an integral part of Python programming language. In OOP, it is similar to the traditional inheritance system in human biological existence. The younger object has all the traits and methods. Through this framework, we can develop classes to use the properties of one another. It helps in getting results by using single code for every class. It also saves time and can simplify the syntax.

Polymorphism- Multiple structures

This framework is an amazing feature of object-oriented programming. It has similar meaning to its name: multiple structures. It means one assignment is completed in many different methods.

Data Abstraction- Central quality of a program

This framework has excellent features through which it gets precise information to use to execute the functionality. There is no need to run a whole program to achieve results. It takes internal commands and run functionalities. We can tag functions with some names and can call them to get the functionality.

Encapsulation- Code and data wrapping together

Encapsulated code and data are an essential part of programming. It restricts the approach and code within specified users. It is done intentionally for using it in combination and keeping it secure.

Object-oriented versus Procedure-oriented Programming languages

Object-oriented	Procedural Programming
Object-oriented programming is the critical thinking approach and utilized where calculation is	Procedural programming utilizes a rundown of instructions to do calculation bit by bit.

finished by using objects.	
It makes the improvement and maintenance easier.	In procedural programming, It isn't difficult to maintain the codes when the undertaking ends up extensive.
It mimics this present reality element. So true issues can be effectively settled through oops.	It doesn't reenact this present reality. It chips away at bit by bit; instructions separated into little parts called capacities.
It gives data hiding. Therefore, it is more secure than procedural dialects. You can't access to private data from anywhere.	Procedural language doesn't give any legitimate method to data binding, so it is less secure.
Example of object-oriented programming	Example of procedural dialects are: C, Fortran, Pascal, VB, and so on.

dialects is C++, Java, .Net, Python, C#, etc.	

Python Class and Objects

A class is basically an assumed element that contains number of objects. It is virtual and gives meaning to us when we look at it with reference to objects and their properties. For example, assume a hospital building. It has rooms, beds, medical equipment, and so on. The hospital building is a class, and all the parts of the building are its objects.

In this area of the instructional exercise, we will talk about creating classes and objects in Python. We will also discuss how to get to a characteristic by using the class object.

Creating classes in Python

Python has a very simple syntax for crating classes. A non-technical individual can make a class by just typing simple commands.

Syntax

 class ClassName:

#statement_suite

Consider the following guide to make a class Employee, which contains two fields as Employee id, and name.

The class likewise contains a capacity show() which is utilized to show the information of the Employee.

Example:

```
class Employee:
id = 10;
name = "ayush"
def display (self):
print(self.id,self.name)
```

Here, self is utilized as a source of a perspective variable which alludes to the present class object. It is consistently the main argument in the capacity definition. Be that as it may, using self is discretionary in the capacity call.

Creating an instance of the class

A class should be instantiated on the off chance that we need to utilize the class characteristics in another class. It can be instantiated by calling the class using the class name.

Example:

```
id number = 10;

name = "John"

print("ID number: %d \nName:
%s"%(self.id,self.name))

emp = Employee()

emp.display()
```

Output:

ID number: 10

       Name: John

Python Constructor

It is a special type of method (function) that is used to initialize the specified members in a class.

There are two types of Constructors:

- Parameterized Constructor

- Non-parameterized Constructor

Its definition is executed when we create the object of this class. Constructors verify that there are measurable resources for the object to perform a task for start-up.

Creating the constructor in Python

In Python, the method __init__ generated the constructor of the class. This method is used when the class is instantiated. We can pass a number of arguments at the time of making the class object, using __init__ definition. Every class should have a constructor, even if it is simply the default constructor.

Example:

```
class Student:

count = 0

def __init__(self):

Student.count = Student.count + 1

s1=Student()

s2=Student()

s3=Student()

print("The number of students:",Student.count)
```

Output:

The number of students: 3

Python Non-Parameterized Constructor Example:

```
class Student:
def __init__(my):
print("It is non parametrized constructor")
def show(my,name):
print("Hello",name)
y = Student()
y.show("Jack")
```

Output:

It is non parametrized constructor

Hello Jack

Parameterized Constructor Example:

```
def __init__(my, firstname):
print(" parametrized constructor")
my.firstname = name
def show(my):
print("Hello",my.firstname)
s = Student("Jack")

s.show()
```

Output:

parametrized constructor

Hello Jack

Python In-built class functions

Python has multiple in-built class functions. Let's try to understand its functionality through an example.

Example:

```
class Workers:

def __init__(my,name,age):

my.name = name;

my.age = age

W = worker("Jack",115,22)

print(getattr(W,'name'))

setattr(W,"age",24)

print(getattr(s,'age'))


delattr(s,'age')

print(s.age)
```

Output:

Jack

24

True

AttributeError: There is no attribute 'age' in Student' object.

Built-in class attributes

A class in Python also contains class attributes (built-in) which give information about the class.

Here is the list of built-in class attributes:

Attribute   Description

__dict__

It is for providing the dictionary containing the information about the class namespace.

__doc__

It is to contain a string that has the class documentation.

__name__

It accesses the class name.

__module__

It accesses the module in which, this class is defined.

__bases__

It is to have a tuple.

Example:

```
def __init__(my,name,roll number,age):
my.name = name;
my.rollbumber = roll number;
m.age = age
def display_details(my):
print("Name:%s, Roll Number:%d,
age:%d"%(my.name,my.roll number))
Y = Student("Jack",10,17)
print(y.__doc__)
print(y.__dict__)
print(y.__module_)
```

Output:

None

{'name': 'Jack', 'Roll number': 10, 'age': 17}

__main__

Python Inheritance

Python inheritance is a very unique feature of the programming language. It improves the usability of the program and development. In this framework, a child class can access the qualities and functionalities of parent class.

Syntax

class derived-class(base class):

<class-suite>

Consider the following syntax.

Syntax

class derive-class(<base class 1>, <base class 2>, ... <base class n>):

<class - suite>

Example:

```
class Animal:
def speak(self):
print("Animal Speaking")
#child class Dog inherits the base class Animal
class Dog(Animal):
```

```python
def bark(self):

print("barking dog")

d = Dog()

d.bark()

d.speak()
```

Output:

barking dog

Animal Speaking

Python Multi-Level inheritance

This inheritance has multiple levels in Python. Similarly, it has in other programming languages. This object-oriented feature is very useful to derive data from one class and to us it in another.

The syntax of multi-level inheritance:

Syntax:

```python
class class1:

<class-suite>

class class2(class1):

<class suite>

class class3(class2):
```

Example:

```
class Animal:
 def speak(self):
print("Speaking Animal")
  #The child class Dog inherits the base class Animal
class Dog(Animal):
def bark(self):
print("barking dog")
#The child class Dogchild inherits another child class Dog
class DogChild(Dog):
def eat(self):
print("Bread eating...")
d = DogChild()
d.bark()
d.speak()
d.eat()
```

Output:

barking dog

Speaking Animal

Bread eating...

Python Multiple inheritance

Python gives the possibility to inherit multiple base classes in the child class.

Syntax

```
class Base1:

<class-suite>

class Base2:

<class-suite>

class BaseN:

<class-suite>
```

Example:

```
class Calculate1:

def Summation(self,a,b):

return a+b;
```

```
class Calculate2:

def Multiplication(self,a,b):

return a*b;

class Derive(Calculate1,Calculate2):

def Divide(self,a,b):

return a/b;

d = Derive()

print(isinstance(d,Derive))
```

Output:

True

Method Overriding

We can give specific implementation of the parent class method in our child class. Using or defining parent class method on a child class is called method over-riding.

Example:

```
class Bank:

def getroi(self):

return 10;

class SBI(Bank):
```

```python
def getroi(self):

return 7;

class ICICI(Bank):

def getroi(self):

return 8;

a1 = Bank()

a2 = SBI()

a3 = ICICI()

print("Bank interest:",a1.getroi());

print("SBI interest:",a2.getroi());

print("ICICI interest:",a3.getroi());
```

Output:

Bank interest: 10

SBI interest: 7

ICICI interest: 8

Data abstraction in Python

Abstraction is a significant part of object-oriented programming. In Python, we can likewise perform data hiding by adding the twofold underscore (___)

as a prefix to the credit that is to be covered up. After this, the property won't be noticeable outside of the class through the object.

Example:

```
class Employee:
count = 0;
def __init__(self):
Employee.__count = Employee.__count+1
def display(self):
print("The number of
employees",Employee.__count)
emp = Employee()
emp2 = Employee()
try:
print(emp.__count)
finally:
1emp.display()
```

Output:

The number of employees 2

AttributeError: 'Employee' object has no attribute '__count'

3. Python Magic Method

Python magic method is defined as the uncommon method that includes "magic" to a class. It starts and finishes with twofold underscores, for instance, _init_ or _str_.

The built-in classes define numerous magic methods. The dir() capacity can be utilized to see the quantity of magic methods inherited by a class. It has two prefixes, and addition underscores in the method name.

It is mostly used to define the over-burden practices of predefined administrators.

init

The _init_ method is called after the making of the class; however, before it came back to the guest. It is invoked with no call, when an instance of the class is made like constructors in other programming dialects. For example, C++, Java, C#, PHP, and so forth. These methods are otherwise called initialize and are called after _new_. Its where you ought to initialize the instance factors.

str

This capacity processes "informal" or a pleasantly printable string portrayal of an object and should restore a string object.

__repr__

This capacity is called by the repr() built-in capacity to figure the "official" string portrayal of an object and returns a machine-discernible portrayal of a kind. The objective of the _repr_ is to be unambiguous.

__len__

This capacity should restore the object's length.

__call__

An object is made callable by adding the _call_ magic method, and it is another method that isn't required as frequently is _call_.

Whenever defined in a class, at that point that class can be called. In any case, in the event that it was a capacity instance itself instead of modifying.

__del__

Similarly, _init_ is a constructor method, _del_ and resembles a destructor. In the event that you have opened a document in _init _, at that point _del_ can close it.

__bytes__

It offers to figure a byte-string portrayal of an object and should restore a string object.

__ge__

This method gets invoked when >= administrator is utilized and returns True or False.

__neg__

This capacity gets required the unary administrator.

__ipow__

This capacity gets approached the types with arguments. For example, a**=b.

__le__

This capacity gets approached correlation using <= administrator.

nonzero

Python Stack and Queue

Python stacks and queue are the most basic functions. They are used to access the data to and to alter it for some purpose. These data structures are famous in computer software world. Queues have a rule FIFO (First In First Out) for sorting data, while stack follows LIFO (Last In First Out) method.

Stack Attributes:

push - It adds a component to the highest point of the stack.

pop - It expels a component from the highest point of the stack.

Tasks on Stack:

Addition – It increases the size of stack.

Cancellation – It is used to decrease the size of stack.

Traversing - It involves visiting every component of the stack.

Qualities:

- Insertion request of the stack is saved.

- Helpful for parsing the activities.

- Duplicacy is permitted.

Code

```
# Code to demonstrate Implementation of

# stack using list

y= ["Python-language", "Csharp", "Androidnew"]

y.push("Javaflash")

y.push("C++lang")

print(y)

print(y.pop())

print(y)

print(y.pop())

print(y)
```

Output:

['Python-language', 'Csharp', 'Androidnew', 'Javaflash', 'C++lang']

C++lang

['Python-language', 'Csharp', 'Androidnew', 'Javaflash']

Javaflash

['Python-language', 'Csharp', 'Androidnew']

Queue Attributes

First-in-First-Out (FIFO) principle allows queue to have elements from both ends. It is open to get in and let go of components.

Basic functionalities in queue:

enqueue – For adding elements.

dequeue – For removing elements from queue.

Qualities

- Insertion request of the queue is protected.

- Duplicacy is permitted.

- Valuable for parsing CPU task activities.

Code

```python
import queue

# Queue is created as an object 'L'

L = queue.Queue(maxsize=10)

# Data is inserted in 'L' at the end using put()

L.put(9)

L.put(6)

L.put(7)

L.put(4)

# get() takes data from

# from the head

# of the Queue

print(L.get())

print(L.get())

print(L.get())

print(L.get())
```

Output:

9

6

7

4

Command line arguments in Python

Python focuses to provide command lines for input parameters that are passed to elements in order to execute functions.

By using getopt module, this operation is executed.

The getopt module of Python

It is very similar to other programming languages. It is used to pass inputs through command lines to get options from the user. It allows a user to input options.

Python Assert Keyword

These keywords inform the programmer about the realities of running the program. It works with conditional commands. When the condition doesn't get fulfilled, it declines with the display of an assertive message on the screen e.g. "no data is available". AssertionErrors are used to define the program properly.

Why Assertion?

It is a highly recommended debugging tool. It keeps the user aware about codes on each step. If some lines of codes have errors or mistakes, it alerts the user with message.

Syntax

assert condition, error_message(optional)

Example:

```python
def avg(scores):
    assert len(scores) != 0,"The List is empty."
    return sum(scores)/len(scores)
scoresb = [67,59,86,75,92]
print("The Average of scoresb:",avg(scoresb))
scores1 = []
print("The Average of scoresa:",avg(scoresa))
```

Output:

The Average of scores2: 75.8

AssertionError: The List is empty.

Python Modules, Exceptions and Arrays

Python modules, exceptions and arrays are an integral part of object-oriented Python programming language. In data science, we use them from time to time to have a better understanding with the usage of code in a logical way. These programming methods are also used in other programming languages, and are a popular framework because of their usage to transform the complexities of programming into simple coding. Let's discuss them one by one.

Python Modules

Python modules are programs that have programming codes in Python. They contain all variables, classes and functions of this unique language. They enable the programmer to organize codes in a proper format that is logically valid. They can be imported to use the functionality of one module for another.

Example:

Now here a module named as file.py will be generated which contains a function func that has a code to print some message on the console.

So let's generate it *file.py.*

#displayMsg prints a message to the name.

def displayMsg(name)

print("Hi "+name);

Now it is required to add this module into the main module to call the method displayMsg() defined in the module named file.

Loading the module in our Python code

In order to utilize the functionality of Python code, the module is loaded. Python provides two types of statements as defined below.

1. The import statement

2. The from-import statement

Python Standard Library- Built-in Modules

There is an unlimited pool of Python Built-in Modules. We will discuss some of the most important modules. These are:

- **random**

- **statistics**

- **math**

- **datetime**

- **csv**

To import any of them, use this syntax:

Import[module_name]

eg. Import random

Random module in Python

This module is used to generate numbers. By using the command random(), we can generate float numbers. The range of these float numbers lies between 0.0 and 1.0.

Here are some important random functions used in random module:

The Function random.randint()

It is for random integers.

The Function random.randrange()

It is for randomly selected elements.

The Function random.choice()

It is for randomly selected elements from non-empty.

The Statistics module of Python

It is a very useful module of Python. It provides numerical data after performing statistics functions.

Here is a list of some very commonly used functions of this module:

The mean() function

It performs arithmetic mean of the list.

For Example:

import statistics

datalist = [5, 2, 7, 4, 2, 6, 8]

a= statistics.mean(datalist)

print("The Mean will be:", a)

Output:

The Mean will be: 4.857142857142857

The median() function

It gives middle value of the list.

Example:

import statistics

dataset = [4, -5, 6, 6, 9, 4, 5, -2]

print("Median of data-set is : % s "

% (statistics.median(dataset)))

Output:

Median of data-set is: 4.5

The mode() function

It provides common data from the list.

Example:

```
import statistics

datasets =[2, 4, 7, 7, 2, 2, 3, 6, 6, 8]

print("Calculated Mode % s" %
(statistics.mode(datasets)))
```

Output:

Calculated Mode 2

The stdev() function

It calculates the standard deviation.

Example:

```
import statistics

sample = [7, 8, 9, 10, 11]

print("Standard Deviations of sample data is % s "

% (statistics.stdev(sample)))
```

Output:

Standard Deviation of sample data is
1.5811388300841898

The median_low()

The median_low function is used to return the low median of numeric data in the list.

Example:

import statistics

simple list of a set of integers

set1 = [4, 6, 2, 5, 7, 7]

Print low median of the data-set

print ("data-set Low median is % s "

% (statistics.median_low(set1)))

Output:

Low median of the data-set is 5

median_high()

The median_high () function is employed to calculate the high median of numeric data in the list.

Example:

import statistics

list of set of the integers

dataset = [2, 1, 7, 6, 1, 9]

print("High median of data-set is %s "

% (statistics.median_high(dataset)))

Output:

High median of the data-set is 6

The math module of Python

This module contains the mathematical functions to perform every mathematical calculation.

Here are two constants as well:

Pie (n): A well-known mathematical constant and is defined as the ratio of circumstance to the diameter of a circle. Its value is 3.141592653589793.

Euler's number (e): It is the base of the natural logarithmic, and its value is 2.718281828459045.

A few math modules which are given below:

The math.log10() function

It calculates base1 0 logarithm of the number.

Example:

```
import math
x=13 # small value of of x
print('log10(x) is :', math.log10(x))
```

Output:

log10(x) is : 1.1139433523068367

The math.sqrt() function

It calculates the root of the number.

Example:

```
import math
x = 20
y = 14
z = 17.8995
print('sqrt of 20 is ', math.sqrt(x))
print('sqrt of 14 is ', math.sqrt(y))
print('sqrt of 17.8995 is ', math.sqrt(z))
```

Output:

```
sqrt of 20 is 4.47213595499958
 sqrt of 14 is 3.7416573867739413
 sqrt of 17.8995 is 4.230780069916185
```

The math.expm1() function

This method calculates e raised to the power of any number minus 1. e is the base of natural logarithm.

The math.cos() function

It calculates cosine of any number in radians.

Example:

```
import math
```

```
angleInDegree = 60
angleInRadian = math.radians(angleInDegree)
print('Given angle :', angleInRadian)
print('cos(x) is :', math.cos(angleInRadian))
```

Output:

Given angle : 1.0471975511965976

cos(x) is : 0.5000000000000001

The math.sin() function

It calculates the sine of any number, in radians.

Example:

```
import math
angleInDegree = 60
angleInRadian = math.radians(angleInDegree)
print('Given angle :', angleInRadian)
print('sin(x) is :', math.sin(angleInRadian))
```

Output:

Given angle: 1.0471975511965976

sin(x) is: 0.8660254037844386

The math.tan() function

It returns the tangent of any number, in radians.

Example:

import math

angleInDegree = 60

angleInRadian = math.radians(angleInDegree)

print('Given angle :', angleInRadian)

print('tan(x) is :', math.tan(angleInRadian))

Output:

Given angle : 1.0471975511965976

 tan(x) is : 1.7320508075688767

The sys module of Python

This module provides access to system-specific functions. It changes the Python Runtime Environment to enable the user to get variables and parameters.

Need to import sys function

First, there is a need to import the sys module in the program before starting the use of functions.

The sys.modules' function

These functions perform some really important tasks on system in Python programming.

- Function of sys.argv: *For arguments*

- Function of sys.base_prefix: *For startup*

- Function of sys.byteorder*: To get byterorder.*

- *Function of sys.maxsize*: To get large integer.

- Function of sys.path*: To set path.*

- Function of sys.stdin*: To restore files.*

- *Function of sys.getrefcount*: To get reference count of an object.

- *Fun tion of sys.exit*: To exit from Python command prompt.

- *Function of sys executable*: Locate the Python in system.

- *sys.platform:* To identify Platform.

The Collection Module of Python

This module plays an important role, as it collects major data formats or data structures, such as list, dictionary, set, and tuple. It improves the functionality of the current version of Python. It is defined as a container that is employed to conserve collections of data, for example, list.

The function of namedtuple() in Collection Module

It produces a tuple object without causing an issue with indexing.

Examples:

John = ('John', 25, 'Male')

print(John)

Output:

('John', 25, 'Male')

OrderedDict() function

It generates dictionary object with key that can overwrite data inside.

Example:

```
import collections
d1=collections.OrderedDict()
d1['A']=15
d1['C']=20
d1['B']=25
d1['D']=30
for k,v in d1.items():
print (k,v)
```

Output:

```
A 15
 C 20
 B 25
D 30
```

Function defaultdict()

It produces an object similar to dictionary.

Example:

```
from collections import defaultdict
number = defaultdict(int)
number['one'] = 1
```

number['two'] = 2

print(number['three'])

Output:

0

Counter() function

It counts the hasbale objects after reviewing the elements of list.

Example:

A = Counter()

Xlist = [1,2,3,4,5,7,8,5,9,6,10]

Counter(Xlist)

Counter({1:5,2:4})

Ylist = [1,2,4,7,5,1,6,7,6,9,1]

c = Counter(Ylist)

print(A[1])

Result:

3

The function deque()

It facilitates addition and removal of elements from both ends.

For Example:

```
from collections import deque

list = ["x","y","z"]

deq = deque(list)

print(deq)
```

Output:

```
deque(['x', 'y', 'z'])
```

Python OS Module

Python OS module provides functions utilized for interacting with the operating system and also obtains related data about it. The OS comes under Python's standard utility modulesPython OS module which allows you to work with the files, documents and directories. Some of OS module functions are as follows:

os.name

It provides the name of the operating system module it imports.

It can register 'posix', 'nt', 'os2', 'ce', 'java' and 'riscos'.

Example:

```
import os
```

print(os.name)

Output:

posix

os.getcwd()

It restores the Current Working Directory (CWD) of the file.

Example:

import os

print(os.getcwd())

Output:

C:\Users\Python\Desktop\ModuleOS

os.error

The functions in this module define the OS level errors in case of invalid file names and path.

Example:

import os

filename1 = 'PythonData.txt'

 f = open(filename1, 'rU')

 text = f.read()

 f.close()

print('Difficult read: ' + filename1)

Output:

Difficult read: PythonData.txt

os.popen()

It opens a file, and it gives back a fileobject that contains connection with pipe.

The datetime Module

It is an imported module that allows you to create date and time objects. It works to conduct many functions related to date and time.

Let's understand it through an example:

Example:

import datetime;

#returns the current datetime object

print(datetime.datetime.now())

Output:

2018-12-18 16:16:45.462778

Python read csv file

The Comma Separated values (CSV) File

It is a simple file format that arranges tabular data. It is used to store data in tabular form ora spreadsheet that can be exchanged when needed. It is in a Microsoft excel supported data form.

The CSV Module Functions in Python

This module helps in reading/writing CSV files. It takes the data from columns and stores it to use in the future.

- The function csv.field_size_limit - *To maximize field size.*

- *The function csv.reader* – To read information or data from a csv file.

- *The function csv.writer* – To write the information or data to a csv file

  These functions have a major role in CSV module.

The Exceptions in Python

Exceptions are actually interruptions that stops the running program. They are mistakes or errors in the code. In Python, these are handled differently.

The Common Exceptions in Python

Here are some common exceptions that may occur in Python. Every Python programmer is very familiar with these errors or exceptions.

- *The exception of ZeroDivisionError:* when a number is divided by zero.

- *The exception of NameError:* when a name is not found.

- *The exception of IndentationError:* when incorrect indentation is given.

- *The exception of IOError:* when Input Output operation fails.

- *The exception of EOFError:* when the end of the file is reached, and still operations are being performed.

Unhandled Exceptions

Example:

```
x= int(input("Enter a:"))

y = int(input("Enter b:"))

z= a/b;

print("x/y = %d"%c)

print("Hello I am a teacher")
```

Output:

Enter a:10

Enter b:0

Traceback (most recent call last):

File "exception-test.py", line 3, in <module>

  c = a/b;

ZeroDivisionError: division by zero

The finally block

It is used to run a code before the try statement.

Syntax

try:

block of code

this may throw an exception

finally:

block of code

this will always be executed

Example:

 try:

 fileptr = open("file.txt","r")

 try:

```
fileptr.write("Hi I am good")

finally:

fileptr.close()

print("file closed")

except:

print("Error")
```

Output:

file closed

Error

The Exception Raising in Python

The raise clause in Python is used to raise an exception.

Syntax

```
Raise exception_class,<value>
```

The Custom Exception in Python

It enables programmers to generate exceptions that have already been launched with the program.

Example:

```
class ErrorInCode(Exception):
```

```python
def __init__(self, data):

self.data = data

def __str__(self):

return repr(self.data)

try:

raise ErrorInCode(2000)

except ErrorInCode as ae:

print("Received error:", ae.data)
```

Output:

> *Received error: 2000*

Python Arrays

Array is a set of elements that are used to work on specific data values. It is advanced level programming that allows users multiple functionality over data structures. Through arrays, code can be simplified, therefore saving a lot of time.

Array Element - Data element stored in array.

Array Index - Position of an element.

Array Representation:

The declaration of array can be done in many different ways.

- Array Index starts with 0.

- Element can be located with the help of its index number.

- The length of the array defines the storage capacity of the elements.

Array operations in Python:

Some of the basic operations in an array are given below:

- *Traverse* – To print all the elements one by one.

- *Insertion* – Addition of element in Index.

- *Deletion* – Deletion of element at index.

- **Search** – *To search the element.*

- *Update* - To update an element at the given index.

Array Generation

array *import* *

MyarrayName = array(typecode, [initializers])

Accessing array elements

The array elements accessibility can be ensured by using the respective indices of those elements.

```
import array as arr
a = arr.array('i', [1, 3, 5, 87])
print("First element:", a[0])
print("Second element:", a[1])
print("Second last element:", a[-1])
```

Output:

First element: 1

Second element: 3

Second last element: 8

Arrays are changeable, and elements can be changed in similar to lists.

A combination of arrays makes the process speedy and saves time. The array can reduce the code's size.

Deletion can be done by using the *del* statement in Python.

The length of an array can be described as the number of elements in an array. It returns an integer value that is equal to the total number of the elements present in that array.

Syntax

len(array_name)

Example:

a=arr.array('d',[1.2 , 2.2 ,3.2,3,6,7.8])

b=arr.array('d',[4.5,8.6])

c=arr.array('d')

c=a+b

print("Array c = ",c)

Output:

Array c= array('d', [1.2, 2.2, 3.2, 3.6, 7.8, 4.5, 8.6])

Example:

import array as arr

x = arr.array('i', [5, 10, 15, 20])

print("First element:", x[0])

print("Second element:", x[1])

print("Second last element:", x[-1])

Output:

First element: 5

Second element: 10

Second last element: 15

4. The Principles Of Algorithm Design

Algorithms are all-important; they are the very foundation of computers and computer science. Your computer may be constructed of hardware items, but without algorithms, it's all a waste of space. The Turing Machine is the theoretical foundation of all algorithms and this was established many years before we even thought about implementing a machine like that using digital logic circuits. The Turing Machine is a model that can translate a set of given inputs into outputs, working to a set of pre-defined rules, much like today's Machine Learning.

Algorithms affect our lives in more ways than we realize. Take page ranking on search engines for example. These are based on algorithms and these allow anyone to search quickly through huge amounts of information. This, in turn, hastens the rate at which new research can be done, new discoveries can be found, and with which innovative technologies can be developed.

Studying algorithms is also essential because it makes us think about problems in specific ways. Our mental abilities sharpen, and we can improve our problem-solving abilities by learning to find and isolate the core components of a problem and define the relationship between them.

In its simplest form, an algorithm is nothing more than a list of instructions to be carried out in sequence. Think of it, in Python terms, as a linear form of do x, then do y, and then do z. However, we can change things and make these algorithms do more by adding if-else statements. By doing that, the direction the action takes then depends on conditions being met, and then we add operations, while statements, for statements, and iteration. To expand our algorithm a bit more, we add recursion which often provides the same result that iteration does even though they are very different. Recursive functions apply the function to inputs that get progressively smaller. The input of one recursive step is the output of the previous one.

Paradigms of Algorithm Design

There are three main paradigms to algorithm design:

- Divide and Conquer

- Greedy

- Dynamic programming

Let's take these one at a time. Divide and conquer is self-explanatory – the problem is broken down into small subproblems and the results of each one combined into an overall solution. This has to be one of the most common techniques to solve problems and is perhaps the most common approach to the design of algorithms.

Greedy algorithms involve optimizing and combining. In short, it means to take the shortest path to the most useful solution for local problems, all the while hoping that somewhere it will all lead to the global solution.

Dynamic programming is most useful when the subproblems start to overlap. This is not the same as the divide and conquers paradigm. Instead of breaking the problem down into individual subproblems, intermediate solutions get cached and then used in a later operation. It does use recursion like divide and conquers but, with dynamic programming, we compare the results at different times. This provides a boost in terms of performance for some types of problems; it can be quicker to retrieve a previous result than it is to go through recalculating it.

Backtracking and Recursion

Recursion is incredibly useful in terms of divide and conquer but it can be hard to see exactly what is going on; each of the recursive calls spins off another recursive call. There are two types of cases at the heart of a recursive function:

- Base case – this tells recursion when it should terminate

- Recursive case – this calls the function the case is in

The calculation of factorials is one of the simplest examples of a problem that results in a recursive solution. The factorial algorithm is responsible for defining 2 cases:

- The base case where n is equal to zero

- The recursive case where n is more than zero. Here is an example of implementation:

When this code is printed, we get 1, 2, 6, 24. For 24 to be calculated, we need the parent call and four recursive calls. On each of the recursions, a copy is made of the method variables and it is stored in memory. When the method has returned, that copy is removed.

It isn't always going to be clear whether iteration or recursion is the best result for a problem. Both repeat sets of operations and both work well with divide and conquer. Iteration keeps on going until the problem has been solved and recursion breaks it down into ever smaller chunks combining the results from each one. Iteration does tend to be better for programmers because control tends to remain local to the loop; with recursion, you get a closer representation to factorials and other like mathematical concepts. Recursive calls are stored in the memory; iterations aren't. All of this leads to trade-offs between memory use and processor cycles, so determination may come down to whether your task is memory or processor intensive.

Backtracking

Backtracking is a type of recursion that tends to be used more for problems like the traversal of tree structures. In these problems, each node presents us with several options and we need to choose one of them. Doing that leads to more options; dependent on the options chosen throughout, we either reach a dead end or a goal state. If the former, we need to backtrack to an earlier node and go down a different route. Backtracking is also a kind of divide and conquers method when we need to do exhaustive searches. More importantly, when we backtrack, we prune off the branches that don't provide any results. Look at this example of backtracking; a recursive approach has been used to generate all the permutations that are possible for a given strength of a given length:

Notice that we have two recursive calls and a 'double list' compression. This results in all the elements of the first sequence being concatenated recursively with the return when n=1. Each of the string elements was generated in the recursive call that came before.

Divide and Conquer - Long Multiplication

Recursion isn't just a clever little trick, but to understand what it can do, we need to compare it to approaches like iteration and we need to be able to understand when to use it for a faster algorithm. In primary math, we all learned an iterative algorithm used for the multiplication of a pair of large numbers. That algorithm was long multiplication involving iterative multiplication and carrying, followed by shifting and addition.

What we want to do is work out whether this procedure really is all that efficient for the multiplication of the numbers. When you multiply two numbers each four digits long, it takes no less than 16 multiplication operations. This method of algorithm analysis, in terms of how many computational primitives are needed, is vital because it provides us with a way of understanding what the relationship is between the time taken to do the computation and the input size to the computation. What we really want to know is, what will happen when the input is massive? We call this topic asymptomatic analysis, otherwise known as time complexity, and it is important when studying algorithms; we will talk about it quite a bit through the course of this section of the book.

A Recursive Approach

As far as long multiplication goes, there is a better way; several algorithms exist for the more efficient operation of multiplying large numbers. The Karatsuba algorithm is one of the best-known long multiplication alternatives and it dates back to 1962. This algorithm takes a very different approach instead of iterative multiplication of single digits, it does recursive multiplication on inputs that progressively get smaller. A recursive program will call itself on each small subset of the parent input.

To build an algorithm, we need to take a large number and decompose it into smaller numbers. The easiest way is to split it into two – one half with important digits and one with less important digits. For example, a number with 4 digits of 2345 would become 2 sets of numbers, each with 2 digits, 23 and 45.

Let's take 2 n digit numbers and write a general decomposition for them. The numbers are x and y and m is a positive integer with a lower value than n:

This does suggest that we are using recursion to multiply the numbers because the process involves multiplication. More specifically, ac, ad, bc, and bd all have smaller numbers than the input making it not inconceivable that the same operation could be applied as a partial solution to the bigger problem. So far, the algorithm has four recursive steps (all multiplication) and it is not yet clear whether this would be more efficient than traditional long multiplication.

So far, we have looked at nothing more than what mathematicians have known for years. However, the Karatsuba algorithm goes a step further and observes that we only really need to know three of the quantities to solve the equation. Those quantities are $z_2=ac$; $z_1=ad + bc$ and $z_0=bd$. We only need to know what the values of a, b, c, and d, are in as much as they contribute to the overall sum and the products required to calculate z_2, z_1, and z_0. This brings about the possibility that we could reduce how many recursive steps are needed and, as it turns out, we can do that.

Because ac and bd have already been reduced to their simplest form, we can't really take these calculations out. What we can do is this:

$$(a+b)(c+d)=ac+bd+ad+bc$$

When ac and bd, calculated previously, are taken away, we are left with the quantity that we need – (ad + bc):

ac+bd+ad+bc-ac-bc=ad+bc

What this shows is that it is perfectly possible to compute ad+bc without having to compute the individual quantities separately.

Below is the Karatsuba algorithm in a Python implementation:

```python
from math import log10, ceil

def karatsuba(x,y):
    # The base case for recursion

    #sets n, which is the number of digits in the highest input number

    #adds 1 if n is uneven

    n = n if n % 2 == 0 else n + 1

    #splits the input numbers

    #applies the three recursive steps

    #performs the multiplication

    return (((10**n)*ac) + bd +
((10**n_2)*(ad_bc)))
```

Just to satisfy ourselves that this really works, there is a test function we can run:

Runtime Analysis

By now, it should be clear that one of the more important sides of algorithm design is gauging how efficient it is in terms of time, or how many operations, and memory. The analysis of the number of operations is called Runtime Analysis. There are several ways to run this and the most obvious is nothing more than a measurement of the time taken for the algorithm to finish. There are problems with this approach; how long it takes depends on what hardware it is run, for a start. Another way, independent of the platform, is to count how many operations it takes, but this also causes problems in that we don't have any definitive way of quantifying operations. This would depend on the programming language used, the style of coding, and how we opt to count the operations. However, we could use this way if we were to combine it with an expectation that the runtime increases as the input size increases and it does it in a specific way. In other words, that there is a relationship mathematically between the input size (n) and the time the algorithm takes to run. There are three principles that guide this, and their importance will become clear as we go on.

First, the principles:

- Making no assumptions about the input data giving us a worst-case analysis

- Ignoring or suppressing lower order terms and constant factors – with larger inputs, the higher-order terms will be dominant

- Focus only on those problems with the large inputs.

The first one is very useful because it provides us with an upper bound that is tight – the algorithm is guaranteed to fail. The second is just about ignoring anything that doesn't contribute majorly to the runtime making work easier and letting us focus on what impacts performance more.

With the Karatsuba algorithm, the square of the input size increased, and so did the number of operations used for multiplication. With a four-digit number, we use 16 operations and with an eight-digit number, we need 64. However, we're not so interested in how an algorithm with small n values behaves so we ignore the factors that only increase linearly or lowly. At the higher n values, the operations that increase fast as n is increased will be the dominant ones.

We'll talk briefly about the merge-sort algorithm here because it is useful to learn about performance at runtime. This is one of the classic algorithms from more than 60 years ago and it is still used today in some of the highly popular sorting libraries. Merge-sort is recursive and uses divide and conquer, which, as you know, means breaking a problem down, sorting the parts recursively, and putting the results together. Merge-sort is an obvious demonstration of this algorithm design paradigm.

Merge-sort has just three steps:

- Sorts the left side of the input array recursively

- Sorts the right side of the input array recursively

- Merges the sorted arrays into one

One typical use is to sort numbers into numerical order. Merge-sort will divide the list in two and work on each side in parallel. Here is the Python code for the algorithm:

The easiest way to determine the running time performance is to start by mapping the recursive calls onto a tree structure with each tree node being a call that works on an ever-smaller subprogram. Each time we invoke merge-sort, we get two recursive calls, so we can use a binary tree to represent this, with each child node getting an input subset. To work out the time the algorithm takes to finish relative to n, we start by working out how much work there is and how many operations are on each tree level.

Keeping our focus on the runtime analysis, on the first level we have two n/2 subproblems; level two gives us four, and so on. So, when does the recursion get to its base case? Simply, when the array is one or zero. To get to a number that is nearly one, we take the number of recursive levels and divide n by 2 that many times. This is the definition of $\log 2$ and, as the first recursive level is 0, the number of levels is $\log 2n+1$.

Let's refine the definitions. Up to now, we have used n to represent the number of elements in an input, referring to how many elements are in the first recursive level, or the length of the first input. What we need to do is be able to know the difference between the initial input length and the input length at each recursive level. For this, we use m i.e. m_j for the input length at recursive level j.

Using recursion trees for algorithm analysis has the advantage of being able to know what is done at each recursive level. Defining the work is the number of operations in relation to the input size. We must measure the performance of an algorithm in a way that is independent of the platform although runtime will depend on the hardware. It is important to count how many operations there are because this is our metric related directly to the performance of our algorithm.

Generally, because we get two recursive calls each time merge-sort is invoked, each level has double the number of calls of the previous one. At the same time, each call is working on an input that is half the size of its parent. To work out how many operations there are, we must know how many operations are used by one merge of two sub-arrays. Look at the Python code above. After the first two recursive calls, we can count the operations – three assignments followed by three while loops. The first loop has an if-else statement and within each is a comparison and an assignment – two operations. This is counted as a set and there is only one set in an if-else, so this set was carried out m times. The last two while loops each have an assignment operation, making for a total of 4m+3 operations for each merge-sort recursion.

Because m has to be at least 1, the number of operations has an upper bound of 7m. This is not an exact science; it all depends on how the operations are counted. We haven't included any increment or housekeeping operations as we are only interested in the runtime growth rate related to n at the high n values.

All this may seem a bit daunting because every call from a recursive call spins off to even more recursive calls and things look as if they exponentially explode. What makes this manageable is as the recursive calls double, the subproblem size halves. These cancel each other out very nicely as we will demonstrate.

To work out the max number of the operations on each tree level, the number of subproblems are multiplied by the number of operations in each of those subproblems, like this:

$2j \times 7(n/2j) = 7n$

What we see here is 2jcancels out how the number of operations there are on each level independently of the level, giving us an upper bound to work with. In our example, it is 7n. This number includes the operations that each recursive call performs on that level only, not on any other. From this, as we get a doubling of the recursive calls for each level, and this is counter-balanced by the subproblem input size halving on each level.

If we wanted to know how many operations there were for one complete merge-sort, we would take the number of operations per level and multiply that by the total number of levels, like this:

$7n(\log 2n + 1)$

Expanding that gives us:

$7n\log 2n + 7$

The key to take from this is that the relationship between input size and running time has a logarithmic component and, if you remember your high-school math, logarithm functions flatten off fast. As x, an input variable, increases in size, so y, the output variable, will increase by progressively smaller amounts.

Asymptotic Analysis

Runtime performance of an algorithm can be characterized in one of three ways:

- Worst-case – using an input that is slow to perform

- Best case – using an input that gives us the best results

- Average case – assuming the input is random

To calculate each one, we must know what the lower and upper bounds are. We looked at using mathematical expressions to represent runtime using multiplication and addition operators. For asymptotic analysis, we need two expressions, one for the best and one for the worst-case.

Big O Notation

The "O" stands for order and denotes that the growth rates are defined as orders of functions. We could say that a function, T(n), is a big O of F(n) and this is defined like this:

T(n)=O(F(n)) if there are constants, n0, and C in a way that:

T(n) C(F(n)) for all n n0

The function of the input size n is g(n) and this is based on all large enough values of n, g(n) being upper bound by a constant multiple of f(n). What we want to do is find the smallest growth rate equal to less than f(n). We are only interested in the higher n values; the variable, n, represents the threshold – below that, we're not interested in the growth rate. T(n) is the function that represents F(n), the tight upper bound.

The notation that reads f(n) = O(g(n)) is telling us that O(g(n)) is a set of functions, within which are all the functions with smaller or equal growth rates than f(n). Below, are the common growth rates from low to high. These are sometimes called a function time complexity:

Complexity	Class Name	Operation Examples
O(1)	Constant	get item, set item, append
O(log n)	Logarithmic	find an element in an array that is sorted

O(n)	Linear	insert, copy, iteration, delete
nLogn	Linear-logarithmic	merge-sort, sorting lists
n2	Quadratic	nested loops, finding the shortest path between nodes
n3	Cubic	Matrix multiplication
2n	Exponential	backtracking

Complexity Classes

Normally, we would be looking for the total running time of several basic operations, but it seems that we can take simple operations and combine their complexity classes to determine the class of combined operations that are somewhat more complex. The goal is to look at the combined statements in a method or a function to find the time complexity of executing multiple operations. The easiest way of combining complexity classes is to add them and this happens when the operations are sequential.

Let's say that we have a pair of operations that insert an element in a list and then proceed to sort the list.

When the item is inserted, it happens in O(n) time while sorting happens in O(nlogn) time. The time complexity can be written as O(n + nlogn). However, because we are focusing only on the high order term, we can work with just O(nlogn).

Let's then assume that we use a while loop to repeat an operation; we would take the complexity class and multiply it by how many times the operation is done. For example, an operation that has a time complexity of O(f(n)) is repeated O(n) times; both complexities are multiplied as follows:

This loop then has a time complexity of O(n2) * O(n) = O(n * n2) = O(n3). All we have done is multiply the operation's time complexity by the number of times that operation was executed. A loop's running time is no more than the combined running time of all the statements in the loop multiplied by the iterations. Assuming both loops will run n times, a single nested loop runs in n2 time.

For example:

    for i in range(0,n):

        for j in range(0,n)

            #statements

Each of these statements is a constant (c) that is
    executed nn times. The running time can thus be
    expressed as;cn n + cn2 = O(n2)

For all consecutive statements in a nested loop, the
    time complexity for each of the statements is
    added and then multiplied by the iterations of
    the statement. For example:

Amortized Analysis

Sometimes we are not bothered so much about the
time complexity of an individual operation;
sometimes we want to know what the average
running time is of a sequence of operations. This is
called amortized analysis and, as you will see later, it
is not the same as the average case analysis because
it doesn't assume anything about the data
distribution of any input values. What it does do is
take the change in the state of the data structures
into account. For example, sorting a list should make
finding operations faster in the future. The amortized
analysis considers the change in the state because
the sequence of operations is analyzed; it doesn't
just aggregate single operations.

What amortized analysis does is determines the
upper bound on runtime and it does this by imposing
each operation in a sequence with an artificial cost.
Each of these costs is then combined. This takes

consideration of the fact that the initial expense of an operation can then make future operations much cheaper.

When there are multiple small operations that are expensive, like sorting, and multiple options that are cheaper, like lookups, using worst-case analysis can give us pessimistic results. This is because worst-case assumes that each of the lookups should compare every element until a match is found.

Up to now, we have assumed that we have random input data and we only looked at how the input size affects the runtime. There are two more common algorithm analyses we can look at:

- Average Case Analysis
- Benchmarking

Average case analysis takes some assumptions about the relative frequency of the different input values and determines the average running time. Benchmarking is when a previously agreed set of inputs is used to measure performance.

Both approaches rely on some domain knowledge. For a start, we would need to know what the expected or the typical datasets are. Ultimately, we will be trying to improve the performance by finetuning to an application setting that is highly specific.

A straightforward benchmarking approach would be to time how long the algorithm takes to finish given different input sizes. This is entirely dependent on what hardware the algorithm is run on; the faster the processor, the better the result. However, the relative growth rates that come with the increases in the input rates will retain the characteristics of the algorithm and not the platform they run on.

5. How To Use Your Python Skills

There are many ways that you can use the skills that you have just learned to be able to try Python and use it for yourself. Once you know how to use Python, you can do all of your own programming, and that will give you the help that you need to be able to get started with your career in programming. Gone are the days where you need to rely on programs that are created by other people or the "expert" help of people who really can't do much to help you. After reading this book, you will be more than just a beginner, and you will be able to use that to your benefit so that you can do everything from providing yourself with a service to making a lucrative income.

Power a Social Media Site

With the capabilities that Python has, you can not only build an entire social media site but also power it.

While many of the other social media sites have moved onto "bigger" languages that are just a few steps up from Python, Instagram still uses Python to power everything that they do. You will be able to do the same, and hopefully, one day have a social media site that is just as famous as Instagram.

Create a Fun Game for Friends

Throughout this book, you learned the way to make different things and give people choices for what they were going to put into your input areas. These are all choices that they can make, but you can benefit by putting them into a game. Whether you want to be a game creator or not is irrelevant. Building a game for your friends to play online (or off!) is a great way to practice your Python skills and have a better chance at building really cool stuff in the future.

In the beginning, you can start with a very basic game. Users are asked input questions, and the output is all based on that information. The better you get at writing Python, the more advanced your games can be. You may even be able to make something that is comparable to your favorite video game. From there, take your skills to a different place and you'll be a true Python master in no time!

Learn Insider Secrets

There are no real secrets of Python, but as you begin to work with more codes and try new things out, you will be able to learn some of the quirks that the language comes with so that you can try new things and you'll be able to find out some of the things that the most advanced Python users have. This is a great way to learn new things, try out new codes, and give yourself a chance at doing more with the Python language so that you can take it to the next level.

You can also use Python if you want to enter any program through the back door. While it isn't necessarily the best hacking language that is available for you to try, it is something that you can get very comfortable with getting the specifics on other programs with. It will give you a chance to do much more than simply creating websites, programs, or other things that can sometimes be complicated for you to figure out.

The Language of Google

The language that Google uses is the same language that you are beginning to learn all about. Google is one of the biggest sites on the Internet and possibly the most-visited around the world depending on which statistics you look at. If something as big as Google continues to use Python, then it is a relatively good language to learn.

One thing that you can do is teach yourself how the programming and the codes of Google work. While I wouldn't necessarily suggest trying to compete with Google, you can try to learn more so that you will be able to give yourself a better chance with the options that you have. One of those options would be to try and get a job with Google. Having Python knowledge will help you get a job at nearly any tech-related industry.

Build on Your Knowledge

For many people who just want to know the basics, Python is the end of the line. For others, though, it can be a simple stepping stone to learning more coding language. The majority of people who know the more complicated methods of writing in different code languages started with Python and continue to use it while they are working on different languages.

One of the best parts of being able to use Python to build on the knowledge that you have is that you will always be able to learn more from what you are doing and what you have done with Python. None of the languages that are present in today's world are exactly the same, but knowing one code language will often help you to have a better chance at learning a different one.

Make Money

You don't need another company to be able to show you what to do. This is something that you can do once you master Python and something that is going to be very lucrative depending on how you market yourself.

How to Make Money with Python

Once you have learned Python and the way to make sure that you are creating the perfect program, you will be able to start making money with it. Some people may be tempted to go to companies or businesses and ask them to hire them, but that is not where the real money is.

If you want to truly make money with Python, you need to go your own way and make sure that you are doing it right.

Follow these steps to launch your Python career and earn yourself some financial freedom:

Practice

You will absolutely need to practice with Python. You should not try to go out on your own and start a career after reading this book. Read it again. Try new things on Python. Use variations. Look for new codes. All of these will help you to practice and will give you a chance to see which aspects of Python you are good at and which ones could stand to have a little more practice.

Remember, though, that you will get better if you practice a lot.

Create

It is necessary to create things with Python for yourself before you are able to create them for other people. Since you have a skill, you will need to use it for your own good first. Try to make some games, design a program, and prepare yourself to do more for other people. Think of things that people may want you to create for them and do them for yourself. This will allow you to keep practicing but will also put your knowledge to work so that you can use it later on when you are listing the work that you did.

List

Create a list of all of the things that you have done with Python. Build a site using Python and make sure that you connect it with the things that you have done. Give yourself a killer domain name and then design the site so that it is seamless. This is your portfolio. It is where you will direct people to when you are talking about your services. It is also where your work will be showcased, so be sure to always show off your best Python programming.

Advertise

Advertising yourself is as simple as advertising a business. Let them know that they need you, not the other way around. If you offer a service that they need and that they can't refuse, you'll be able to advertise yourself much more easily. It is a good idea to try and make sure that you are doing what you can to advertise yourself in a positive light. Use social media, networking opportunities, and even chances offline to advertise the fact that you are able to do programming. Always remember to include the link to your portfolio so that they can see the work that you have done.

Prove Value

Some people may balk at the prices that you are charging them especially if they have never tried to hire a programmer before. Make sure that you show them why it costs so much to hire you. They will be much easier to retain if you can prove that you are valuable.

Negotiate

The chances are that you are going to have to negotiate especially when you are first getting started with your Python programming career. There is nothing wrong with this even if you think that you are worth more than what someone wants to pay you for the work that you are doing. Keep all of this in mind when you start to forget why you were doing it in the first place. The negotiation process can be tricky, but you'll be able to do the most if you do negotiate in the beginning.

Collect

Sit back and collect on the money that you can make from programming. You stand to have a very lucrative career if you make sure that you always do the best work possible, you provide people with a reason to want to hire you, and you show them that you are extremely valuable when it comes to the services that you offer. Are you ready for financial freedom thanks to Python?

6. Development Tools

As with every work environment, to increase our productivity in Scientific Computing there are several tools beyond the programming language. In this chapter we will talk about the most important tools of Python.

IPython

The interactive use of Python is extremely valuable. Other environments geared toward scientific computing, such as Matlab™, R, Mathematica™, among others, use interactive mode as their primary mode of operation. Those who want to do the same with Python can greatly benefit from IPython.

IPython is a very sophisticated version of the Python shell designed to make interactive use of the Python language more aware..

First steps

To start IPython, type the following command:

1 $ ipython [options] archives

Many of the options that control IPython's operation are not passed on the command line; they are specified in the IPythonrc file within the /.IPython directory.

Four IPython options are considered unique and should appear first, before any other options: -gthread, -qthread, -wthread, -pylab. The first three options are for the interactive use of modules in the construction of GUIs (graphical interfaces), respectively GTK, Qt, WxPython.

These options start IPython on a separate thread to allow interactive control of graphics. This option will execute from pylab import on startup, and allows graphs to be displayed without having to invoke the show () command, but will execute scripts that contain show () at the correct time.

After one of the four options above has been specified, the regular options may follow in any order. All options may be abbreviated to the shortest unambiguous form, but must be case sensitive (as in Python and Bash languages, by the way). One or two hyphens may be used in specifying options.

All options can be set to be turned off (if enabled by default).

Due to a large number of existing options, we will not list them here. consult the IPython documentation to learn about them. However, some options may appear throughout this section and will be explained as they arise.

Magic Commands

One of the most useful features of IPython is the concept of magic commands. In the IPython console, any line beginning with the% character is considered a call to a magic command. For example, %autoindent turns on automatic indentation within IPython.

There is an option that is enabled by default in IPythonrc, called automagic. With this function, magic commands can be called without %, i.e. autoindent is understood as % autoindent. User-defined variables can mask magic commands.

Therefore, if I set a variable autoindent = 1, the word autoindent is no longer recognized as a magic command but as the name of the variable I created. However, I can still call the magic command by placing the% character at the beginning.

The user can extend the magic command set with their own creations. See the IPython documentation on how to do this.

The magic command% magic returns an explanation of the existing magic commands.

%Exit Exits the IPython console.

%Pprint Turns text formatting on / off.

%Quit Exit IPython without asking for confirmation.

%alias Give me a synonym for a command.

You can use %1 to represent the line on which the alias command was called, for example:

1 In [2]: alias all echo " Input between parenthesis: (% l) "

2 In [3]: all Hello World

3 Input between parenthesis: (Hello world)

%autocall Turns on / off mode that lets you call functions without parentheses. For example: fun 1 becomes fun (1).

%autoindent Turns on / off auto-indentation.

%automagic Auto magic on / off.

%bg Executes a background command on a separate thread. For example:%bg func (x, y, z = 1). As soon as execution starts, a message is printed on the console informing you of the job number. Thus, you can access job result # 5 through the jobs.results [5] command.

IPython has a task manager accessible through the job object. For more information on this object, type jobs ?. IPython lets you automatically complete a partially typed command. To see all methods of the job object try typing jobs.following the <TAB> key.

%bookmark Manages the IPython bookmark system. To learn more about bookmarks type% bookmark ?.

%cd Changes directory.

%colors Change the color scheme.

%cpaste Pastes and executes a preformatted clipboard block. The block must be terminated by a line containing --.

%dhist Print directory history.

%ed Synonym for% edit

%edit Opens an editor and executes the edited code on exit. This command accepts several options, see the documentation.

The editor to be opened by the% edit command is whatever is set in the $ EDITOR environment variable. If this variable is not clear, IPython will open vi. If you do not specify a file name, IPython will open a Temporary file for editing. The% edit command has some conveniences.

For example, if we define a fun function in an edit session when exiting and executing code, this function will remain clear in the current namespace. Then we can just type %edit fun and IPython will open the file containing it, automatically placing the cursor on the relevant line. When you leave this editing session, the edited function will be updated.

1 In [6]: %ed

2 IPython will make a temporary file named:/tmp/ipython_edit_GuUWr_.py

3done. Executing edited code.. .

4   Out [6]: "def fun():\ n   p r in t ` fun'\ n   \ ndef fun():\ nprint 'fun'\ n"

5

6 In [7]: fun()

7 fun

8

9 In [8]: fun()

10 fun

11

12 In [9]: % ed fun

13done. Executing edited code.. .

%hist Synonym for% historic.

%history Prints the command history. Previous commands can also be accessed via the _i <n> variable, which is the only historical command.

1 In [1]: %hist

2 1: _ip.magic ("%hist")

3

4 In [2]: %hist

5   1: _ip.magic ("%hist")

6   2: _ip.magic ("%hist")

IPython has a sophisticated session registration system. This system is controlled by the following magic commands:

%logon, %logoff, %logstart and %logstate. For more information see the documentation.

%lsmagic Lists the available magic commands.

%macro Give a set of command lines as a macro for later use: % macro test 1 2 or %macro macro2 44-47 49.

%p Synonym for print.

%pdb turns on / off interactive debugger.

%pdef Prints the header of any callable object. If the object is a class, it returns information about the class's constructor.

%pdoc Prints the docstring of an object.

%pfile Prints the file where the object is set.

%psearch searches for objects in namespaces.

%psource prints the source code of an object. The object must have been imported from a file.

%quickref shows a quick reference guide

%quit exits IPython.

%r repeats the previous command.

%rehash updates the synonym table with all entries in

$ PATH. This command does not check to execute permissions and whether the entries are even files. %rehashx does this, but is slower.

%rehashdir adds the executables from the specified directories to the synonym table.

%rehashx updates the thesaurus with all executable files in $ PATH.

%reset resets the namespace by removing all user names.

%run runs the specified file inside IPython as a program.

%runlog runs files as logs.

%save saves a set of lines to a file.

%sx runs a command on the Linux console and captures its output.

%store stores variables to be available in a future session.

%time times the execution of a command or expression.

%timeit times the execution of a command or expression using the timeit module.

%unalias removes a synonym.

%upgrade upgrades the IPython installation.

%who prints all interactive variables with a minimum of formatting.

%who_ls returns a list of all interactive variables.

%whos is similar to% who, with more information about each variable.

To top it off, IPython is an excellent interactive working environment for scientific computing, especially when invoked with the -pylab option. The numpy main package is also exposed in pylab mode. Numpy sub-packages need to be imported manually.

Code Editors

When editing Python programs, a good code editor can make a big difference in productivity. Due to the significance of the blanks for the language, an editor that maintains consistent code indentation is very important to avoid bugs.

It is also desirable for the editor to know Python's rules of indentation, for example: indent after:, indent with spaces rather than tabs. Another desirable feature is the colorization of the code to emphasize the language syntax. This feature dramatically increases the readability of the code.

Editors that can be successfully used for editing Python programs fall into two basic categories: generic editors and Python-specialized editors. In this section, we'll look at the key features of some editors in each category.

Generic Editors

There are a number of text editors available for the Gnu / Linux environment. The vast majority of them meet our basic requirements for automatic indentation and colorization. I selected some that stand out in my preference for usability and versatility.

Emacs: Incredibly complete and versatile editor, it works as an integrated development environment. Must have python-mode installed. For those with no prior experience with Emacs, I recommend that the Easymacs1 package be installed as well. This package makes the Emacs interface much easier, especially for adding standard CUA keyboard shortcuts. You can also use IPython within Emacs.

Scite: Lightweight and aware editor, supports Python well (runs the script with <F5>) as well as several other languages. It allows you to configure C and Fortran compilation commands, which makes it easier to develop extensions. Completely configurable (Figure 4.1).

Ideal for use in conjunction with IPython (% edit command).

Jedit: I have included Jedit in this list as it supports Jython development (see Section 5.5). Aside from that, it is a very powerful editor for java and not as heavy as Eclipse.

Kate / Gedit Standard editors of KDE and Gnome respectively. Good for casual use, Kate has the advantage of a built-in console.

Specialized Publishers

Python publishers tend to be more of the IDE (integrated development environment) type, offering features that only make sense for managing midsize to large projects, but too much for editing a simple script.

Boa-Constructor: Boa-constructor is an IDE, aimed at projects wishing to use WxPython as a graphical interface. In this respect it is perfect, allowing visual construction of the interface,

Gnu Nano Editor

generating all the code associated with the interface. It also features an excellent debugger for Python programs and supports extension modules written in other languages, such as Pyrex or C .

Eric: Eric is also a Python IDE with the PyQt interface. It has functional integration with the Qt Designer interface generator, making it easy to develop graphical interfaces with this tool. It also has a great debugger. In addition Eric offers many other functions, such as integration with version control, version control systems, storage generators, etc.

Pydev (Eclipse): Pydev is an IDE for Python and Jython developed as an Eclipse plugin. For those who already have experience with the Eclipse platform, it may be a good alternative, otherwise it may be much more complicated to operate than the alternatives mentioned above. In terms of functionality, it matches Eric and Boa-constructor.

IDE Boa-Constructor

Software Version Control

When developing software on any scale, we experience a process of progressive improvement in which software goes through various versions. In this process, it is very common, at a certain stage, to recover some functionality that was present in an earlier version, and which for some reason has been deleted from the code.

Another challenge in the development of scientific products (software or others) is teamwork around the same object (often a program). Usually each team member works individually and presents their results to the team in regular meetings. What to do when modifications developed by different members of the same team become incompatible? Or even when two or more employees are working on different parts of a program but need each other to work?

The type of tool we will introduce in this section seeks to solve or minimize the above problems and can also be applied to the collaborative development of other types of documents, not just programs. Since this is a Python-based book, let's use a version control system developed entirely in Python Mercurial 2.

In practice the mechanism behind all version control systems is very similar. Migrating from one to another is a matter of learning new names for the same operations. In addition, the daily use of the version control system involves only two or three commands.

IDE Eric

Understanding Mercurial

Mercurial is a decentralized version control system, meaning there is no notion of a central server where code is deposited.

Diagram of a Mercurial Repository

Code repositories are directories that can be cloned from one machine to another.

So what does a repository consist of? To simplify our explanation, consider that the repository has already been created or cloned from someone who created it. We'll see how to create a repository from scratch later.

The archive contains the complete project history. The working directory contains a copy of the project files at a certain point in time (for example, in revision 2). It is in the working directory that the researcher works and updates the files.

After a commit, as the working directory sources did not correspond to the latest project revision, Mercurial automatically creates a script in the file. With that we have two lines of development going in parallel, with our working directory belonging to the branch started by revision 4.

Mercurial groups changes sent by a user (via commit) into an atomic changeset, which constitutes a review.

Ana's Repository

But since Mercurial allows the same project to be developed in parallel, the revision numbers for different developers could differ. Therefore each revision also receives a global identifier consisting of a forty digit hexadecimal number.

In addition to ramifications, merge between branches can occur at any time. Whenever there is more than one branch under development, Mercurial will name the most recent revisions of each branch (heads). Among these, the one with the largest revision number will be considered the tip of the repository.

Example of use:

In these examples, we will explore the most common operations in a collaborative development environment using Mercurial. Let's start with our first developer, called Ana.

Our second developer, Brad, has just joined the team and clones the repository Ana5.

1 $ hg clonessh:// machine of ana/project my project

2 requesting all changes

Note: We assume here that Ana's machine is running a ssh server

Modifications by Brad

Modifications of Ana

3 adding change sets

4 adding manifests

5 adding File changes

6 added 4 change sets with 4 changes to 2 Files

Valid URLs:

file://

http://

https://

ssh://

static-http://

After the above command, Brad will receive a complete copy of Ana's file, but his working directory, my project, will remain independent.

Brad then decides to pull Ana's repository to synchronize it with his own.

1 $ hg pull

Updated Brad Repository

2   pulling from ssh://machineofana/project

3 searching for changes

4 adding change sets

5 adding manifests

6 adding File changes

7 added 1 change sets with 1 changes to 1 Files

8 (run 'hg heads 'to see heads, 'hg merge 'to merge)

The hg pull command, if not specifying the source, will pull from the source from which the local repository was cloned. This command will update the local file, but not the working directory.

As Ana's changes were the last ones added to Brad's repository, this revision becomes the tip of the Archive.

Brad now wants to merge his development branch with the tip of his Archive that corresponds to the modifications made by Ana. Usually, after pulling modifications, we run a hg update to synchronize our working directory with the newly updated Archive. So Brad does that.

1 $ hg update

2 this update spans a branch affecting the following Files:

3hello.py (resolve)

Brad's Repository after the Merger

4 aborting update spanning branches!

5 (use 'hg merge' to merge across branches or 'hg update −C' to lose changes)

Due to the ramification in the Brad Archive, the update command does not know which branch to merge the existing modifications into Brad's working directory. To solve this, Brad will need to merge the two branches. Fortunately this is a trivial task.

1 $ hg merge tip

2 merging hello.py

In the merge command, if no revision is specified, the working directory is a branch head and, because there is only one other head, the two heads will be merged. Otherwise a revision must be specified.

Ready!

Creating A Repository

To create a repository from scratch, you only need one command:

1 $ hg init

When the directory is created, a directory named .hg is created within the working directory. Mercurial will store all repository information in the .hg directory. The contents of this directory should not be changed by the user.

Additional Information

Of course, many other things can be done with a version control system. The reader is encouraged to consult the Mercurial documentation to find out. For quick reference, use the hg help -v <command> command with any command from the list below.

add add the specified archive (s) in the next commit.

addremove Add all new files, removing the missed before.

annotate Shows information about file line modifications.

archive Creates an unversioned (compressed) file from a specified revision.

backout Reverses the effects of a previous modification. branch Changes or shows the name of the current branch.

branches List all branches of the repository.

bundle **Creates a compressed file containing all modifications not present in another repository.**

cat Returns the specified file as it was in a given revision.

clone Replicates a repository.

commit Files all modifications or specified files.

copy Copies the specified files to another directory on the next commit.

diff Shows differences between revisions or between specified files.

Export Print header and differences for one or more modification sets.

grep Search for words in specific files and revisions.

heads Show current heads.

help Show help for a command, extension, or command list.

identify Print information about the current working copy.

import **Imports an ordered set of updates (patches). [This command is the counterpart of Export.]**

incoming Shows new sets of modifications existing in a given repository.

init **Creates a new repository in the specified directory. If the directory does not exist, it will be created.**

locate Finds files.

log Shows revision history for the repository as a whole or for some files

manifest Returns the manifest (controlled file list) of the current or other revision.

merge Merges the working directory with another revision.

outgoing Shows set of modifications not present in the destination repository.

parents Show the parents of the working or revision directory.

paths Show symbolic path names.

pull Pulls updates from the specified source.

push **Sends modifications to the specified destination repository. [It is the counterpart of pull.]**

recover Undoes a broken transaction.

remove **Removes the files specified at the next commit. rename Renames files; Equivalent to copy + remove.**

revert Revert files to the state they were in a given revision.

rollback Undoes the last transaction in this repository.

root Prints the root of the current working directory. serve Exports the directory via HTTP.

showconfig Shows the combined configuration of all hgrc files.

status Shows modified files in the working directory.

tag Adds a marker for the current or other revision.

tags Lists repository bookmarks.

tip Shows the tip revision.

unbundle Applies a modification file.

update Updates or merges the working directory.

*Verify*Verifies the integrity of the repository.

version Returns version and copyright information.

7. The Best Python Libraries To Use With Data Science

Now that we know a bit about the basics that come with the Python language, it is important that we spend some time learning the best libraries and extensions that we are able to add into the mix to make sure that Python is going to work the way that we would like for data science. The regular library that comes with Python can do a lot of amazing things, but it is not going to be able to handle all of the graphing, mathematics, and the machine learning that we need with data science.

The good news here though is that there are a few other libraries that we are able to work with that utilize Python and can help with machine learning and data science together. All of these are going to help us handle tasks in a slightly different manner so take a look at them and how they are meant to work with Python and data science. The best libraries that can help you to get this work done will include:

NumPy and SciPy

If you want to do any kind of work with machine learning or data science with Python, you have to make sure that you work with the NumPy and the SciPy library. Both of these are going to be the basis of many of the other libraries that we are going to talk about here, which is why it is likely that when you work with data science, you are going to also add in a bit of library as well.

First, we will look at NumPy, which is going to stand for Numeric and Scientific Computation. This is a useful library because it is going to lay down some of the basic premises that we need for doing any kind of scientific computing with data science in Python. This library can also help us to get ahold of some functions that have been precompiled for us, and it is fast for handling any numerical and mathematical routine process that you would like to do.

Then there is also the Scientific Python library, which we call SciPy, that goes along with NumPy in many cases. This is the kind of library that you want to work with to add in some kind of competitive edge to what you are doing in machine learning. This happens when you work to enhance some of the useful functions for things like regression and minimization to name a few.

Matplotlib

As you are going through data science and Python, there are going to be times when you will want to work with a graph or a chart or some other kind of visual. This is going to make it easier to see the information that is found in the text, in a glance and the matplotlib will be able to make some of these graphs for you in no time.

The matplotlib extension is going to provide us with all of the parts that we need to take the info and turn it into the visualizations that you need for your data. This library is going to work with pretty much any of the different types of visualizations that you need from a histogram, bar charts, error charts, line graphs, and more.

The Scikit-Learn library

The Scikit-Learn is the library that we are going to take a look at next. This is a great one to go with when it comes to machine learning. This is because the package that comes with this library is going to provide us with a lot of machine learning algorithms and more that we can use to really get data science to work. It is going to include a lot of different parts that can ensure we analyze the information that is fed into the algorithm in a proper manner.

One other benefit that we are going to see when it comes to this kind of library is that it is easy to distribute, which means it works well in commercial and academic kind of settings, and there are not a lot of dependencies that go with it. The interface is concise and consistent, which make it easier to work with, and you will find that the most common of the machine learning algorithms are already inside, making it easier to create some of the models you need for data science.

Pandas

The next library in Python that you want to work with to make machine learning and data science do what you would like. Pandas are going to stand for the Python Data Analysis Library, which helps us to do a lot of the work that is needed in the Python world. This is an open-sourced tool that helps us with some of the data structures that are needed to do data analysis. You can use this library to add in the right tools and data structures to make sure your data analysis is complete, and many industries like to work with this one to help out with some different processes like finance, statistics, engineering, and social science.

This Pandas library is going to be really adaptable, which makes it really great for getting a ton of work done in less time. It can also help you work with any kind of data that you are able to bring in, no matter what kind of source you are getting that info from, making it a lot easier to work with. This library is going to come with many different features that you can enjoy and some of the best ones are going to include:

1. You can use the Pandas library to help reshape the structures of your data.

2. You can use the Pandas library to label series, as well as tabular data, to help us see an automatic alignment.

3. You can use the Pandas library to help with heterogeneous indexing of the info and it is also useful when it comes to systematic labeling of the data as well.

4. You can use this library because it can hold onto the capabilities of identifying and then fixing any of the data that is missing.

5. This library provides us with the ability to load and then save data from more than one format.

6. You can easily take some of the data structures that come out of Python and NumPy and convert them into the objects that you need to Pandas objects.

TensorFlow

TensorFlow, one of the best Python libraries for data science, is a library that was released by Google Brain. It was written out mostly in the language of C++, but it is going to include some bindings in

Python, so the performance is not something that you are going to need to worry about. One of the best features that comes with this library is going to be some of the flexible architecture that is found in the mix, which is going to allow the programmer to deploy it with one or more GPUs or CPUs in a desktop, mobile, or server device, while using the same API the whole time.

Not many, if any, of the other libraries that we are using in this chapter, will be able to make this kind of claim. This library is also unique in that it was developed by the Google Brain project, and it is not used by many other programmers. However, you do need to spend a bit more time to learn the API compared to some of the other libraries. In just a few minutes, you will find that it is possible to work with this TensorFlow library in order to implement the design of your network, without having to fight through the API as you do with other options.

The Keras library

If you are looking for a Python library that can handle data science and data analytics that is also easy for the user to work with, then this is the library for you. It is able to handle a lot of the different processes that come with the other libraries, but it keeps in mind the user, rather than the machine when it comes to designing the interface and the other parts

that you use within this coding library. The user experience is easy, the interface is designed to only need a few clicks to get the processes done and it all comes together to make data science and machine learning as easy as possible.

This library is going to work a lot of the modules that are needed for machine learning. You can work with a module that is on its own, or you can combine together a few modules in order to get the results that you would like. There is a lot of flexibility that comes with using this kind of library, and that is one of the many reasons that so many programmers like to use it when completing work with Python data science.

These are just a few of the different libraries that you are able to use along with the Python coding language to get some of your data science and machine learning work done. These libraries all work on slightly different types of processes when it comes to data science, which is going to make them so much easier to work with overall. Take a look at each one, and see just how they can all come together to provide you with the results that you want in your data analytics project.

8. Lists And Dictionaries

We have learned quite a lot ever since we started with this book. We have gone through operators, we learned about various data types, and we also looked at loops and statements. During all of this, we did mention the word 'list' and represented these with a square bracket instead of curly or round brackets. This chapter will now explore and explain what exactly lists are. We will also come across the term "dictionaries" and hopefully, by the end of this chapter, we should be familiarized with the core concepts of these and how they are vital to programming of any kind.

Remember, this book is aimed only for absolute Python beginners. For more advanced references, you are encouraged to seek appropriate knowledge in books or on online learning platforms specific to your requirements.

A Look into What Lists Are

Let us go ahead and create an imaginary family that comprises of Smith, Mary, their daughter Alicia, and their son Elijah. How would we do that? Begin by creating a variable named family as shown below:

----

family = ['Smith', 'Mary', 'Alicia', 'Elijah']

Using the [] brackets, we provided the data to this variable. Now, this specific variable holds more than one name within it. This is where lists come to the rescue. Through listing, we can store as many values within a variable as we like. In this case, we can stick to four only.

If you now use the print command to print 'family', you should see the following:

======

['Smith', 'Mary', 'Alicia', 'Elijah']

======

The values or names stored within the brackets are called as items. To call on the item or to check what item is stored on a specific index number, you can use the method we had used earlier in strings.

----

print(family[0])

======

Smith

======

Instead of showing 'S', the complete name was shown. Similarly, if you use the other functions such as the len() function, it would provide you with the length of the list. In this case, it would should you that there are four items in this list. Let us try that out for ourselves.

----

print(len(family))

=====

4

=====

You can use the [x:y] where x and y are ranges you can set. This can be helpful if the list you are working on contains hundreds of entries. You can only filter out the ones you would like to view. You can jump straight to the end of the list by using [-1] to see the last entry. The combinations are endless.

Here is a little brain-teaser. Suppose we have numerous numbers in a list, around 100. They are not listed chronologically and we do not have time to scroll through each one of them. We need to find out which of these numbers is the highest. How can we do that?

This is where lists, loops, and if statements come together. How? Let us look into it right away:

```
numbers = [312, 1434, 68764, 4627, 84, 470, 9047,
98463, 389, 2]

high = numbers[0]

for number in numbers:
    if number > high:
        high = number

print(f"The highest number is {high}")
```

======

The highest number is 98463

======

Time to put our thinking cap on and see what just happened.

We started out by providing some random numbers. One of these was surely the highest. We created a variable and assigned it the first item of the list of numbers as its value. We do not know whether this item holds the highest value.

Moving ahead, we initiated a 'for' loop where we created a loop variable called number. This number would iterate each value from numbers. We used an 'if' statement to tell the interpreter that if the loop variable 'number' is greater than our currently set highest number 'high', it should immediately replace that with the value it holds.

Once the program was run, Python sees we assigned 'high' a value of the first item which is 312. Once the loop and if statement begin, Python analyzes if the first item is greater than the value of the variable 'high'. Surely, 312 is not greater than 312 itself. The loop does not alter the value and ends. Now, the 'for' loop restarts, this time with the second item value. Now, the value has changed. This time around, when the 'if' statement is executed, Python sees that our variable has a lower value than the one it is currently working on. 312 is far less than 1434. Therefore, it executes the code within the statement and replaces the value of our variable to the newly found higher value. This process will continue on until all values are cross-checked and finally the largest value is maintained. Then, only the largest value will be printed for us.

2-D Lists

In Python, we have another kind of list that is called the two-dimensional list. If you are someone who is willing to master data sciences or machine learning, you will need to use these quite a lot. The 2-D list is quite a powerful tool. Generally, when it comes to maths, we have what are called matrixes. These are arrays of numbers formed in rectangular form within large brackets.

Unlike your regular lists, these contain rows and columns of values and data as shown here:

----

matrix = [

    [19, 11, 91],

    [41, 25, 54],

    [86, 28, 21]

]

In an easier way, imagine this as a list which contains a number of lists inside. As illustrated above, each row is now acting as a separate list. Had this been a regular list, we could have printed a value using the index number. How do you suppose we can have the console print out the value of our first item within the first list?

----

print(matrix[0][0])

Using the above, you can now command interpreter to only print out the first value stored within the first list. The first zero within the first [] tells the interpreter the number of list to access. Following that is the second bracket set which further directs the search to the index number of the item. In this case, we were aiming to print out 19 and thus, 19 will be our result.

Take a moment and try to print out 25, 21, and 86 separately. If you were able to do this, good job.

You can change the values of the items within the list. If you know the location of the said item, you can use the name of the variable followed by the [x][y] position of the item. Assign a new number by using the single equal to mark and the value you wish for it to have.

The 2-D lists are normally used for slightly advanced programming where you need to juggle quite a lot of values and data types. However, it is best to keep these in mind as you never know when you may actually need to use them.

List Methods

Somewhere in the start, we learned about something called methods. These are extra methods which are available that can be used with the said variable or object. So far, we have seen how to use the .lower or the .upper methods for strings. Those methods change the input of the user to either lower or upper case. For lists, things are a little different.

To start off, let us go back to the PyCharm and create our own list of random numbers. Let's use the following number sequence:

```
----------

numbers = [11, 22, 33, 44, 55, 66, 77]

----------
```

We are not going to print this out to our console. Instead, we would like to see what possible methods are available for us to use. In the next line, type the name of the variable followed by the dot operator ".". to access the methods.

Quite a lot, aren't they? We won't be needing all of them right now. We will just focus on the ones which are more commonly used and that every beginner should know. Let us type the append method.

The append method allows us to add an entry or a value to the list under the selected variable. Go ahead and add any number of your choice. Done? Now try and print the variable named 'numbers' and see what happens.

You should be able to see a number added at the end of the list. Good, but what if you don't wish to add a number at the end? What if you want it to be somewhere close to the start?

To do that, we need a method called insert.

----

numbers.insert()

In order for us to execute this properly, we will need to first provide this method with the index position where we wish for the new number to be added. If you wish to add it to the start, use zero or if you wish to add it to any other index, use that number. Follow this number by a comma and the number itself.

Now, if you print the numbers variable, you should be able to see the new number added exactly where you wanted.

----

numbers.insert(2, 20)

print(numbers)

=====

[11, 22, 20, 33, 44, 55, 66, 77]

=====

Similarly, you can use a method called remove to delete any number you wish to be removed from the list. When using the remove method, do note that it will only remove the number where it first occurred. It will not remove the same number which might have repeated later on within the same list as shown here:

----

numbers = [11, 22, 33, 44, 55, 66, 77, 37, 77]

numbers.remove(77)

print(numbers)

=====

[11, 22, 33, 44, 55, 66, 37, 77]

=====

For any given reason, if you decide you no longer require the list content, you can use the clear command. This command does not require you to pass any object within the parentheses.

----

numbers.clear()

Using another method, you can check on the index number of a specific value's first occurrence.

----

numbers.index(44)

If you run the above, you will get '3' as a result. Why? The index position of three contains the number 44 in the list we used earlier. If you put in a value that is not within the defined list values, you will end up with an error as shown here:

=====

```
print(numbers.index(120))
```

ValueError: 120 is not in list

=====

There is another useful method that helps you quite a lot when you are dealing with a bunch of numbers of other data types. In case you are not too sure and you wish to find out whether a specific number exists within a list, you can use the 'in' operator as shown:

```
numbers = [11, 22, 33, 44, 55, 66, 77, 37, 77]

print(43 in numbers)
```

What do you think the result will be? An error? You might be wrong. This is where the result will show 'False'. This is a boolean value and is indicating that the number we wanted to search for does not exist in our list. If the number did exist, the return boolean value would have been 'True'.

Let us assume that we have a large number of items in the list and we wish to find out just how many times a specific number is being used or repeated within the said list. There is a way we can command Python to do it for us. This is where you will use the 'count' method.

In our own list above, we have two occurrences where the number 77 is used. Let us see how we can use this method to find out both the instances.

----

print(numbers.count(77))

The result will now state '2' as our result. Go ahead and add random numbers to the list with a few repeating ones. Use the count method to find out the number of occurrences and see how the command works for you. The more you practice, the more you will remember.

Now we have seen how to locate, change, add, clear, and count the items in the list. What if we wish to sort the entire list in ascending or descending order? Can we do that?

With the help of the sort method, you can actually have that carried out. The sort() method by default will only sort the data into ascending order. If you try and access the method within a print command, the console will show 'none' as your return. To have this done correctly, always use the sort method before or after the print command. To reverse the order, use the reverse() method. This method, just like the sort() method, does not require you to pass any object within the brackets.

Tuples

In Python, we use lists to store various values and these values can be accessed, changed, modified, or removed at will, whenever we like. That certainly might not be the best thing to know if you intend to use data that is essential in nature. To overcome that, there is a kind of list that will store the data for you but after that, no additional modification will be carried out, even if you try and do it accidentally or intentionally. These are called tuples.

Tuples are a form of list which are very important to know when it comes to Python. Unlike the square bracket representation for lists, these are represented by parentheses ().

----

numbers = (19, 21, 28, 10, 11)

Tuples are known as immutable items. This is because of the fact that you cannot mutate or modify them. Let us deliberately try and modify the value to see what happens.

As soon as you type in the dot operator to access append, remove, and other similar methods, you should see this instead:

```
numbers = (19, 21, 28, 10, 11)
numbers.
    m count(self, x)                                    tuple
    m index(self, x, start, end)                        tuple
    m __add__(self, x)                                  tuple
    f __annotations__                                   object
    p __class__                                         object
    m __contains__(self, x)                             tuple
    m __delattr__(self, name)                           object
    f __dict__                                          object
    m __dir__(self)                                     object
    m __eq__(self, o)                                   object
    m __format__(self, format_spec)                     object
Press Ctrl+ to choose the selected (or first) suggestion and insert a dot afterwards Next Tip  ⋮
```

Tuples simply do not have these options anymore. That is because you are trying to modify a value that is secure and locked by Python. You can try another method to see if you can forcefully change the value by doing this:

----

numbers = (19, 21, 28, 10, 11)

numbers[0] = 10

```
print(numbers)
```

======

```
numbers[0] = 10
```

TypeError: 'tuple' object does not support item assignment

======

See how the error came up? The program cannot carry out this change of value, nor can it append the value in any way.

While most of the time you will be working with lists, tuples come in handy to ensure you store values which you know you really don't wish to change accidentally in the future. Think of a shape that you wish to create and maintain throughout the game or website as uniform. You can always call on the values of a tuple and use the values when and where needed.

The only way these values might be changed is if you purposely or unintentionally overwrite them. For example, you had written the values of a tuple within the code and move on hundreds of lines ahead. At this point, you might have forgotten about the earlier values or the fact that you wrote these values previously. You start writing new values by using exactly the same name and start storing new values within them. This is where Python will allow you to overwrite the previously stored values without providing you any errors when you run the program.

The reason that happens is because Python understands that you may wish for a value to change later on and then stay the same for a while until you need to change them yet again. When you execute the program, the initially stored values will continue to remain in use right up until the point where you want them to be changed. In order to do that, you can simply do the following:

```
numbers = (1, 2, 3, 4, 5)

print(numbers)

numbers = (6, 7, 8, 9, 10)

print(numbers)
```

=======

```
(1, 2, 3, 4, 5)

(6, 7, 8, 9, 10)
```

=======

The number values have changed without the program screaming back at us with an error. As long as you know and you do this change on purpose, there is absolutely nothing to worry about. However, should you start typing the same tuple and are about to rewrite it, you will be notified by PyCharm about the existence of the same tuple stored before. Can you guess how? Go ahead and try writing the above example in PyCharm and see how you are notified.

PyCharm will highlight the name of the tuple for you, and that is an indication that you have already used the same number before. If this was the first occurrence, PyCharm will not highlight the name or the values for you at all.

Another Useful Feature: Unpacking

Since we just discussed tuples, it is essential to know about a feature that has further simplified the use of tuples for us. Unpacking is of great help and is quite useful, too. Suppose you have a few values stored in a tuple and you wish to assign each one of them to another variable individually. There are two ways you can do that. Let us look at the first way of doing so and then we will look at the use of unpacking for comparison.

First method:

```
----------

ages = (25, 30, 35, 40)

Drake = ages[0]

Emma = ages[1]

Sully = ages[2]
```

```
Sam = ages[3]
```

If you print these values now, you will see the ages accordingly. This means that the values stored within these individual variables were successfully taken from the tuple as we wanted. However, this was a little longer. What if we can do all of that in just one line?

Second method:

```
ages = (25, 30, 35, 40)

Drake, Emma, Sully, Sam = ages
```

Now this looks much more interesting. Instead of using a number of lines, we got the same job done within the same line. Each individual variable still received the same age as the first method and each can be called upon to do exactly the same thing. This is how unpacking can work miracles for us. It saves you time and effort and allows for us to maintain a clean, clear, and readable code for reference.

With that said, it is now time for us to be introduced to one of the most important elements within Python that is used both by beginners and experts almost every single time.

Dictionaries

There are times you will come across certain information that is unique and holds a key value. Let us assume that you have to design a software that can store information about customers or clients. This information may include and is not limited to names, numbers, emails, physical addresses, and so on. This is where dictionaries will come into play.

If you had thought that dictionary in Python would be like your everyday dictionary for languages we speak, you might not have been completely wrong here. There is a similarity that we can see in these dictionaries. Every single entry that is made is unique. If an entry tries to replicate itself or if you try to store the same value again, you will be presented with an error.

So how exactly do we use dictionaries? For that, let us switch back to our new best friend, the PyCharm, and start typing a little.

Come up with an imaginary person's name, email address, age, and phone number. Don't start assigning these yet, as we would like to use the dictionary here to do the same. Ready? Okay, let us begin.

```
user_one = {      #Dictionaries are represented by {}

    'name': 'Sam',

    'age': 40,

    'phone': 123456789,

    'married': False

}
```

We have entered some information about a virtual character named Sam. You can use the print command and run the dictionary named 'user_one' and the system will print out these values for you.

For dictionaries, we use the colon : sign between values. The object name is placed in a string followed by the colon sign. After that, we use either a string, a number (integer or float), or a boolean value. You can use these to assign every object with its unique key pair. In case you are confused, key pair is just another way of saying the value that is assigned to the object. For example, the key pair for 'name' is 'Sam'.

Now, let us try and see what happens if we add another 'married' value. As soon as you are done typing, the system will highlight it straight away. Note that you can still type in the new value and the system will continue to function. However, the value it will use will be the latest value it can find.

This means that if you initially set the value for married to False and later change it to True, it will only display True.

```
user_one = {   #Dictionaries are represented by {}
    'name': 'Sam',
    'age': 40,
    'phone': 123456789,
    'married': False,
    'married': True
}
print(user_one['married'])
```

=======

True

=======

When it comes to calling values from the dictionary, we use the name of the string instead of the index number. If you try and run the index number zero, you will be presented with a 'KeyError: 0' in the traceback. Can you guess why that happens?

Dictionaries store values which are unique. If you use a number or a name that does not exist within the defined dictionary, you will always end up with an error. You will need to know the exact name or value of the information you are trying to access.

Similarly, if you try to access 'Phone' instead of 'phone', you will get the same error as Python is case-sensitive and will not identify the former as an existing value.

Dictionaries can be updated easily should the situation call for it. Let us assume that we got the wrong phone number for our client stored in 'user_one', we can simply use the following procedure to update the entry right away:

----

user_one['phone'] = 345678910

print(user_one['phone'])

You should now be able to see the new number we have stored. There's one little thing you may have noticed right about now when you did this. See the crazy wiggly lines which have appeared? These are here to suggest you rewrite the value instead of updating it separately to keep the code clean. PyCharm will continue to do this every now and then where it feels like you are causing the code to grow complicated. There is no reason for you to panic if you see these lines. However, if the lines are red in color, something is surely wrong and you may need to check on that.

Similarly, if you wish to add new key information to your dictionary, you can do so easily using almost the same process as shown here:

```
----------

user_one['profession'] = 'programmer'

----------
```

It is that easy! Try and print out the information now and you should be able to see this along with all previous entries available to you.

Lastly, you can use a method called 'get' to stop the program from coming back with an error in case you or your program user enters a wrong or a missing value when calling upon a dictionary. You can also assign it a default value like a symbol to notify yourself or the user that this value does not exist or is not identifiable by the program itself. Here is a little example where the user has tried to find out information about 'kids'. We have provided it with a default value of 'invalid':

```
print(user_one.get('kids', 'invalid'))
```

If you run this through, you will be presented with a result that shows an object named 'invalid'. We will make use of this feature in a more meaningful way in our test.

9. How To Handle Unstructured Data With Text Mining

Many times, the data that we are going to work with is going to come to us in an unstructured form. While there can be a lot of valuable information that is hidden in that unstructured data, it is often a big pain to deal with. It is not organized, the formatting is often different based on where you get the information, and it can take a lot of time to get this data ready to go through one of your models or algorithms

This doesn't mean that we want to avoid the unstructured data completely. Our modern world is full of a ton of data, and most of it is going to be unstructured. If you really want to be able to figure out about your data and what is inside of it, and you want to answer some of those big business questions that are important to you, then you have to spend time working with unstructured data.

This means that we need to have some kind of plan in place to help deal with some of the unstructured data that you have. it is not going to be as smooth cut and as easy as what we can see with structured data. But when we are able to combine together a few of the options that we use with data science, specifically what we can do with text mining, we will

376

be able to organize that unstructured data in a manner that is easy to read through, and can give us the results that we would like in the end. So, let's get started.

What is Text Mining

The first thing that we need to take a look at in this kind of process is the idea of text mining. This is often going to be referred to as text data mining and it is going to be the process of extracting and analyzing data when it comes to us in the form of large amounts of text data that is unstructured. The analyzing of text data is part of this process, or we can call it text analytics. Text mining is going to help us to perform a process that is able to identify keywords, topics, patterns, and concepts, as well as some other important attributes, to the data that we are working with.

Then it will extract and analyze the important parts of the data from all of the unstructured text data that we do not need. This analysis can help us to really find some of the valuable insights, the ones that would be hard to identify without some help from text mining.

When we look at the large amounts of data that most companies are collecting on a daily basis, taking the time to manually identify the information that you need from that huge amount of data is impossible.

So, being able to use text mining is a great lifesaver for these businesses. This process can actually go through and find the important information that you need, and then you can use this with your algorithms and other options to get the results that you would like.

As the years have gone on, the process of text mining has definitely become more practical and most companies that are working with a data science project are going to use it.

This is mainly because of the big data that we are using today. Those who are using this big data, including data scientists, businesses, and more, will find that they can use this text mining, and deep learning, to make it easier to analyze a very large set of data that is not structured in order to get the important predictions and insights out of it that pertain to them.

Text mining is able to extract and analyze all of the facts, relationships, and assertions that are found in the source of data, as long as they relate to the information that you are working with. This process is going to take that data and turn it into a structured form of data. Now, there are going to be a few different methods that the data scientist is able to use to make this happen including visualization with the help of mind maps, charts, and HTML tables, integration with the structured data that you are already storing in a database, and other machine learning systems that are set up to do more of the classification that you are looking for.

As we work through this, you may find that the sources of analyzing and mining are going to be diverse, and it often depends on where you were able to get your data in the first place. Things like medical records, social network posts, call center logs, comments on surveys, emails from the customer, and even corporate documents can all be mined to figure out what important information is there.

Basically, anything that is full of text-based data that could also help the business to learn more about themselves, their customers, and their competition can be used in data mining.

There are a few different technologies that are going to come into play to help us sort through this information and make sure that it all fits together.

For example, in addition to working with the process of text mining, we can also work with artificial intelligence and natural language processing technologies to make sure that we are able to transform some of the key content that is found in various text documents into insights that are quantitative and actionable.

How Can Text Mining Help?

We have already spent a bit of time talking about the importance of text mining and what it is able to do for our business and all of the data that we are holding onto. Text mining is going to work in the same manner as we see with the process of data mining, but the focus is going to be more of the text rather than on the structured data. This makes it easier for us to handle and process a lot of the more complex and unstructured forms of data that most businesses are collecting in data science.

The first step that we need to do in the text mining process is to make sure that we can organize the data. We have to do this with regards to both quantitative and qualitative analysis. This is why we are going to bring out the technology for natural language processing to make this all work.

Text mining is going to include a few different parts that have to all come together to make sure that this process does what we are expecting. Some of the tasks that text mining are able to handle for us include:

1. Information identification and retrieval. This means that it is able to collect the data from all of the sources that you want to use and they will analyze it.

2. Apply the text analytics: This means that we are going to use different methods, including statistical methods or natural language processing to help with things like speed tagging.

3. Named entity recognition. This means that the program will be able to identify some of the named text features the process name as categorizations.

4. Disambiguation. This means that we will focus on clustering.

5. Document clustering. This is used to help us identify sets of similar text documents.

6. Identify nouns and other terms that are going to end up referring to the same object, and then find out the relationship and the fact among the entities and some of the other information that is in the text.

7. Then we can perform a sentiment analysis as well as quantitative text analysis.

8. Finally, we can work to create an analytic model that is able to help us to generate the right business strategies and figure out the actions that we are able to take in here.

What Can Text Mining Do?

The best example that we are able to see with text mining is the sentimental analysis. This is an analysis that is able to track the review or the sentiment of a customer about a company and a product in a process that is known as opinion mining. In this kind of analysis, we are able to collect text from social networks, online reviews, and other sources of data and then perform our own NLP in order to identify the positive or the negative feedbacks that we see with the customers.

Another common use of all of this is going to be things like marketing to figure out how the customer will respond to things, biomedical applications to help with clinical studies, security applications, and even with things like fraud management in a bank or another financial institution.

We can even see this happen with scientific literature mining for a publisher to search through the data on an index retrieval system, how to classify a website, blocking out emails that are spam, figuring out when an insurance claim is going to be fraudulent, and examining some of the corporate documents that need to be looked over as part of the electronic discovery process.

The Advantages of Text Mining

The next thing that we need to take a look at is the advantages of text mining. There are a lot of benefits that come with using this kind of technique in your business and understanding how this works is going to make a big difference in your business and how you will work with text mining.

The first benefit is fraud detection. Insurance companies and banks will find that it can help with detecting fraud before this issue happens. It is a good way to figure out the behavior of your customers to determine which way to move your business. It can help with things like risk management so that the business is able to make some smart decisions that will actually benefit them rather than cause harm. And it can work with finishing up a scientific analysis as well.

This is just the beginning of what we are able to see when it comes to working with text mining though. In addition, text mining, when it is used with the right processes, can help a company to detect issues and then resolve these issues before they have the potential to become a big problem, which could negatively affect your company.

Text mining can help you to take a look at some of the communication and reviews from your customers in order to learn what the customer is telling us.

Companies are then able to use this information to learn the best ways to improve the customer experience by identifying the features that are required for the customer.

It can also come in and help with other factors that are going to help to increase the sales and then the revenues and the profits of the company so that they can continue growing over time.

We can even take the idea of text mining a step further and see how we are able to use this in the healthcare industry. For example, this type of process is able to come into play to help us identify the diseases that a patient may have, and it could be a great way to diagnose a lot of the diseases, often before a doctor is able to do it.

More about Text Mining

To help us perform the process of text mining, it is important to have people on your team with skills for data analysis and have a good understanding of statistics. Other skills that the data scientist should have in order to complete this process including natural language processing, machine learning algorithms, deep learning algorithms, knowledge about how to work with databases, and information about frameworks of big data processing. It is also a good option to know how to program in a coding language as well to get some of the work done.

The scope of text mining is going to be interesting as well. Text mining is really a field that is growing like crazy, so the scope is promising in the future. The amount of text data is growing all of the time, and social media platforms are going to generate a lot of text data. We have to be able to mine all of this text data in order to get some real insights into the different domains that are present.

The target audience for working with and learning more about this technology is going to be professionals who would like to identify the valuable insights that the huge amount of unstructured data for companies for purposes that are varied. For example, it is possible for a company to use this to increase their sales and see more profits, to help with detecting fraud, to learn more about their customers, and to even perform scientific analysis that can put them in the lead of others.

In conclusion, there are a lot of different parts that we need to consider when it comes to text mining. Some of the things that we need to remember when it comes to this part of data science include:

1. Text mining is often going to be known as text data mining. This is the process of extracting and then analyzing data from a

large amount of text data that is not structured.

2. Text mining work is going to include things like information retrieval or the identification of information, text analytics, named entity recognition, document clustering, identifying nouns or other keywords, and more among the information that we have in our text. We are then able to perform a sentiment analysis and a quantitative text analysis before creating an analytic model that will help to generate good business strategies that we can follow.

3. Text mining is going to help with things like healthcare, customer behavior, scientific analysis, risk management, and fraud detection to name a few

4. To help us perform this process of text mining, people need to have a variety of skill to get it done. This can include knowledge of deep learning and machine learning algorithms, natural language processing, database knowledge, big data processing frameworks, statistics, and data analysis.

5. It is a field is going to grow fast and will continue to do this as the field of big data

continues to grow as well. This means that the scope that comes with text mining is promising in the future, and it is likely to continue growing more and more.

Working with text mining is going to be very important when we work with some of the unstructured data that comes up in our analysis. This process is going to help us to mine through the large amounts of text that we are working with, ensuring that we are able to see some results out of this data and that we are actually able to use it for our needs as well.

10. Variable Scope And Lifetime In Python Functions

Variables and parameters defined within a Python function have local scope implying they are not visible from outside. In Python, the variable lifetime is valid as long the function executes and is the period throughout that a variable exists in memory. Returning the function destroys the function variables.

Example

Start IDLE.

Navigate to the File menu and click New Window.

Type the following:

def function_my()

   marks=15

print("The value inside the function is:", marks)

marks=37

function_my()

Print"The value outside the function is:",marks)

   Function Types

They are broadly grouped into user-defined and built-in functions. The built-in functions are part of the

Python interpreter while the user-defined functions are specified by the user.

Exercise

Give three examples of built-in functions in Pythons

Function Argument

Calling a function requires passing the correct number of parameters otherwise the interpreter will generate an error.

Illustration

Start IDLE.

Navigate to the File menu and click New Window.

Type the following:

```
def salute(name,message):
    """This function welcomes to
    the student with the provided message"""
    print("Welcome",salute + ', ' + message)
welcome("Brenda","Lovely Day!")
```

Note: The function welcome() has two parameters. We will not get any error as has been fed with two arguments. Let us try calling the function with one argument and see what happens:

```
welcome("Brenda")    #only one argument passed
```

Running this program will generate an error saying "TypeError: welcome() missing 1 required positional argument. The same will happen when we pass no arguments to the function.

Example 2

Start IDLE.

Navigate to the File menu and click New Window.

Type the following:

welcome()

The interpreter will generate an error "typeerror: welcome() missing 2 required positional arguments".

Keywords Arguments in Python

Python provides a way of calling functions using keyword arguments. When calling functions using keyword arguments, the order of arguments can be changed. The values of a function are matched to the argument position-wise.

Note:

In the previous example function welcome when invoked as welcome("Brenda", "Lovely Day!"). The value "Brenda" is assigned to the argument name and "Lovely Day!" to msg.

Calling the function using keywords

Start IDLE.

Navigate to the File menu and click New Window.

Type the following:

welcome(name="Brenda", msg="Lovely Day!")

Keywords not following the order

Welcome(msg="Lovely Day!", name="Brenda")

Arbitrary Arguments

It may happen that we do not have knowledge of all arguments needed to be passed into a function. Analogy: Assume that you are writing a program to welcome all new students this semester. In this case, you do not how many will report.

Example

Start IDLE.

Navigate to the File menu and click New Window.

Type the following:

```
def welcome(*names):
"""This welcome function salutes all students in the names tuple."""
    for name in names:
        print("Welcome".name)
welcome("Lucy","Richard","Fridah","James")
```

The output of the program will be:

Welcome Lucy

Welcome Richard

Welcome Fridah

Welcome james

Recursion in Python

The definition of something in terms of itself is called recursion. A recursive function calls other functions.

Example

Python program to compute integer factorials

Start IDLE.

Navigate to the File menu and click New Window.

Type the following:

Exercise

Write a Python program to find the factorial of 7.

Python Anonymous Function

Some functions may be specified devoid of a name and these are called anonymous functions. The lambda keyword is used to denote an anonymous function. Anonymous functions are also referred to as lambda functions in Python.

Syntax

lambda arguments: expression.

Lambda functions must always have one expression but can have several arguments.

Example

Start IDLE.

Navigate to the File menu and click New Window.

Type the following:

```
double = lambda y: y * 2
# Output: 10
print(double(5))
```

Example 2

We can use inbuilt functions such as filter () and lambda to show only even numbers in a list/tuple.

Start IDLE.

Navigate to the File menu and click New Window.

Type the following:

```
first_marks = [3, 7, 14, 16, 18, 21, 13, 32]
```

```python
fresh_marks = list(filter(lambda n: (n%2 == 0) ,
first_marks))

# Output: [14, 16, 18, 32]

print(fresh_marks)
```

Lambda function and map() can be used to double individual list items.

Example 3

Start IDLE.

Navigate to the File menu and click New Window.

Type the following:

```python
first_score = [3, 7, 14, 16, 18, 21, 13, 32]

fresh_score = list(map(lambda m: m * 2 ,
first_score))

# Output: [6, 14, 28, 32, 36, 42, 26, 64]

Print(fresh_score)
```

Python's Global, Local and Nonlocal

Python's Global Variables

Variables declared outside of a function in Python are known as global variables. They are declared in global scope. A global variable can be accessed outside or inside of the function.

Example

Start IDLE.

Navigate to the File menu and click New Window.

Type the following:

```
y= "global"
def foo():
    print("y inside the function :", y)
foo()
print("y outside the function:", y)
```

Explanation

In the illustration above, y is a global variable and is defined as a foo() to print the global variable y. When we call the foo() it will print the value of y.

Local Variables

 A local variable is declared within the body of the function or in the local scope.

Example

Start IDLE.

Navigate to the File menu and click New Window.

Type the following:

```
def foo():
```

```
    x = "local"
```

foo()

print(x)

Explanation

Running this program will generate an error indicating 'x' is undefined. The error is occurring because we are trying to access local variable x in a global scope whereas foo() functions only in the local scope.

Creating a Local Variable in Python

Example

A local variable is created by declaring a variable within the function.

def foo():

Start IDLE.

Navigate to the File menu and click New Window.

Type the following:

```
    x = "local"

    print(x)
```

foo()

Explanation

When we execute the code, the output will be:

Local

Python's Global and Local Variable

Using both local and global variables in the same code.

Example

Start IDLE.

Navigate to the File menu and click New Window.

Type the following:

```
y = "global"
def foo():
    global y
    x = "local"
    y = y * 2
    print(y)
    print(x)
foo()
```

Explanation

The output of the program will be:

global global

local

Explanation

We declared y as a global variable and x as a local variable in the foo(). The * operator issued to modify the global variable y and finally, we printed both y and x.

Local and Global Variables with the same name

Start IDLE.

Navigate to the File menu and click New Window.

Type the following:

```
y=6
def foo():
y=11
    print("Local variable y-", y)
foo()
Print("Global variable y-", y)
```

Python's Nonlocal Variables

A Python's nonlocal variable is used in a nested function whose local scope is unspecified. It is neither global nor local scope.

Example

Creating a nonlocal variable.

Start IDLE.

Navigate to the File menu and click New Window.

Type the following:

```
def outer():
    y = "local variable"
    def inner():
        nonlocal y
        y = "nonlocal variable"
        print("inner:", y)
    inner()
    print("outer scope:", y)
Outer()
```

Global Keyword in Python

There are rules when creating a global keyword:

A global keyword is local by default when we create a variable within a function.

It is global by default when we define a variable outside of a function and you do not need to use the global keyword.

The global keyword is used to read and write a global variable within a function.

The use of global keyword outside a function will have no effect.

Example.

Start IDLE.

Navigate to the File menu and click New Window.

Type the following:

```
number = 3      #A global variable
def add():
    print(number)
add()
```

The output of this program will be 3.

Modifying global variable from inside the function.

```
number=3                  #a global variable
def add():
    number= number + 4    # add 4 to 3
    print(number)
add()
```

Explanation

When the program is executed it will generate an error indicating that the local variable number is referenced before assignment. The reason for encountering the error is because we can only access the global variable but are unable to modify it from inside the function. Using a global keyword would solve this.

Example.

Start IDLE.

Navigate to the File menu and click New Window.

Type the following:

Modifying global variable within a function using the global keyword.

```
number = 3          # a global variable
def add():
    global number
    number= number + 1 # increment by 1
    print("Inside the function add():", number)
add()
print("In main area:", number)
```

Explanation

When the program is run, the output will be:

402

Inside the function add(): 4

In the main area: 4

We defined a number as a global keyword within the function add(). The variable was then incremented by 1, variable number. Then we called the add () function to print global variable c.

Creating Global Variables across Python Modules

We can create a single module config.py that will contain all global variables and share the information across several modules within the same program.

Example.

Start IDLE.

Navigate to the File menu and click New Window.

Type the following:

Create config.py

x=0

y="empty"

Then create an update.py file to modify global variables

Import config

config.x=11

config.y="Today"

Then create a main.py file to evaluate the changes in value

import config

import update

print(config.x)

print(config.y)

Explanation

Running the main.py file will generate:

11

Today

Python Modules

Modules consist of definitions as well as program statements.

An illustration is a file name config.py which is considered as a module. The module name would be config. Modules are sued to help break large programs into smaller manageable and organized files as well as promoting reusability of code.

Example: Creating the First module

Start IDLE.

Navigate to the File menu and click New Window.

Type the following:

Def add(x, y):

"""This is a program to add two

numbers and return the outcome"""

outcome=x+y

return outcome

Module Import

The keyword import is used to import.

Example

Import first

The dot operator can help us access a function as long as we know the name of the module.

Example

Start IDLE.

Navigate to the File menu and click New Window.

Type the following:

first.add(6,8)

Explanation

import statement in Python

The import statement can be used to access the definitions within a module via the dot operator.

Start IDLE.

Navigate to the File menu and click New Window.

Type the following:

```
import math
print("The PI value is", math.pi)
```

Import with renaming

Example

Start IDLE.

Navigate to the File menu and click New Window.

Type the following:

```
import math as h
   print("The PI value is-",h.pi)
```

Explanation

In this case, h is our renamed math module with a view helping save typing time in some instances.

When we rename the new name becomes valid and recognized one and not the original one.

From...import statement Python.

It is possible to import particular names from a module rather than importing the entire module.

Example

Start IDLE.

Navigate to the File menu and click New Window.

Type the following:

from math import pi

Print("The PI value is-", pi)

Importing all names

Example

Start IDLE.

Navigate to the File menu and click New Window.

Type the following:

from math import*

print("The PI value is-", pi)

Explanation

In this context, we are importing all definitions from a particular module but it is encouraged norm as it can lead to unseen duplicates.

Module Search Path in Python

Example

Start IDLE.

Navigate to the File menu and click New Window.

Type the following:

import sys

sys.path

Python searches everywhere including the sys file.

Reloading a Module

Python will only import a module once increasing efficiency in execution.

print("This program was executed")

import mine

Reloading Code

Example

Start IDLE.

Navigate to the File menu and click New Window.

Type the following:

import mine

import mine

import mine

Mine.reload(mine)

Dir( ) built-in Python function

For discovering names contained in a module, we use the dir() inbuilt function.

Syntax

Dir(module_name)

Python Package

Files in python hold modules and directories are stored in packages. A single package in Python holds similar modules. Therefore, different modules should be placed in different Python packages.

Data types in Python

☐   Numbers

The presence or absence of a decimal point separates integers and floating points. For instance, 4 is integer while 4.0 is a floating point number.

On the other hand, complex numbers in Python are denoted as r+tj where j represents the real part and t is the virtual part. In this context, the function type() is used to determine the variable class. The Python function instance() is invoked to make a determination of which specific class function originates from.

Example

Start IDLE.

Navigate to the File menu and click New Window.

Type the following:

number=6

  print(type(number))#should output class int

print(type(6.0))#should output class float

complex_num=7+5j

print(complex_num+5)

print(isinstance(complex_num, complex))#should output True

Important: Integers in Python can be of infinite length. Floating numbers in Python are assumed precise up to fifteen decimal places.

Number Conversion

This segment assumes you have prior basic knowledge of how to manually or using a calculator to convert decimal into binary, octal and hexadecimal. Check out the Windows Calculator in Windows 10, Calculator version Version 10.1804.911.1000 and choose programmer mode to automatically convert.

Programmers often need to convert decimal numbers into octal, hexadecimal and binary forms. A prefix in Python allows denotation of these numbers to their corresponding type.

Number SystemPrefix

Octal'0O' or '0o'

Binary'0B' or '0b'

Hexadecimal'0X or '0x'

Example

print(0b1010101)#Output:85

print(0x7B+0b0101)#Output: 128 (123+5)

print(0o710)#Output:710

Exercise

Write a Python program to display the following:

a.0011 11112

b.7478

C.9316

Type Conversion

Sometimes referred to as coercion, type conversion allows us to change one type of number into another. The preloaded functions such as float(), int() and complex() enable implicit and explicit type conversions. The same functions can be used to change from strings.

Example

Start IDLE.

Navigate to the File menu and click New Window.

Type the following:

int(5.3)#Gives 5

int(5.9)#Gives 5

The int() will produce a truncation effect when applied to floating numbers. It will simply drop the decimal point part without rounding off. For the float() let us take a look:

Start IDLE.

Navigate to the File menu and click New Window.

Type the following:

float(6)#Gives 6.0

ccomplex('4+2j')#Gives (4+2j)

Exercise

Apply the int() conversion to the following:

a.4.1

b.4.7

c.13.3

d.13.9

Apply the float() conversion to the following:

e.7

f.16

G.19

☐ *Decimal in Python*

Example

Start IDLE.

Navigate to the File menu and click New Window.

Type the following:

(1.2+2.1)==3.3 #Will return False, why?

Explanation

The computer works with finite numbers and fractions cannot be stored in their raw form as they will create an infinite long binary sequence.

☐   *Fractions in Python*

The fractions module in Python allows operations on fractional numbers.

Example

Start IDLE.

Navigate to the File menu and click New Window.

Type the following:

import fractions

print(fractions.my_fraction(2.5))#Output 5/2

print(fractions.my_fraction(4))#Output 5

print(fractions.my_fraction(2,5))#output 2/5

Important

Creating my_fraction from float can lead to unusual results due to the misleading representation of binary floating point.

Mathematics in Python

To carry out mathematical functions, Python offers modules like random and math.

Start IDLE.

Navigate to the File menu and click New Window.

Type the following:

import math

print(math.pi)#output:3.14159....

print(math.cos(math.pi))#the output will be -1.0

print(math.exp(10))#the output will be 22026.4....

print(math.log10(100))#the output will be 2

print(math.factorial(5))#the output will be 120

Exercise

Write a python program that uses math functions from the math module to perform the following:

a.Square of 34

b.Log1010000

c.Cos 45 x sin 90

D.Exponent of 20

Random function in Python

Start IDLE.

Navigate to the File menu and click New Window.

Type the following:

```
import math
print(random.shuffle_num(11, 21))
y=['f','g','h','m']
print(random.pick(y))
random.anypic(y)
print(y)
Print(your_pick.random())
```

Lists in Python

We create a list in Python by placing items called elements inside square brackets separated by commas. The items in a list can be of mixed data types.

Start IDLE.

Navigate to the File menu and click New Window.

Type the following:

```
list_mine=[]#empty list
```

list_mine=[2,5,8]#list of integers

list_mine=[5,"Happy", 5.2]#list having mixed data types

Exercise

Write a program that captures the following in a list: "Best", 26,89,3.9

Nested Lists

A nested list is a list as an item in another list.

Example

Start IDLE.

Navigate to the File menu and click New Window.

Type the following:

list_mine=["carrot", [9, 3, 6], ['g']]

Exercise

Write a nested for the following elements: [36,2,1],"Writer",'t',[3.0, 2.5]

Accessing Elements from a List

In programming and in Python specifically, the first time is always indexed zero. For a list of five items, we will access them from index0 to index4. Failure to access the items in a list in this manner will create index error. The index is always an integer as using other number types will create a type error. For nested lists, they are accessed via nested indexing.

Example

Start IDLE.

Navigate to the File menu and click New Window.

Type the following:

list_mine=['b','e','s','t']

print(list_mine[0])#the output will be b

print(list_mine[2])#the output will be s

print(list_mine[3])#the output will be t

Exercise

Given the following list:

your_collection=['t','k','v','w','z','n','f']

a.Write a Python program to display the second item in the list b.Write a Python program to display the sixth item in the last

C.Write a Python program to display the last item in the list.

11. Future Of Python

Increasing Popularity of Python

Python is ruling the world of modern technology and due to its uniqueness it has left other languages like C++, Java, etc. far behind. Python, with its great utility, has a promising and bright future. Python has gone though 25 years of continuous amendments with improved and better-updated versions so that it can serve as the fastest and most reliable programming language. Python provides the best quality, which is why it catches the eye of every developer. Over 126,000 websites have utilized Python. A plethora of decision-making systems for predictive analysis have developed applications using Python. It is the language of today and the future, as well.

Profiles of Python developers

Python developers are as assorted as the language and its applications. Python clients vary broadly in age, yet most of its users are in their 20s, and a quarter are in their 30s. Strikingly, nearly one-fifth of Python clients are under the age of 20. It can be clarified, by the way, that numerous under-studies use Python in schools and colleges, and it's a common first language for many computer programmers.

According to the recent survey, almost 65% of software engineers are moving towards Python language as a career. As Python is a simple and easy to learn language, many newcomers are adopting this high-level language to make their fortune from this new field of Data Science. It is a widespread practice nowadays and every software engineer is looking to learn the libraries, methods, and use of Python to become a data scientist. 30% of engineers that have under two years of expert experience have started using Python as their primary programming language.

General Python utilization

Right around four out of five Python designers state it's their primary language. Different research demonstrates the quantity of Python engineers, which are using it as primary language. In Stack Overflow's review, Python fame has expanded from 32% in mid-2017 to 38.8% by the end of that year.

Python utility with Other Languages:

Python is being used by all developers now who were only focusing on other high-level languages just a year ago. This trend is changing because of the evolution of Data Science.

According to a survey, JavaScript is utilized by 79% of web engineers, yet just 39% of those are engaged with Data investigation or Artificial Intelligence.

Some important companies that use Python as Data Science:

Google

Google is considered the biggest IT giant and has supported Python from its start. Google utilizes Python in their web crawler.

Facebook

Facebook is keen in utilizing Python in their Production Engineering Department.

Instagram

Instagram's engineering team revealed in 2016 that the world's most massive deployment of the Django web framework driven by them is completely written in Python.

Netflix

Netflix utilizes Python in a very similar manner to Spotify, depending on the language to power its data analysis on the server-side.

Dropbox

This cloud-based storage system employs Python in its desktop client.

10.2 Factors behind the Python growth in Modern World

Growth of Python is becoming prominent and is improving day by day. Software engineers and developers prefer this language due to its versatility and ease of use. Various other factors that are behind its growth are as follows:

1. Good support and community

Programming languages often face support issues. They lack complete documentation to help programmers when problems arise. Python has no such issues and is well supported. A plethora of tutorials and documentation is available to assist the programmers in the best possible ways. It has a good and active community whose function is to support developers. Experienced programmers help the beginners and a supportive atmosphere has been created.

2. Easy to Code and Write

If we compare Python to other programming languages like Java, C or C++, Python possesses a readable and straightforward code. Coding is expressed in a relatively easy manner to allow beginners to understand it quickly.

To learn the advanced level of python programming, a lot of time and effort is required, but for beginners, it is an easy task. Users can quickly identify the purpose of code, even after a quick glance.

3. Python is the Language of Education

Python is an easy language to use. It possesses functions, expressions, variables, and all other elements that students can easily understand and practice. It is the standard programming language for the Raspberry Pi, a PC structured training. Colleges teach Python in PC sciences, as well as to arithmetic understudies. Also, Matplotlib (a prominent Python library) is utilized in subjects at all levels to express complex data. Python is one of the quickest developing languages on Codecademy, as well, and thus is anything but difficult to learn remotely.

4. Simple to Code and Write

Python has an elementary coding and syntax structure. In comparison to other high-level programming languages like Java, C, or C++, Python has a straightforward and discernible code. The code is communicated in a simple way, which can be mostly deciphered even by a novice software engineer.

5. Python Is Perfect For Building Prototypes.

Python not only allows the users to write less code, it also provides the utility to build prototypes and ideas very quickly. Brainstorming or ideation is an essential aspect of web development, which is mostly overlooked. The capability to think about prototypes that can function faster becomes much more pivotal.

4. Integration and execution is quick

Python is considered as high-class language. It is the quickest language when it comes to execution and integration and saves quite a lot of time for programmers. With projects like PyPy and Numba, the speed is enhanced even more, making it the fastest language with each passing day.

5. Python has a Standard Library

Python contains libraries that eliminate the burden of composing a code by the programmer. These libraries possess a large quantity of built-in functions and already available codes. Therefore, code can easily be generated instead of having to be created.

6. Cross-Platform Language

One of the most prominent features of Python Programming Language is that it is accessible to cross-platforms. It supports highly efficient operating systems such as Linux, Windows, Ubuntu, and more.

Thus, one can undoubtedly keep running a product without agonizing over framework support. It very well may be translated in the language with the assistance of a convenient component that makes it easy to utilize. To sum things up - compose code on the Mac and run it smoothly on Windows.

7. Provides a plethora of tools

It contains a vast standard library collection, which reduce the effort for writing codes or functions. Libraries in Python always have pre-written codes in them.

Some of the tools are as follows: Tkinter (a GUI development), file format, built-in function, custom Python interpreter, internet protocols and support, module, etc. This extensive collection increases the usefulness of Python as a programming tool for data science.

8. Python is Free

Python is an open-source language and its free to use. Guido van Rossum has run Python since its creation. It is Open Source and GPL excellent. The creator of this language had a vision to keep it free for all the programmers of the world. However, open-source programming has officially changed the world. Python has no hidden cost or sale-able modules, and this makes it an ideal device for all to utilize.

9. Career Opportunities Associated With Python

In this powerful present-day world where everything changes at a quick rate, the prevalence of Python never seems to stop. Today, Python Certification is very popular. It has a lot of libraries that help data investigation, control, and representation. In this manner, it has advanced as the most favored language and viewed as the "Following Big Thing" and an "Absolute necessity" for Professionals.

With a wide range of programming languages, Python has outperformed different languages. Vocation openings related to Python have additionally developed fundamentally as its fame has expanded. Numerous IT organizations are searching for more applicants with experience and aptitudes in Python programming languages. Python has shown to be the best vocation for software engineers and now is the time - sooner rather than later.

Conclusion

We have covered the basics of Python programming language. The constructs we have learned so far, such as loops, expressions, and conditions, should be enough to help you further your career in Python development. What we have covered is enough to help you understand Python examples.

Although not everything has been covered, we have tried to provide you with a refresher in Python that you can build on it to become an excellent programmer. Python is one of the top four widely used programming language. As it has increased in popularity, its main focus on the quality of code and readability, plus the associated impact on developer productivity, appears to have been the driving force to Python success.

If you experience difficulties with some of the concepts discussed in this book, it is good if you can explore other introductory resources to help you understand. Or you can even consult with an experienced Python developer.

In general, you should master the basics of python discussed inside this book, master the language syntax, and then start to deepen your knowledge on specific features of python. Keep in mind that great programmers don't stop learning. So make a point always to learn something new in Python every day.

KALI LINUX

THE COMPLETE GUIDE TO LEARN LINUX FOR BEGINNERS AND KALI LINUX, LINUX SYSTEM ADMINISTRATION AND COMMAND LINE, HOW TO HACK WITH KALI LINUX TOOLS, COMPUTER HACKING AND NETWORKING.

Introduction

When you think of hacking, you may imagine something along the lines of someone violently smashing a keyboard, zooming in on things while controlling someone else's computer, and saying things like "I'm in" or "Hack engaged." Or maybe the word hacking makes you think of breaking into someone's Instagram account.

A History of Hacking

Hacking has been around since as early as the 1960s when, in 1961, a group of MIT students hacked their model trains hacking to modify their functions. That is where the term comes from. So the term hacking is not even directly related to computers! Originally, hacking meant to explore and improve something.

In the 1970s, phone hackers, or "phackers," made their debut when they exploited operational characteristics in phones to gain access to free phone calls, although they were fairly rare. At the time, computer hackers were not yet popular because so few people had personal computers.

This changed in the 1980s when personal computer use gave birth to the first computer hackers. This is no surprise, since when there's a product, there is always someone out there willing to mess with the product to their advantage. Likewise, when there's someone to mess with the product, there is someone to protect it. The birth of computer hacking led to the birth of ethical hacking, as well. The '80s was the decade we first saw hackers breaking into systems to use them for personal gain.

This new type of crime naturally called for new legislation. In 1986, the Federal Computer Fraud and Abuse Act was first written. The Act made it a crime for anyone to access a computer used by a financial institution, a government agency, or any organization involved in foreign commerce or communication. This was mainly prompted by the increase in PC use by the general public.

The 1990s was marked by the first high-profile arrests related to hacking. Kevin Mitnick, Kevin Poulsen, Robert Morris, and Vladimir Levin were among the first to get arrested for stealing property software as well as leading digital heists. This was also when the term crackers, meaning those that "crack" into digital encryption codes (e.g. passwords and such), began to be used.

During the late 2000s, the hacking of major companies like eBay, Amazon, and Microsoft often dominated the headlines. This was particularly true when news broke in early 2000 that the International Space Station's system had been breached by 15-year-old Jonathon James.

1. Ethical Hacker

In the real-world examples, you would call an ethical hacker the firefighter of the group; they put out fires and save innocent lives. They are, more often than not, hired by a government or a law agency to protect data and resolve any harm caused to individuals or businesses. A small business can also hire an ethical hacker to protect the company's data used maliciously or attacked by a malicious hacker.

Unethical Hacker - The Cracker

The unethical hacker, also known as the cracker, is the criminal that gets his information and assets illegally by getting into a device without the owner's knowledge or consent. The intent of this hacking is malicious. This type of hacker causes financial harm, steals confidential data, embezzles funds, disrupts businesses, and spreads incorrect data, among other things.

The Grey Hat

Then there is the hacker who isn't completely ethical or unethical; he's the person that steals to feed the poor. He falls in the gray area between the two other types of hackers. This gray area is where the name grey hat stems from. An example of a grey hat hacker would be a hacker who is hired to protect a particular database and then uses that access to confidential data for personal gain. You may not consider them criminals, but they won't be getting any medals soon. Then you have your "hacktivists," groups such as Anonymous, that use hacking for political and social messages. Finally, there are the "kiddies," or non-skilled people who use already-made tools to gain access to systems. This is when you guess someone's Facebook password because you want to see if they were where they said they were last night.

Types of Hacking

As you can tell, hacking isn't as simple as guessing someone's password and logging into their accounts.

There are actually numerous types of hacking that you need to be familiar with.

Phishing

The concept of phishing comes from the everyday activity of fishing. These types of hacks use email or sometimes phone to pose as a legitimate institution to obtain important information that can hurt an individual or a business. Hence, they throw the hook to "fish" for a victim. This usually works by first telling the victim they're a trusted organization, then asking for confidential data.

The first phishing lawsuit was filed in 2004 against a Californian teenager who created a copy of the website called "America Online" where he retrieved credit card information from visitors. One of the first and most popular phishing emails was the infamous "Nigerian Prince" email, which was an email from a "prince" who was stuck and needed your help to get back to his millions. Today, most of us don't fall for the Nigerian Prince scam, but phishing is still alive and problem for millions of internet users. The prevalent phishing -emails are mostly easy to spot.

They share a sense of urgency, unusual sender and suspicious hyperlinks. It is when a website is copied and looks like the real thing that things can get complicated. Banking websites can often be targets of phishing because of their extensive access to credit card numbers and sensitive information.

Virus

The purpose of a virus is to corrupt resources on websites. Just like in a human body, the virus can change forms, corrupt the "healthy" programs, and self-propagate. And just like in with us, there are plenty of viruses that can attack your malware.

Topher Crypter Virus is one of the most dangerous types of viruses because of its ability to completely take over the computer, leading to the spread of further viruses. A famous example of a Topher Crypter is the Trojan Virus.

Metamorphic Virus can write, rewrite, and edit its own code. It is the most infectious virus, and it can do massive damage to the computer and data if not detected early.

Polymorphic Virus is similar to a metamorphic virus, but it copies itself; where the metamorphic virus can rewrite its code, the polymorphic just copies its original code with slight modifications.

Macro Virus is written in the same language as software programs such as Microsoft Word or Excel. It starts an automatic sequence of actions every time the application is opened.

Cluster Virus makes it appear as though every program in the system is affected when, in fact, it is only in the one program in the system. It causes the illusion of a cluster and can be removed by figuring out the original "carrier" of the virus.

Tunneling Virus works against antiviruses. It sits in the background and sits under the antivirus. When an antivirus detects virus, the antivirus will try to re-install itself only to install itself as the tunneling viruses.

Stealth Virus uses its mechanism to avoid any detection by antiviruses. The stealth virus will hide in the memory and hide any changes it has made to any files.

Extension Virus will hide in a website or browser extension and create changes through there.

Cookie Theft

Cookies are files stored on your computer used by your browser to save useful information about the websites you visit or any actions you take. Session cookies are temporary and erased once you close your browser. Certain cookies persist in your browser until you yourself erase them or they expire (which could take years). These are called persistent cookies.

Websites use cookies to modify your browsing experience in order to make it tailored to your needs as well as for proper ad placement. Cookie thefts are used by hackers in order to gain access to that information. Cookies are one of the most natural methods of hacking, they can be stolen through public Wi-Fi networks!

UI Redress

UI redress, also called clickjacking, is masking a click in order to gain clicks for a different website. A user might think they are clicking on a straightforward link, but due to clickjacking, they will be redirected to a completely different website. The hacker is "hijacking" clicks. This can get out of control quickly as users will click links that say things such as "win a free vacation," and they will be redirected to a sharing page, causing the clickjacking to spread massively over social media or email.

DNS Spoofing

Domain name server spoofing is an attack in which the domain name is taken over by redirecting the clicks to a fraudulent website. Once there, the users are led to believe they are logging in with their account names and passwords into the original website, but in reality, they are giving away their information to the hacker performing the DNS spoofing. There are a few methods to perform DNS spoofing such as Man in the Middle (where interaction among the server and user is sidetracked) or DNS server compromise (where the server is directly attacked).

The above examples are all types of hacking used by malicious hackers, but ethical hacking also works with them. In order to prevent and "heal" these attacks, the ethical hackers must know how they work, and this is why ethical hackers have to be educated on all the types and methods of hacking used.

Becoming a hacker takes skill, and the ironic part is that both unethical and ethical hackers will use the same education and tools. The only difference is that one will use their "powers" for evil and the other for good (or something in between). It's like a modern-day equivalent of the classic superhero-villain duo Batman and Joker. In order to be a successful ethical hacker, you have to understand malicious hacking as well.

2. The Meaning of Ethical Hacking And Types

Ethical Hacking is an approved routine with regards to bypassing framework security to distinguish potential information ruptures and dangers in a system. The organization that claims the framework or system permits Cyber Security specialists to perform such exercises so as to test the framework's safeguards. In this manner, not at all like pernicious hacking, this procedure is arranged, affirmed, and all the more significantly, legitimate.

Ethical programmers plan to examine the framework or system for powerless focuses that pernicious programmers can abuse or decimate. They gather and break down the data to make sense of approaches to fortify the security of the framework/organize/applications. Thusly, they can improve the security impression so it can all the more likely withstand assaults or redirect them.

The act of Ethical hacking is designated "White Hat" hacking, and the individuals who perform it are called

White Hat programmers. As opposed to Ethical Hacking, "Dark Hat" hacking portrays works on including security infringement. The Black Hat programmers utilize unlawful procedures to bargain the framework or obliterate data.

Not at all like White Hat programmers, "Dim Hat" programmers don't request authorization before getting into your framework. Be that as it may, Gray Hats are additionally not quite the same as Black Hats since they don't perform hacking for any close to home or outsider advantage. These programmers don't have any malevolent expectation and hack frameworks for entertainment only or different reasons, more often than not advising the proprietor about any dangers they find. Dark Hat and Black Hat hacking are both unlawful as the two of them establish an unapproved framework break, despite the fact that the goals of the two sorts of programmers vary.

The most ideal approach to separate between White Hat and Black Hat programmers is by investigating their intentions. Dark Hat programmers are inspired by malevolent goal, showed by of individual increases, benefit, or provocation; though White Hat programmers search out and cure vulnerabilities, in order to keep Black Hats from exploiting.

Different approaches to draw a differentiation between White Hat and Black Hat programmers include:

Procedures utilized: White Hat programmers copy the strategies and techniques pursued by malevolent programmers so as to discover the framework inconsistencies, recreating all the last's means to discover how a framework assault happened or may happen. On the off chance that they locate a powerless point in the framework or system, they report it quickly and fix the imperfection.

Lawfulness: Even however White Hat hacking pursues indistinguishable procedures and strategies from Black Hat hacking, just one is legitimately worthy. Dark Hat programmers violate the law by entering frameworks without assent.

Possession: White Hat programmers are utilized by associations to enter their frameworks and identify security issues. Dark cap programmers neither possess the framework nor work for somebody who claims it.

Jobs and Responsibilities of an Ethical Hacker

Ethical Hackers must pursue certain rules so as to perform hacking legitimately. A decent programmer knows their obligation and clings to the majority of the Ethical rules. Here are the most significant principles of Ethical Hacking:

An Ethical programmer must look for approval from the association that possesses the framework. Programmers ought to acquire total endorsement before playing out any security appraisal on the framework or system.

Decide the extent of their evaluation and make known their arrangement to the association.

Report any security breaks and vulnerabilities found in the framework or system.

Keep their revelations secret. As their motivation is to verify the framework or system, Ethical programmers ought to consent to and regard their non-divulgence understanding.

Eradicate all hints of the hack in the wake of checking the framework for any defenselessness. It keeps malignant programmers from entering the framework through the distinguished provisos.

Ethical Hacking is a difficult territory of concentrate as it requires dominance of everything that makes up a framework or system. This is the reason affirmations have turned out to be well known among yearning Ethical programmers.

With applicable Ethical Hacking confirmations, you can propel your vocation in cybersecurity in the accompanying ways:

Confirmed people realize how to configuration, fabricate, and keep up a safe business condition. In the event that you can exhibit your insight in these zones, you will be precious with regards to examining dangers and formulating successful arrangements.

Ensured cybersecurity experts have better pay prospects contrasted with their non-confirmed friends. As per Payscale, Certified Ethical Hackers procure a normal compensation of $90K in the U.S.

Confirmation approves your aptitudes in the field of IT security and makes you progressively detectable while applying for testing work jobs.

With the developing occurrences of security breaks, associations are putting gigantically in IT security and lean toward affirmed contender for their association.

New companies need profoundly talented experts experienced in repulsing digital dangers. A confirmation can enable you to show your IT security abilities to acquire lucrative occupations at new businesses.

In this day and age, cybersecurity has turned into a drifting subject of expanding enthusiasm among numerous organizations. With noxious programmers discovering more current approaches to break the barriers of systems consistently, the job of Ethical programmers has turned out to be progressively significant over all parts. It has made a plenty of chances for cybersecurity experts and has motivated people to take up Ethical hacking as their profession. Along these lines, on the off chance that you have ever thought about the potential outcomes of getting into the cybersecurity space, or even simply upskilling, this is the ideal time to do as such. What's more, obviously the most proficient method for achieving this is by getting guaranteed in Ethical hacking, and the most ideal approach to do that is to let Simplilearn help you accomplish it! Look at them now, and join the battle for secure frameworks

3. Pick Your Hat

Remember in the *Harry Potter* series when the sorting hat sorts you into which house you're supposed to be in (Slytherin for the bad ones, Gryffindor for the brave ones, etc.). Hacking hats are similar to this, only you're your own sorting hat, and you can switch sides. Let's learn what each means.

To understand the hats hackers metaphorically wear, we must first understand the ethical standards in the hacker communities.

Hacker Ethics

Richard Stallman of the Free Software Foundation, as well as one of the creators of the copyleft concept had the following to say about hacking:

"The hacker ethic refers to the feelings of right and wrong, to the ethical ideas this community of people had—that knowledge should be shared with other people who can benefit from it, and that important resources should be utilized rather than wasted."

The general principles of hacker ethics are:

1. Access to computers must be universal and unlimited

2. All information must be free

3. Encourage decentralization

4. Judge, according to hacks, not according to diplomas, economic stance, race, gender, religion, etc.

5. Create art and beauty with computers

6. Change your life for the better

Black Hat Hacker

The term black hat hacker is derived from old Western movies where the bad guys wore black hats, and the good guys wore—you guessed it—white hats.

The freshest looking color black gets all the bad rap. Villains often wear only black, and then there's death, dark magic and black cats—all associated with dark and evil things. Black hat hackers are thus the ones we hear about in the media the most, the ones using their "powers" for evil.

The black hat hacker is the one that finds security flaws to gain access and uses them for their malicious intents. These can be financial—such as gaining information about credit cards so you can access assets and accounts—or purely informational. Black hat hackers gain access to personal files of celebrities, and they are the ones that will go shopping with your card or even access files from large corporations for larger-scale hacks. Black hat hackers can cause significant damage to an individual or a business, compromising a website or even shutting down security systems.

Black hat hackers range from a kid spreading viruses to major league hackers obtaining credit card passwords. Sometimes, malicious hackers work outside the internet and obtain information through phones by calling and pretending to be a legitimate company. One of the infamous non-computer scams hackers use is pretending to be the IRS or CRS and calling people threatening to take legal action because they haven't paid their taxes. A good rule of thumb to recognize spot this scam is to look for a sense of urgency, like—it has to be paid right here, right now, through your credit card—and the instalment of fear—"if you don't pay this right now you will go to jail!"

Black hat hackers have their conventions, like Comic Con but for hacking. The two famous ones are DefCon and Black Hat. These conventions, however, are often attended by white hat hackers, as well, to learn from the black hats and gain information on anything necessary to know. It's fascinating how close these two worlds have to stay to learn from each other to take each other down.

There are plenty of notorious black hat hackers to choose from, but some stand out even amongst the crowd. Of course, many of the best never got caught, but among those who did get caught are:

Albert Gonzales - He has been accused of the most significant ATM theft in history in the years between 2005 and 2007. When he was arrested, the authorities found $1.6 million cash in his possession as well as $1 million cash around his property, so naturally, he has been sentenced to 20 years in federal prison.

Vladimir Levin - He transferred $10 million from Citibank bank accounts to his own all while hanging out in his apartment. He was discovered when his accomplices tried to withdraw funds from different bank accounts around the world and pointed to him when they were caught. He was arrested and tried for merely three years, and most of the funds have been recovered (apart from $40,000). Media portrayed Levin as a biochemist and a scientist with a Ph.D., but in the later years, it was revealed he was an administrator with not much formal education. Goes to show how sensationalistic it can all get with no actual evidence.

George Hotz - In 2007, at just 17, he was the first person to unlock the iOS security system, and in 2010 he hacked into the Sony system, which resulted in a massive and famous Sony lawsuit. This resulted in the hacking group Anonymous hacking Sony and the most costly security break up to date. He continued to release jailbreak technology up until 2010 when he finally crossed over to the white hat side or more of a gray area.

Johnathan James (aka c0mrade) - At 16 years old, Johnathan became the first person in the United States to go to juvenile prison for cybercrime. At the age of 15, he had broken into the security systems of NASA and the Department of Homeland Defense and stole a software worth over $1 million. He broke into the Defense Threat Reduction Agency and intercepted messages from employees. Johnathan committed suicide at 28, and a past suicide note indicated it may have had something to do with him being implicated in another hacking situation.

Gary McKinnon - McKinnon, from Scotland, hacked into NASA, the US Army, the Air Force, and the Navy systems searching for information about UFOs that he believes the US government is hiding. At one point, a message appeared on all of the computers in the US Army saying "your security system is crap." He has been accused of the largest ever hack of United States government computers, but he was never extradited to the US. The reasons for not doing so was his Asperger's syndrome. Theresa May believed extraditing him would cause more harm than good and that the extradition would be a breach of human rights.

Kevin Mitnick - He started hacking at age 12 by bypassing the punch system in the Los Angeles public bus system. In 1979, at age 17, he gained access to its unauthorized network; following that, he was convicted and sentenced to prison before being given supervised discharge. When he was nearing the end of his probation, he hacked into Pacific Bell computers and fled. He became a fugitive for two and a half years. After a very public pursuit, he was arrested in 1995 on several counts of wire fraud and possession of unauthorized devices. He has been depicted in several movies, books, and comic books, and to this day, he is the most famous black hat hacker.

Hacker Hierarchy

Much like the rest of the world, the hacker world has its own divisions. One of those divisions within the black hat hacker community is based on your hacking skills:

Newbies - They have access to hacker tools but are not very aware of how the programs work.

Cyberpunks - Also known as Green Hat Hackers, they are newbies with more ambition to become coders. They use other tools, but they actively learn to code.

Coders - These are the people who write the programs other hackers use to infiltrate systems.

Cyberterrorists - They infiltrate systems to profit illegally; they are at the top of the hacker food chain.

White Hat Hacker

White hat hackers are what they call the good guys of the hacking industry. They break into systems and do pretty much the same things the black hat hackers do, only the reason behind white hacker hacks is security. They expose vulnerabilities to create higher standards of security before the black hat hackers can take advantage of the system's weaknesses

Often, a former black hat hacker turns white-hat hacker, but you rarely see the opposite. White hat hackers are also known as ethical hackers. In the simplest terms, an ethical hacker tests security networks by pretending to be a malicious hacker to see where the weaknesses are. This means anything from emailing the staff to ask for passwords to testing complicated security systems. This is the reason many black hat hackers switch sides, they get to do the same thing but without the fear of legal prosecution.

Ethical hacking is evident in the US military as well. One of the first instances of ethical hacking was actually conducted by the US Air Force. The idea of ethical hacking didn't come from the Air Force, however. Dan Farmer and Wietse Venema, two programmers, first created the idea of ethical hacking, even if they didn't call it that. Their idea was to raise security on the internet as a whole. Farmer started a software called Computer Oracle and Password System (COPS) designed to identify security weaknesses. Venema designed a Security Administrative Tool for Analyzing Networks (SATAN) that became an accepted method for auditing computer and network security.

Other famous ethical hackers include:

Kevin Mitnick - Yes, the same Kevin Mitnick that was a fugitive is now a famous white hat hacker. After his infamous black hat days, he now works as a consultant and for the FBI. He also acts as a public speaker and teaches classes in universities.

Joanna Rutkowska - She is a cybersecurity researcher focused on Qubes OS. In 2006, she attended a black hat conference and exposed vulnerabilities in Vista Kernel. In 2009, she prevented an attack targeting Intel systems including the Trusted Execution Technology.

Charlie Miller - He is known for exposing vulnerabilities in Apple as well as being the first to locate MacBook Air bug. He spent years working for Uber, and at some point, he even worked for the National Security Agency (NSA). In 2014 he hacked a Jeep Cherokee and managed to control its brakes, steering wheel and acceleration remotely.

Greg Hoglund - He is an author, researcher, and specialist in computer forensics. He contributed to software exploitation and online game hacking and has patented methods for fault injections for white hat hacking purposes. He also founded the popular rootkit.com, a website devoted to the subject of rootkits (collection of computer software designed to enable access that is not otherwise allowed). White hat hackers have a harder job and get a lot less credit, but the work they do is a lot more fulfilling and, in the end, legal. While as a black hat hacker some get "cool points," white hat hacking is as equally as interesting. The coolest thing about white hat hacking is all the freedom you get to enjoy because you're not being prosecuted and arrested.

Grey Hat Hackers

Nothing is black and white, and neither are the hacker hats. There is a group of hackers who fall between black and white hackers, called grey hat hackers. So what exactly are grey hat hackers?

They are the hackers who won't always abide by the laws or ethical standards, but they don't have the malicious intents that the black hat hackers do. The term was first coined at a black hat convention DEFCON by a hacker group L0pht, and it was first publicly used in a New York Times interview in 1999.

Lopht described themselves as a group who support the ethical reporting and exposing vulnerabilities but disagree with the full disclosure practices that dominate the white hat communities.

They were also referred to as white hat hackers by day and black hat hackers by night.

It is still not clear as to what a grey hat hacker is because the term is so broad. The general idea is that it is a hacker who will break the law to improve security. You can think of them as the chaotic good of the group.

Some examples of grey hackers are:

Dmitry Sklyarov - In the early 2000s, the Russian citizen, along with his employer, ElcomSoft, caught the attention of the FBI for an alleged violation of the DMCA (Digital Millennium Copyright Act). Sklyarov visited the US to give a presentation called eBooks Security and was arrested on his way back because he had violated the DMCA. The complaint was that Sklyarov and his company illegally obtained copy protection arrangements by Adobe. The US government eventually dropped all charges against him in exchange for his testimony against ElcomSoft.

Julian Assange - Julian Assange, the creator of WikiLeaks, a non-profit that publishes news leaks, is perhaps the clearest example of a grey hat hacker. He began hacking at age 16 and went on to hack NASA, the Pentagon, and Stanford University. He created WikiLeaks in 2006, and it remains an ethical grey area. Some argue that Assange is merely exposing the corruption of elite corporations, while others argue that the work he is doing is illegal and corrupt. One of the most notorious documents released by WikiLeaks is the video of US soldiers shooting 18 civilians from a helicopter in Iraq. Assange has been fleeing the law for years, and he is currently. He is being charged on 17 different counts, and many argue the charges are not valid and a symbol of the end of free journalism.

Loyd Blankenship - Also known as the The Mentor, Blankenship is a well-known writer and hacker. He was a member of different hacker groups including the Legion of Doom. He is the author of the *Hacker Manifesto* and *GURPS Cyberpunk*, which is a cyberpunk roleplaying sourcebook written for Steve Jackson Games. That book landed Blankenship in hot water because it was believed he illegally accessed Bell South and that this would help other groups commit similar hacks.

Guccifer - Guccifer is a Romanian hacker that targeted celebrities. He was the man behind the Hillary Clinton email leak that some argue ultimately caused her downfall in the 2016 presidential elections and got Donald Trump elected. Before Clinton, Guccifer accessed the emails of Romanian starlets. He then moved onto US Secretary of State Colin Powel and George W. Bush.

Anonymous - This is a well-known hacktivist group that has been in the news recently. They are widely known for their attacks against government agencies, institutions, corporations, and the Church of Scientology, but the Anonymous resume list can go on for days. Several people have been arrested for involvement in Anonymous cyberattacks, but to this day, the group still operates.

Hacker hats are all about what you ultimately want to stand for. The idea is the same—penetrate security measures made by individuals and companies. The ethical standpoint behind the hacking decides which hat you want to choose for yourself.

If you are just looking to have some fun testing systems, then stick with the clear-cut white hat hacking. I mean, stick with it in general because it will keep you out of jail.

4. Programming Linux

Programming on Linux is being used for creating interfaces, applications, software and programs. Linux code is often used for the desktop, embedded systems as well as for real-time programs. Linux is an open source OS kernel which is compatible with Perl, C++, Java and various other languages of programming.

How does Linux work?

Linux functions as the kernel of an OS which can also be distributed and shared freely. An operating system or OS is that interface which helps in connecting the users with the hardware of computer and also supports the running of the applications and programs. Kernel is nothing but the OS core as it manages all the communication between the components of hardware and software.

What are the functions of the Linux programmers?

Starting off with Linux programming employ tools such as GBU compiler and also debugger which helps in creating applications for the storage of data, construction of GUI and also script writing. More advanced form of applications related to Linux allows the programmers to develop software related to Linux, optimize the programs which are already existing and also write new programs with various complex form of features such as multiprocessing, multi-threading, inter-process communication and also interaction of hardware device.

Uses of Linux

Linux is being widely used today in various servers, system of computer security and architecture of computer system. It is also widely used in the real-time programs along with the embedded systems of the PDAs and cell phones. Linux programming has also resulted in various applications.

How to develop the modules of Kernel?

Right before you start off with core programming in Linux, the best way of increasing your knowledge along with expertise of Linux programming is to start working on the kernel module. The modules are developed independently which works with the Linux kernels for functioning as a compact operating system. The kernel modules consist of various things such as drivers of devices for the several peripheries of hardware, file managers and other low-level features of the OS. The only barrier that comes at the entry of kernel module is much lower in rate than there are for working on the kernel of Linux. There are several modules which are being developed by various individuals and teams. So, it can be concluded that there is no specific gatekeeper at the entry of development.

Logical Breakdown of Programming in Linux

When you are using some of the major forms of operating system then you are interacting indirectly to the shell. If you are using Linux Mint, Ubuntu or any other proper distribution of Linux, you will be interacting with the shell every single time when you will be using the terminal. Let us discuss about the breakdown of programming in Linux which consists of Linux shells along with scripting of shell. So, right before we start, you will need to get acquainted with some of these terminologies:

- *Kernel*
- *Shell*

- *Terminal*

What is a kernel?

Kernel is nothing but a program related to computer systems which act as the core of the operating system. It comes with overall control over all the elements in a system. It helps in managing various resources of the systems based on Linux:

- Management of files

- Management of processes

- Management of I/O.

- Management of memory

- Management of the devices and various other components

A complete system of Linux can be broken down like: Kernel + installation scripts + other scripts of management + GNU system libraries and utilities.

What is a shell?

A shell is a special type of user program which helps in providing a proper interface to the users for using the services related to an operating system. The shells accept commands which are readable by humans from the users and then converts those into something which can be understood by the kernel. It can be regarded as the interpreter of command language which helps in executing the commands which are read from the devices of input like keyboard or from the files in the system. A shell starts when a user logs into the system or starts with a terminal.

A shell can be easily classified into two different categories:

- *Graphical shell*
- *Command line shell*

The graphical shells provide various means for the purpose of manipulating the programs which are based on the GUI or graphical user interface by letting the operations like closing, opening, resizing and moving windows, along with switching the focus in between the windows. Ubuntu OS along with Windows OS can be regarded as great examples which provide the GUI to the users for the purpose of interacting with various programs.

Shells can be accessed by the users by using the CLI or command line interface. A special type of program in Linux known as the terminal is provided for typing in the commands of the humans like ls, cat and many others and further which are being executed. The final result is then displayed directly on the terminal which can be seen by the user. Suppose you execute the command ls along with the option –l. This will be listing all the available files within the present working directory in a form of long listing.

Working along with the command line shell might turn out to be a bit difficult if you are a beginner only because of the fact that it is tough to memorize a bunch of commands at the same time. It is highly powerful in nature and it also allows the users to store all the commands within a specific file and then execute all of them together. In this way, any form of repetitive task can be made automatic easily. All of these files are generally known as Shell Scripts in the Linux systems.

In a Linux system, there are various types of shells which are available for the users:

• BASH: Also known as Bourne Again Shell, it is being widely used in the systems which are based on Linux. It is being used as the default shell of login in the Linux systems. If you want you can also install this in the Windows operating system.

• CSH: Also known as the C shell, it uses the syntax of the C shell and its usage is more or less similar to the programming language of C.

• KSH: Also known as the Korn shell, it is the base of the POSIX Shell standard.

Each of the shells functions in the same way but all of them understand various commands and also provides various built-in functions.

Scripting of Shell

In general, the shells are interactive in nature which means that they can accept the commands as inputs from the users and can also execute the same. However, it might happen that you need to or want to execute a whole bunch of commands in a routine manner, so you will need to type all the commands every time within the terminal. As the shells can also take in the commands in the form of inputs from the files, you can also write the commands within a file and then execute the same in the shell for avoiding the task of repetition. All these files are known as Shell Programs or Shell Scripts. The shell scripts are somewhat similar in structure with the batch file which can be found in MS-DOS. Each of the shell scripts is saved with the extension of .sh file such as yourscript.sh.

The shell scripts also come with syntax like all other languages of programming. In case you are already acquainted with any of the languages of programming like C, C++ or Python, it will be easier for you to start with shell scripting. The shell scripts consist of:

• Shell Keywords: It includes else, if, break and many others

• Shell Commands: It includes ls, cd, echo, touch, pwd and many others

• Control Flow: It includes if..then..else, shell and case loops and many others

You can use shell scripts for avoiding the repetitive work and thus opting for automation. It also helps in monitoring of the system. It also allows the addition of various new functionalities to the shells.

Programming in Linux Using C

Linux is turning out to be a heaven of programming for all the developers. It is mainly because of the open source nature of Linux and also being a completely free operating system. Turbo C compiler is the old form of compiler which has been used for compiling programs. The same job can be done on Linux for creating a new environment of programming. Let's have a look at how to get started with programming in Linux by using C for writing, compiling and running programs based on C.

Programming in Linux using C++

C can be regarded as a language of programming which is of procedural nature. It was developed in between 1969 and 1973 by Dennis Ritchie. Initially, it was developed as a programming language for the systems for the purpose of writing up a complete operating system. The main features of the C++ language come with low-level accessing of system memory, a very simple and easy set of keywords and a very clean style. All these features make the C++

language very much suitable for all sort of system programming such as operating system or even development of compiler. The very first step includes installation of some tools of development along with several applications like GCC, GNU, C++ compiler for the task of compiling the program and for executing the overall code in Linux. C and C++ are somewhat similar and for understanding C++ let us first have a look at C.

If you want you can also verify the installed set of tools by using the command:

cc -v.

Let us now consider a very easy C program file which is named as Sort.c:

```
int main( void )
{
 printf( "Hello! Sort\n" );
return 0;
}
```

For compiling this easy program you can use:

cc filename.c -0 executable_file_name

In this command, the filename.c is the C program file and -0 option has been used for showing up the errors in the code. In case there is no form of error in the code, it will generate an executable form of file named as executable_file_name.

cc Sort.c -0 sortoutput

In this, sortoutput is the file which is executable in nature and it is being generated. So, you can execute the same like:

./sortoutput

For program files related to C++

C++ is a programming language which has been developed for the general purpose of programming and is being widely used today for the purpose of competitive programming. It comes with object-oriented, imperative and generic program features. You can run C++ on various OS platforms such as Linux, Windows, Mac, Unix and many others. Right before we start programming by using C++ you will be needing a proper environment which needs to be set up on your computer system for the purpose of compiling and running your C++ based programs successfully. You can verify all your installed tools on C++ by using this command:

g++ -- version

Let us consider a very simple C++ program:

```
// main function

// where the execution

// of program starts

int main()

{

// print Hello Universe!

cout<< "Hello Universe!\n";

return 0;

}
```

For compiling this entire code you can use:

g++ filename.cpp -0 executable_file_name

Here in this command, filename.cpp is the file of C++ program and -0 option has been used for showing out the errors within the code. In case no error has been found, it will generate an executable form of file named as executable_file_name.

g++ sort.cpp -0 sortoutput

Here in this command, sortoutput is the executable form of file which is being generated. So, you can execute the same such as:

./sortoutput

Installing compiler for C++ in Linux

If you are using Linux based system such as CentOS, Red Hat, Fedora or something else, you can type in this command as the root for installing the compiler of C++:

yum install –y gcc-c++*

In order to verify that the compiler of GCC has been installed properly in the system use:

rpm –qa | grep –i c++

You can also use the which command as:

which c++

Writing the first C++ based program on Linux

- *From the terminal window, open up a new file for the purpose of editing by using the command vim as:*

vim hello.cc

- *Within the vim editor, you can now type your C++ program or code.*
- *After you are done with writing the program, save and then exit the file.*
- *For compiling the new program of C++, you will need to type this command in the terminal:*

c++ hello.cc

If the compilation process runs without any error, no form of output is going to be printed on the screen.

- *An executable form of file will be created within the present directory with a.out as the default name.*
- *For running this same program, you can execute the executable file which has been generated in a similar way you execute any of the executables of Linux.*

How to specify name meant for the executable which has been generated?

Compiling the programs of C++ without any of the specifying options will be producing an executable form of file with the name a.out. In case you want to specify a particular name for the executable of your choice you have two ways: first, is to rename the a.out default after it has been created and second, is to specify the filename of the executable at the time of compilation by using the option –o.

c++ hello.cc –o /opt/hello.run

Executing the system commands from programs of C++

It is very much important to be able to communicate with the compiling system by executing the commands of OS when needed. The system() function will be allowing you to run the commands of the system from the code of C++. For the ease of the compiler to recognize all these functions properly and for compiling in the proper way, stdlib.h library file is required to be invoked.

Bottom line

- *For writing down C or C++ based programs on the machines based on Linux, you will need the GCC compiler.*
- *All the C++ programs are saved and written as .cc format of files.*
- *All the resulting form of executable can also be executed in a similar way the Linux or Unix executables are being executed.*
- *The system function is being used for running the commands of the system from the code of C++.*
- The g++ and c++ command both compile and link with the source files of C++.

Programming in Linux Using Python

For appending any of the items to the bottom of the list use append(). For removing any of the items from the list, you can easily pass the particular element to the method remove() or the proper position of the item in the list as pop(). For displaying the complete list of the available methods for any object you can use Ctrl+space after you have typed in the item name along with a dot.

Programming in Linux Using Java

Java is one of the most popular languages of programming which is being widely used for the purpose of developing software for almost everything starting from cell phones to the cable TV boxes and extending its use to the large systems of enterprise information. The overall concept behind writing the source code of Java, compiling the same and then running it is more or less the same across most of the OS.

Java is a programming language which was originally developed by the Sun Microsystems. It falls under the category of compiled form of programming language in which the programmer writes up the source code and then submits the same to the compiler which will be checking out the syntaxes of the program and will generate a complete file which you can run. For instance, when you are using Google Chrome web browser, you are in true sense running all the programs which have been generated from a compiler which is used by the software developers.

To a wide extent, the programming languages of the past needed you to re-compile all the source code for every new OS in which you wanted to run your program on. For instance, a program which has been compiled for running in Windows will not be running on a system which has Linux in it unless and until if it has been re-compiled. Given the wide differences in the OS and the elements of hardware, this process was very difficult and complicated to carry out. One of the major motivations for the programming language of Java was the motivation of being able to write only one single set of source code and then provide the resulting program with the ability to run on some different set of operating systems or environments of operation.

Java comes with write once and then run anywhere capability only because of the way in which the compiler translates the entire source code in a particular file known as Byte Code file which can then run under any form of supported JRE or Java Runtime Environment.

The development process of Java involves these steps:

- Write down the Java source code and then save the same in one or more than one plain text files.

All of these files generally come with .java format at the end.

- Run the compiler of Java (javac) for compiling the source code which you have written into a file of Byte Code. The Byte Codes generally have .class at end of the name of the file.

- Run the program after submitting the byte code to a JRE.

Downloading Java Development Kit

5. The Hacking Process

The hacking process generally involves coming up with a plan on how the attack will take place. For starters, you should come up with a plan on how to collect information that will come in handy when facilitating the attack. The main importance of the plan is to ensure that the attack will be well-coordinated and there will be no mishaps in the process. Also, the plan ensures that the ethical hacker is confident about what they are doing. The ethical attackers also handle their duties very seriously. For starters, you may start by testing a program that is present on the client's computer; in the process, you may also outline, define, and document your goals. The testing phase is important since you will be able to come up with the testing standards and you will also gain some familiarity with the tools that you are supposed to use during the ethical hacking process. In this chapter, we will also investigate how a good hacking environment can be created since it will help to ensure that the hacking process will be successful. Ethical hackers cannot hack into a system without the authorization of the target or client.

Coming Up with Your Goals

Hackers should come up with goals that are implementable. As an ethical hacker, your main goal is to make sure that you have discovered all the vulnerabilities that are present within the system. If there are any vulnerabilities, the ethical hacker will then come up with techniques that will be used to seal all the loopholes so that the external attackers cannot hack into the system and corrupt it in different ways. The goal formation process involves the following steps:

1. Always define your specific goals. The goals should also align with the objectives of the business/client. As an ethical hacker, make sure that you have investigated the goals that the management is trying to achieve as well as your end-goals.
2. Make sure that you have also formulated a schedule that will guide you from the start to the end of the project. The hacking

490

timeline should also comprise of specific dates and time. For instance, some attacks cannot take place during business hours since there is a lot of traffic because of the employees and a DoS (Denial of Service) attack should be avoided through all means possible.

The goal formation process may take a lot of time; however, it will be worth it. The goals are meant to offer some guidance. As an ethical hacker, you may also refer to your goals from time to time to ensure that you are on the right track.

Determining the Specific System that You Will Hack

There may be many web applications that should be tested and they cannot be tested at a go since the system may crash in the process. Make sure that the hacking project has been broken down accordingly so that the attack may also be easily manageable. You may also start by carrying out an analysis so that you can be able to investigate the specific systems that you will test first. The main questions that you should ask yourself include:

1. Which systems are critical? There are some systems that can be accessed without the need of any authorization and that means that when an external attacker gets hold of these systems, there will be a lot of trouble and the business may also incur some losses.
2. Which systems can be attacked easily?
3. Which specific systems have not been documented?

After you have formulated your goals, you will be able to decide the specific systems that you will start to test. The main reason why goals are important is because they will help you to actualize your expectations and you will be able to investigate whether they are achievable. Also, the goals will help you to make sure that you can come up with a timeline and you will also estimate the amount of resources that you need when performing the attack.

The devices that you can test include:

1. Switches and Routers - The switches usually connect the computers on one network. The

routers will also connect many networks together.

2. Web applications and database servers.
3. Firewalls.
4. E-mails and files.
5. Bridges and wireless access points.
6. Laptops, workstations, and tablets.
7. Client and server operating systems.
8. The mobile devices are used to store confidential pieces of information.

When dealing with a small network, you can easily test everything. You can test the emails and the web servers. Also, make sure that the ethical hacking process is also flexible. Make sure that you have started with the networks and systems that are highly vulnerable. Some of the factors that you should consider include:

1. The applications that are present within the system.
2. The operating system that is being used.
3. The amount of sensitive information that has been stored within the system and network.

The Attack Tree Analysis

The attack tree analysis is used by attackers when formulating an attack. It is in the form of a flow chart that helps to outline how the attack will be carried out. Security teams usually use the attack tree when performing some risk analysis that is critical. To improve your hacking skills, you should make sure that you are able to plan an attack and also handle it in a methodological manner.

The main challenge that is present is the time that is needed when formulating the attack tree. Also, you should possess the necessary expertise when formulating the attack tree. Nowadays, there are some tools that can be used to formulate the attack tree. You can use the SecurITree tool to formulate the attack tree.

The ethical hacking process is also advancing as compared to the assessment of the present vulnerabilities. As an ethical hacker, you should make sure that you possess a lot of knowledge about varying systems. For example, you can start by looking for some information about the target. Also, you can use varying ethical hacking techniques. At times, you may be undecided and that means that you should assess the system thoroughly to make sure that there is enough visibility. You can also focus more on the firewall.

Formulating the Testing Standards

In an instance whereby there is some form of miscommunication, the system can crash easily when the ethical hacking process is taking place. Make sure that you have come up with testing standards so that you may avoid some challenges. Some of the standards include:

1. When are you performing the tests? Is there a specific time?
2. Which tests are being performed?
3. How will you perform each test and which IP address will you use?
4. The specific amount of knowledge that you possess about the systems that you are going to test.
5. Which are the best steps to take after you have discovered that there are some vulnerabilities within the system.

Some of the practices that you should utilize during the ethical hacking process include:

Timing

The timing is very important and it should also apply during the ethical hacking process. When you carry out some tests, you must make sure that the business process that are going on within the organization are not affected in any way. There are harmful situations that you should also avoid through all means possible including miscommunication. The DoS (Denial of Service) attacks should also be avoided, especially when dealing with an e-commerce site that has high traffic. If there are many people who are involved in handling the project, it is best to agree on the timing so that the end goals can be easily achieved.

It is good to make sure that the ISP (Internet Service Provider) is knowledgeable about the ethical hacking attack that is about to take place. After making sure that they are aware, you can go ahead and assess the vulnerabilities that are present within the system and the ISP (Internet Service Provider) will not try to block the traffic after suspecting that there is some malicious behavior that is taking place.

Make sure that the testing timeline is made up of short-term dates and the tests should be carried out at intervals. Make sure that the milestones are also outlined. The timelines and all the data should be keyed into a spreadsheet so that it can also offer some guidance.

Specific Tests

As an ethical hacker, your services may be required at some point, especially when carrying out penetration tests. Some of the tests include cracking the passwords so that you may be able to gain access to some of the web applications. In some instances, you may need to collect some information that will come in handy when facilitating the attack and that means that you should carry out a social engineering attack. You may need to carry different tests and you should make sure that you have not revealed any information about the tests that you are about to carry out. The documentation process is important since it will help to get rid of the miscommunication that may come about in the future. In some instances, you may have to make sure that you collect some evidence through the use of screenshots. Also, you may lack the knowledge to handle some tests, but that does not mean that the tests cannot take place. In such an instance, you should use the automated tools since you may also be unable to learn more about some of the tests that you should conduct.

About the Blind and Knowledge Assessments

During the testing phase, make sure that you possess enough knowledge about the system and the network. The possession of such knowledge may not be necessary; nevertheless, you should make sure that you possess some basic knowledge about the system that you are about to test and you will also be able to protect yourself by ensuring that there are no digital footprints that can be used to trace back to the individual who facilitated the attack. When you want to learn more about a specific organization, the process is not tough in any way. You just need to carry out a survey as a formality so that you can understand how the system operates and you can go ahead and plan the attack. After carrying out some background research, you will not carry out the attack blindly. When you carry out an assessment, some of the techniques that you have used will depend on the specific needs that you possess.

The best approach that you can use during the hacking process is to make sure that you have come up with a plan that will come in handy when facilitating multiple attacks. Also, as a client, you should make sure that the hacker that you have hired does not harbor any malicious motives. Some of the hackers may have a limited scope depending on the end result that they expect. Also, ensure that the network administrators cannot detect that there is a test that is being carried out. As an attacker, to avoid being caught, you may use social engineering attacks. If a system is being accessed by many people, when they discover that there is an attack taking place, they may change their habits and that means that the expected results will not be accurate. If you want to inform people about the attack, make sure that only the key players such as the IT experts can get a hold of such information.

Location

The tests that you are carrying out as an ethical hacker should dictate the location of where you will carry out the ethical hacking process. The major goal is to make sure that the system has been tested at a location that can be easily accessed by malicious users. The major challenges, in this case, include being unable to determine whether there is someone within the organization who has hacked into the system; as a result, always make sure that all the present loopholes have been sealed. Also, you may combine different tests and they can also be executed both externally and internally.

You can carry out different tests, including cracking the passwords and also assessing the network within the target organization. In some instances, you should also seek the services of another professional who has knowledge about how to hack into a system. Some of the gadgets that you can also test include routers, firewalls, web applications, and servers. When carrying out an external attack, make sure that your internet connection is stable. You may also have to use the external proxy servers. Make sure that you have assigned a specific IP address to the computer that will be used during the vulnerability assessment process. Also, ensure that you have accessed the network outside the firewall. The internal tests are easy and you will only need to have access to the network physically as well as the organization's servers. In some instances, you can also use a cable modem.

How to Handle the Vulnerabilities in the Network

When it comes to handling the vulnerabilities that are within the network, you should make sure that you have come up with sensible techniques that you can use to seal all the loopholes that are within the organization. The hacking process cannot take place forever since the system will be at the risk of crashing. Ensure that you have followed a certain path until you will no longer be able to access the system. You may have some doubts and, in such cases, make sure that you have referred to the goals that you had outlined before you started the ethical hacking process. After discovering some loopholes, make sure that you have contacted the right personnel so that they can also handle the problem fast. If some of these problems are not fixed on a timely basis, some of the external attackers may take advantage of these loopholes and they can also cause some damage that is irreversible. The staff within the company should also make sure that they have not violated any of the employment arrangements within the company.

Silly Assumptions

When you start to assume things, there is a high likelihood that you will not be able to achieve your objectives. There are many assumptions that people make when they are about to hack into a system and they include:

1. You may assume that the networks are available during the testing phase.
2. You may assume that you know all the risks that are present
3. You may also assume that you have all the tools that you need during the testing phase.

4. You may also assume that some of these tools will also minimize the chances of the network crashing.

Make sure that you have documented all the assumptions that you may be having before the ethical hacking process commences.

How to Select the Tools that You Will Use to Carry Out the Vulnerability Assessment

There are some factors that you should consider before you can choose the security assessment tools that you will use during the vulnerability assessment process. For starters, you must consider the tests that you are supposed to run. The ethical hacking tests can also be conducted using a network. When you perform the tests comprehensively, ensure that you have selected the tools appropriately.

Make sure that you have an in-depth understanding of all the tools that you are going to use when scanning for the vulnerabilities. The tools are accompanied by a manual which may be in the form of a Readme file. Make sure that you have opened the file so that you can learn more about how the tools operate and how they should be installed. There are message boards that can also help you to learn more about the tools that are offered by Kali Linux.

Some tools are quite hazardous since they can also affect the health of the network. Make sure that you are very careful when using some of these tools. Also, ensure you have in-depth knowledge about the options that are available. During the ethical hacking phase, do not try to use any tools that you are not conversant with since you may end up causing more harm than good. For instance, you may initiate a DoS (Denial of Service) attack abruptly. Some data may also be lost in the process. If some of the tools that are available for free do not prove to be worth it, you can purchase the commercial versions of the tools since they will be more effective. The main point to note is that some of these commercial tools are quite expensive, but their functionality is superb. Commercial tools ensure that you have gotten value for your money.

6. Kali Linux Tools

In this section, we will go through the different types of tools that are available in Kali Linux. The tools can be classified as per the tasks that are achieved by using them. The classification is as follows:

- Exploitation Tools

- Forensics Tools

- Information Gathering Tools

- Reverse Engineering Tools

- Wireless Attack Tools

- Reporting Tools

- Stress Testing Tools

- Maintaining Access Tools

- Sniffing and Spoofing Tools

- Password Attack Tools

Let us now go through the tools available in each category one by one to understand their specific purpose.

Exploitation Tools

If you consider a network over the Internet, which has a set of computers running on it, there are many applications in each system that can make that system vulnerable. This can happen due to many reasons such as bad code, open ports on the servers, etc., which make these systems easily accessible. This is where exploitation tools come into the picture. They help you target and exploit such vulnerable machines. But you are not an attacker, and therefore, these tools will help you identify and patch these vulnerabilities. Let us go through the available exploitation tools in Kali Linux one at a time.

Armitage

Developed by Raphael Mudge, Armitage is a graphical user interface front-end, which is to be used with the Metasploit framework. It is a tool that is available in the graphical form, and it is easy to use as it recommends exploits on a given system. The tool is open-source and free to use. It is mostly popular for the data it can provide about shared sessions and the communication it provides through a single instance of Metasploit. A user can launch scans and exploits on a system using Armitage, which will give the user data about available exploits. This, combined with the advanced tools available in the Metasploit framework, gives a user control over a vulnerable system.

The Backdoor Factory (BDF)

The Backdoor Factory known as BDF is a Kali Linux tool that is used by researchers and security professionals. Using this tool, a user can slide in their desired code in the executable binaries of system files on application files. The tool executes the code without letting the system know that there is something additional happening along with the regular system or application processes.

The Browser Exploitation Framework (BeEF)

As the name suggests, if you want to perform penetration testing on browsers, the Browser Exploitation Framework should be your go-to tool. Using this tool, you can also target a browser on the client-side if there are vulnerabilities present in it.

Commix

Commix is a Kali Linux tool which allows users to test web applications. It has been very useful to set up test environments for web developers, penetration testers, and researchers. It performs injections into a web application and allows a user to identify bugs and errors. The tool has been developed in Python.

Crackle

The Crackle tool is a Kali Linux tool, which is used as a brute force utility. It can detect and intercept traffic between Bluetooth devices. The pairing code used between Bluetooth devices is mostly 4-6 digits and is in an encrypted format. Crackle can decrypt these codes, and you can then intercept all communication that happens between the Bluetooth devices.

JBoss-Autopwn

JBoss-Autopwn is a penetration-testing tool used in JBoss applications. The Github version of JBoss Autopwn is outdated, and the last update is from 2011. It is a historical tool and not used much now.

Linux Exploit Suggester

The Linux Exploit Suggester tool provides a script that keeps track of vulnerabilities and shows all possible exploits that help a user get root access during a penetration test.

The script uses the uname -r command to find the kernel version of the Linux operating system. Additionally, it will also provide the -k parameter through which the user can manually enter the version for the kernel of the Linux operating system.

sqlmap
The sqlmap Kali tool is a free and open-source tool that is used for penetration testing. Using this tool, you can detect vulnerabilities in SQL databases and therefore, perform SQL injections. The detection engine on this tool is extremely powerful, and it has a range of tools that can perform extreme penetration allowing a user to fetch information such as data from databases, database fingerprinting, etc. It can also give the user access to the file system in the operating system, thereby allowing the user to execute commands.

Yersinia
The Yersinia tool available in Kali Linux can be used to detect vulnerabilities in network protocols such that a user can take advantage of them. The

framework of this tool is solid for testing and analyzing deployment of systems and networks. The attacks using this tool are layer-2 attacks that can be used to exploit the weaknesses in a layer-2 network protocol. Yersinia is used during penetration tests to start attacks on network devices such as DHCP servers, switches, etc. which use the spanning tree protocol.

Cisco Global Exploiter

The Cisco Global Exploiter (CGE) tool is a security testing exploit engine/tool that is simple yet fast and advanced. There are 14 vulnerabilities that are known to exist in Cisco routers and switches. This tool can be used to exploit those vulnerabilities. The Cisco Global Exploiter is basically a perl script, which is driven using the command line and has a front-end that is simple and easy to use.

Forensics Tools

In this section, we will go through the Kali Linux tools that are available to be used in the Forensics domain.

chkrootkit

The chkrootkit tool can be used during a live boot of a system. It helps identify if there are any rootkits that are installed on the system. The tool helps in hardening the system and lets a user ensure that it is not vulnerable to a hacker. The tool can also be used to perform a system binary scan which lets a user know if there are any modifications made to the stock rootkit, string replacements, temporary deletions, etc. These are just a few of the things that this little tool can do. It looks like a fairly simple tool, but the power it possesses can be invaluable to a forensic investigator.

p0f

The p0f tool is used when you want to know the operating system if a host that is being targeted. You can do this just by intercepting transmitted packages and analyzing them. It does not matter if the system has a firewall or not, the tool will still fetch you the information on the operating system. The tool is amazing as it does not lead to any extra traffic on the network, and its probes are not mysterious at all. Given all these features, p0f in the hands of an advanced user can help detect the presence of firewalls, use of NAT devices, and the presence of load balancers as well.

pdf-parser

The pdf-parser tool can be used to parse a PDF file and identify all the elements used in the file. The output of the tool on a PDF file is not a PDF file. It is not advisable for textbook cases of PDF files, but it gets the job done. The use case of this tool is mostly to identify PDF files that may have scripts embedded into them.

Dumpzilla

The Dumpzilla tool is developed in Python. This tool extracts all information that may be of interest to forensics from web browsers like Seamonkey, Mozilla Firefox, and Iceweasel.

ddrescue

The ddrescue tool is often termed as a savior tool. It is used to copy data from one-block devices such as a hard disk drive to another block device. It is, however, called a savior because while copying data, it will copy all the good parts first, which helps to prevent read errors on the source block device.

The ddrescue tool's basic operation is completely automatic which means that once you have started it, you do not need to wait for any prompts like an error, wherein you would need to stop the program or restart it.

By using the mapfule feature of the tool, data will be recovered in an efficient fashion, as it will only read the blocks that are required. You also have the option to stop the ddrescue process at any time and resume it again later from the same point.

Foremost

There are times when you may have deleted files on purpose or by mistake and realized that you needed them later. The Foremost tool is there to rescue you. This tool is an open-source tool that can be used to retrieve data off of disks that have been completely formatted. The metadata around the file may be lost, but the data retrieved will be intact. A magical feature is that even if the directory information is lost, it can help retrieve data by reference to the header or footer of the file, making it a fast and reliable tool for data recovery.

An interesting fact is that Foremost was developed by special agents of the US Air Force.

Galleta

The Galleta tool helps you parse a cookie trail that you have been following and convert it into a spreadsheet format, which can be exported for future reference.

Whenever a cybercrime case is ongoing, cookies can be used as evidence. But understanding cookies in their raw format is a challenging task. This is where the Galleta tool comes handy as it helps in structuring the data fetched from cookie trails and can be then run through other software to decode the data further. This software needs the input of the date to be in a spreadsheet format, and that is exactly what Galleta feeds into this software.

Information Gathering Tools

The prerequisite for any attack is information. It becomes very easy to target a system when you have sufficient information about the system. The success rate of the attack is also on the higher side when you know everything about the target system. All kinds of information are useful to a hacker, and nothing can be considered as irrelevant.

The process of information gathering includes:

- Gathering information that will help in social engineering and, ultimately, in the attack

- Understanding the range of the network and computers that will be the targets of the attack

- Identifying and understanding all the complete surface of the attack, i.e., processes, and systems that are exposed

- Identifying the services of a system that are exposed and collecting as much information about them as possible

- Querying specific service that will help fetch useful data such as usernames

We will now go through Information Gathering tools available in Kali Linux one by one.

Nmap and Zenmap

Ethical hacking is a phase in Kali Linux for which the tools NMap and ZenMap are used. NMap and ZenMap are basically the same tools. ZenMap is a Graphical Interface for the NMap tool that works on the command line.

The NMap tool, which is used for security auditing and discovery of network, is a free tool. Apart from penetration testers, it is also used by system administrators and network administrators for daily tasks such as monitoring the uptime of the server or a service and managing schedules for service upgrades.

NMap identifies available hosts on a network by using IP packets that are raw. This also helps NMap identify the service being hosted on the host, which includes the name of the application and the version. Basically, the most important application it helps identify on a network is the filter or the firewall set up on a host.

Stealth Scan

The Stealth Scan is also popularly known as the half-open scan or SYN. It is called so because it refrains from completing the usual three-way handshake of TCP. A SYN packet is sent by an attacker to the target host, who then acknowledges the SYN and sends a SYN/ACK in return. If a SYN/ACK is received, it can be safely assumed that the connection to the target host will complete and the port is open and can listen to the target host. If the response received is RST instead, it is safe to assume that the port is closed or not active on the target host.

braa

braa is a tool that is used for scanning mass Simple Network Management Protocol (SNMP). The tool lets you make SNMP queries, but unlike other tools that make single queries at a time to the SNMP service, braa has the capability to make queries to multiple hosts simultaneously, using one single process. The advantage of braa is that it scans multiple hosts very fast and that too by using very limited system resources.

Unlike other SNMP tools that require libraries from SNMP to function, braa implements and maintains its own stack of SNMP. The implementation is very complex and dirty. Supports limited data types, and cannot be called up to standard in any case. However, braa was developed to be a fast tool, and it is fast indeed.

dnsmap

dnsmap is a tool that came into existence originally in 2006 after being inspired by the fictional story "The Thief No One Saw" by Paul Craig.

A tool used by penetration testers in the information gathering stage, dnsmap helps discover the IP of the target company, domain names, netblocks, phone numbers, etc.

Dnsmap also helps on subdomain brute force, which helps in cases where zone transfers of DNS do not work. Zone transfers are not allowed publicly anymore nowadays, which makes dnsmap essential.

Fierce

Fierce is a Kali tool that is used to scan ports and map networks. Discovery of hostnames across multiple networks and scanning of IP spaces that are non-contiguous can be achieved by using Fierce. It is a tool much like Nmap, but in the case of Fierce, it is used specifically for networks within a corporation.

Once the target network has been defined by a penetration tester, Fierce runs a whole lot of tests on the domains in the target network and retrieves information that is valuable and which can be analyzed and exploited by the attacker.

Fierce has the following features.

- Capabilities for a brute-force attack through custom and built-in test list

- Discovery of name servers

- Zone transfer attacks

- Scan through IP ranges both internal and external

- Ability to modify the DNS server for reverse host lookups

Wireshark

Wireshark is a Kali tool that is an open-source analyzer for network and works on multiple platforms such as Linux, BSD, OS X, and Windows.

It helps one understand the functioning of a network, thus making it of use in government infrastructure, education industries, and other corporates.

It is similar to the tcpdump tool, but Wireshark is a notch above as it has a graphical interface through which you can filter and organize the data that has been captured, which means that it takes less time to analyze the data further. There is also an only text-based version known as tshark, which has almost the same amount of features.

Wireshark has the following features.

- The interface has a user-friendly GUI

- Live capture of packets and offline analysis

- Support for Gzip compression and extraction

- Inspection of the full protocol

- Complete VoIP analysis

- Supports decryption for IPsec, Kerberos, SSL/TLS, WPA/WPA2

URLCrazy
URLCrazy is a Kali tool that tests and generates typos and variations in domains to target and perform URL hijacking, typo squatting, and corporate espionage. It has a database that can generate variants of up to 15 types for domains and misspellings of up to 8000 common spellings. URLCrazy supports a variety of

keyboard layouts, checks if a particular domain is in use and figures how popular a typo is.

Metagoofil

Metagoofil is a Kali tool that is aimed at retrieving files such as pdf, xls, doc, ppt, etc.which are publicly available for a company on the Internet. The tool makes a Google search to scan the Internet and download such files to the local machine. The tool then extracts the metadata of these files using libraries such as pdfminer, hachoir, etc. The output from this tool is then fed as input to the information-gathering pipeline. The inputs include usernames, server or machine names, and software version, which help penetration testers with their investigation.

Ghost Phisher

Ghost Phisher is a Kali tool, which is used as an attack software program and also for security auditing of wired and wireless networks. Ghost Phisher is developed in the Python programming language. The program basically emulates access points of a network, therefore, deploying its own internal server into a network.

Fragroute

Traffic moving towards a specific system can be intercepted and modified with the use of the Fragroute tool in Kali Linux. In simple words, the packets originating from the attacker system known as frag route packets are routed strategically to a destination system. Attackers and security personnel use it to bypass firewalls. Information gathering is a use case for fragroute and is therefore widely used by attackers or penetration testers.

Reverse Engineering Tools

We can learn how to make and break things from something as simple as a Lego toy to a car engine simply by dismantling the parts one by one and then putting them back together. This process wherein we break things down to study it deeply and further improve it is called Reverse Engineering.

The technique of Reverse Engineering in its initial days would only be used with hardware. As the process evolved over the years, engineers started applying it to software, and now to human DNA as well. Reverse engineering, in the domain of cyber security, helps understand that if a system was breached, how the attacker entered the system and the steps that he took to break and enter into the system.

While getting into the network of corporate infrastructure, attackers ensure that they are utilizing all the tools available to them in the domain of computer intrusion tools. Most of the attackers are funded and skilled and have a specific objective for an attack towards which they are highly motivated. Reverse Engineering empowers us to put up a fight against such attackers in the future. Kali Linux comes equipped with a lot of tools that are useful in the process of reverse engineering in the digital world. We will list down some of these tools and learn their use.

Apktool
Apktool is a Kali Linux tool that is used in the process of reverse engineering. This tool has the ability to break down resources to a form that is almost the original form and then recreate the resource by making adjustments. It can also debug code that is small in size, step by step. It has a file structure,

which is project-like, thus making it easy to work with an app. With Apktool, you can also automate tasks that are repetitive in nature, like the building of an apk.

Dex2jar

Dex2jar is a Kali tool, which has a lightweight API and was developed to work with the Dalvik Executable that is the .dex/.odex file formats. The tool basically helps to work with the .class files of Java and Android.

It has the following components.

- Dex2jar has an API that is lightweight, similar to that of ASM.

- dex-translator component does the action of converting a job. It reads instructions from dex to the dex-ir format and converts it to ASM format after optimizing it.

- Dex-ir component, which is used by the dex-translator component, basically represents the dex instructions.

- The dex-tools component works with the .class files. It is used for tasks such as modifying an apk, etc.

diStorm3

diStorm is a Kali tool which is easy to use the decomposer library and is lightweight at the same time. Instructions can be disassembled in 16 bit, 32 bit and 64-bit modes using diStorm. It is also popular amongst penetration testers as it is the fast disassembler library. The source code, which depends on the C library, is very clean, portable, readable, and independent of a particular platform, which allows it to be used in embedded modules and kernel modules.

diStorm3 is the latest version which is backward compatible with diStorm64's old interface. However, using the new header files is essential.

edb-debugger

edb debugger is a Kali tool which is the Linux equivalent for the popular Windows tool called "Olly debugger." It is a debugging tool with modularity as one of its main goals. Some of its features are as follows.

- An intuitive Graphical User Interface

- All the regular debugging operations such as step-into, step-over, run and break

- Breakpoints for conditions

- Basic analysis for instructions

- View or Dump memory regions

- Address inspection which is effective

- Generation and import of symbol maps

- Various available plugins

The core that is used for debugging is integrated as a plugin so that it can be replaced when needed as per requirement.

The view of the data dump is in tabbed format. This feature allows the user to open several views of the memory at a given time while allowing you to switch between them.

Jad Debugger

Jad is a Kali Linux tool that is a Java decompiler and the most popular one in the world. It is a tool which runs on the command line and is written in the C++ language. Over the years, there have been many graphical interfaces which have been developed which run Jad in the background and provide a comfortable front end to the users to perform tasks such as project management, source browsing, etc. Kali Linux powers Jad in its releases to be used for Java application debugging and other processes of reverse engineering.

JavaSnoop

JavaSnoop is a Kali Linux tool that allows testing of Java application security. By developing JavaSnoop, Aspect has proved how it's a leader in the security industry in providing verification services for all applications and not just web-based applications.

JavaSnoop allows you to begin tampering with method calls, run customized code, or sit back and see what's going on the system by just attaching an existing process such as a debugger.

OllyDbg

OllyDbg is a Kali Linux tool which is a debugger at a level of a 32-bit Assembler developed for Microsoft Windows. What makes it particularly useful is its

emphasis on code that is in binary in times when the source is not available.

OllyDbg brags of the following features.

- Has an interactive user interface and no command-line hassle

- Loads and debugs DLLs directly

- Allows function descriptions, comments and labels to be defined by the user

- No trash files in the registry or system directories post installation

- Can be used to debug multi-threaded applications

- Many third-party applications can be integrated as it has an open architecture

- Attaches itself to running programs

Valgrind
Valgrind is a tool in Kali Linux tool which is used for profiling and debugging Linux based systems. The tool allows you to manage threading bugs and

memory management bugs automatically. It helps eliminate hours that one would waste on hunting down bugs and therefore, stabilizes the program to a very great extent. A program's processing speed can be increased by doing detailed profiling on the program by using Valgrind too. Suite for debugging and profiling Linux programs. The Valgrind distribution has the following production-quality tools currently.

- Memcheck which detects errors in memory

- DRD and Helgrind which are two other thread error detectors

- Cachegrind is a branch prediction and cache profiling tool

- Callgrind is a branch detection profile and a call-graph generating cache profiler

- Massif which profiles heaps

- Three experimental tools are also included in the Valgrind distribution.

- SGCheck which detector for stack or global array overrun

- DHAT which is a second profiler for heap and helps understand how heap blocks are being used

- BBV which basic block vector generator

Reverse Engineering plays an important role where manufacturers are using it to sustain competition from rivals. Other times reverse engineering is used to basically figure out flaws in software and re-build a better version of the software. Kali Linux provides tools which are known in the reverse engineering domain. In addition to the tools that we have discussed, there are many 3rd party reverse engineering tools as well but the ones we have discussed come installed in the Kali Linux image.

7. Malware And Cyber Attacks

In this chapter, we start talking about *malware types*, and later on we will discuss *Cyber Attacks*. For starters, we will discuss Viruses, Trojans, Worms, Ransomware and other types of programs that were badly designed. But first of all, let us answer the following question:

1) What is a Malware ?

A *malware* (aka. malicious software) is a malicious software program designed to steal, destroy, or corrupt data stored on our devices.

Many people use the *generic term of the virus*, which is not necessarily correct because there can be many types of dangerous programs. Here below (only) a part of them:

1) *Virus*
2) *Trojans*
3) *Worms*
4) *Ransomware*
5) *Spyware*
6) *Adware*

7) and many more (Rootkit, time bombs, backdoor, etc.)

Here is the picture below on **Wikipedia**, the proportion (in 2011) of malware from the Internet. Since then, many things have changed or changed, but it's interesting to have such a hierarchy with the most common types of malware.

And now take some of these malware and discuss them in more detail:

1) Viruses

A virus is a program with which we are all accustomed to. Whether we had the computer infected with a virus or that we heard / seen someone else, we know that these viruses can be really dangerous for us (and especially for our data stored on the computer - the most important element for us).

Virus programmers take advantage of existing vulnerabilities in different operating systems (especially Windows) and write software to take advantage of them (and users of these devices).

2) Trojans

A Trojan is a type of program designed to appear for the benefit of the person who uses it, but there is a malicious code behind that has other intentions altogether. These types of programs are most common in the Internet (as you could see in the picture above) and are used to being easily masked in front of an inexperienced user. So in the (first) run of the program, the trojan is installed and will hide, doing its job "quietly". The term Trojan comes from the story of the Trojan horse in Greek mythology, exposed in the movie [Troy].

3) Worms

A worm is a form of malware that once it infects a device (PC, laptop, server, etc.) will do its best to expand and infect others on the network. Thus, a worm manages to *slow networks* and the connected devices (by using CPU and RAM resources) and even the network, because infected computers will generate abnormal traffic.

4) Ransomware

A more popular type of malware lately is ransomware, whose purpose is to *encrypt the hard disk* (or SSD) victims and to request a cash *redeem* for the decryption key.

5) Adware

There are programs that once installed on a device (or in the browser) will start to show commercials (annoying).

6) Spyware

Spyware are programs designed to extract certain data from users. They are not meant to hurt (by consuming resources) or affect the victim in any way, but simply extract data and send them to "mother servers" (those who have initiated "espionage").

First, you need to be aware of the existence of such programs, after which you have to take protection / prevention measures against them.

In this situation, anti-virus programs are very welcome because they contain very large databases (called signatures) that check every program / file on your operating system (Windows, Linux or Mac).

Now you can also know that Windows has the highest number of malware (viruses, Trojans, ransomware, etc.). Why? Because Windows is the most widely used operating system in the world, and hackers have something to "steal." That's why the main focus of attackers and cyber-security companies is on Windows.

The Mac and Linux are also not free from malware, but their number is not that big. They have been designed with a higher degree of security in mind and operate completely differently from Windows.

Examples of Cyber Attacks

These hacking methods are very common, and each one serves a particular purpose.

What is a Cyber Attack?
A cyber attack is a means by which a person (with evil intentions) takes advantage of the *vulnerabilities*

existing on a particular system (server, computer, network equipment, application, etc.).

Here are some of the most common attacks on the Internet:

1) *MITM*-Man *in* the Middle

2) *DoS*-Denial *of* Service

3) *DDoS*-Distributed *Denial of* Service, check this link: http://www.digitalattackmap.com/

4) *SQLi*-SQL injection

5) *XSS*-Cross-Site Scripting

In addition, there are many more in the Internet world, but to illustrate some, we will only focus on the top 3. So let's take the first type of attack, MITM, and discuss it in more detail about it (and show you some ways you can make such attacks - but please do it in an ethical way), after which will go further with the discussion and discuss DoS and DDoS.

After all, in we will discuss web security and other types of attacks: SQL injections and XSS.

What is a MITM (Man In The Middle) attack ?

MITM is a type of cyber attack in order to listen to the traffic of users connected to the same network.

What this means? It means that if you go to a café in town, someone can connect with you to the same Wi-Fi, and from just a few commands you can see all your conversations on Facebook, Google, etc.

That's how it is, but do not worry because things are not that simple. Why? Because the vast majority of our Internet connections are secured (*HTTPS instead of HTTP*;)), instead it does not mean that there can be no one listening to your traffic.

To avoid such situations, I recommend that you use a VPN in public places.

There are several ways you can do MITM (I will list below just a few of the many possibilities below):

- MAC Spoofing
- ARP Spoofing
- Rogue DHCP Server
- STP Attack
- DNS Poisoning

These are some of the most common. In the following I will discuss some of these and I will give you some practical examples of how to do it.

1) MAC Spoofing

The term spoofing comes from deceiving, and in this case it refers to the deception of at least one device in the network by the fact that a certain computer is given as another computer (or even Router) using its MAC address.

This can be done very easily using a program that changes your MAC address with a PC to see its traffic. Here's an example (https://windowsreport.com/mac-address-changer-windows-10/) on Windows 10 about how to change your MAC address, but in my opinion the process is much more complex, compared to Linux:

 # ifconfig eth0 down

 # macchanger -m 00:d0:70:00:20:69 eth0

 # ifconfig eth0 up

First, we stop the interface (eth0 in this example), then we use the *macchanger* command that helps us with the *MAC address change*, and the -m argument lets us specify an address. For verification, use the command: *#ifconfig*

PS: If you want to *generate a random MAC*, then use: *#macchanger -r eth0*

2) ARP Spoofing

ARP Spoofing works in a similar way to MAC spoofing, just as the attacker uses the ARP protocol to mislead the entire network about having the MAC address X (which is actually the Router). Thus, all network devices that want to reach the Internet will send the traffic to the attacker (which will redirect it to Router). In this situation, the attacker can see all the traffic passing through him using a traffic capture program such as Wireshark.

To initiate such an attack first we must *start the routing process on Linux* so that traffic can be sent from the victim to the Router and vice versa (through us, the "attackers"):

 # echo "1" > proc/sys/net/ipv4/ip_forward

 # cat /proc/sys/net/ipv4/ip_forward

Now we are *redirecting* the traffic to the port we want to listen to:

 # iptables -t nat -A PREROUTING -p tcp -- destination-port 80 -j REDIRECT --to-port 8181

After which we need to install the program:

> # sudo apt-get update
>
> # sudo apt-get install *dsniff*

And now we can give the command to start the attack:

 # sudo arpspoof -i *eth0* -t *192.168.1.3 192.168.1.1*

 # sudo arpspoof -i *eth0* -t *192.168.1.1 192.168.1.3*

- -i eth0: is the interface on which we will start the attack

- -t 192.168.1.3: is the IP of the victim (the device we want to attack - CHANGE with an IP from your network)

- 192.168.1.1: is the Router IP (CHANGE the Router IP to your Router)

Virtually these two orders, send fake packages to the two devices informing them that traffic has to pass through the attacker. Now all you have to do is open Wireshark and see how the victim's traffic "passes through you".

Here is another need for an element that will facilitate the *DECRYPTION of traffic*. Why? Because much of the Internet traffic is encrypted.

With this tool we will use: *SSLstrip* (removes the security element, SSL), and the command to decrypt HTTPS traffic in HTTP is:

sudo python *sslstrip.py -l 8181*

This command will listen to traffic on port 8181 and try to decrypt it. After that, you can start Wireshark and see the encrypted traffic (however, I suggest you start Wireshark and when the traffic is encrypted to see the difference).

PS: At a simple search on Google you will find SSLstrip;)

To write the result to a file (from the terminal) you can use a tool similar to Wireshark called *Ettercap*. Once you install it on Linux you can give the following command:

 # *sudo* ettercap –i eth0 –T –w /root/scan.txt – M arp /192.168.1.3 /

The arguments used in the command are:

- -i eth0: the interface on which traffic is listened

- -T : to launch command execution over the terminal

- -M : Man in middle mode

- -w : writing data to a file

- 192.168.1.3: the victim's IP address

8. Virtual Private Networks To Help

The next thing that we need to take a look at is the Virtual Private Network. The VPN is going to be a means of extending a local network to the external nodes so that these nodes are going to become a part of the local network. This practice is going to have a lot of legitimate uses, including allowing the network of a corporate in disparate geographical areas to help them connect and share resources in a secure manner. Of course, it would also provide hackers with a big advantage so that they can join in with a network of a target server if they know how to work with this network in the right manner.

VPN's and Tunneling

The power of a VPN is going to lie in a practice that is known as tunneling. Instead of connecting to a destination server through the internet via a service provider, the user is going to establish an encrypted connection to the VPN server, which is then going to help get them connected with their destination. Although the ISP is able to see whether the user is connected to a known VPN server IP address, it is not able to read through all of the encrypted traffic that happens here either.

When a request is sent from the user over to the server of the VPN, then the VPN is going to decrypt the request (which is going to include the headers for the destination), and then it will relay it through the internet. When packets are sent back to the VPN, this will be encrypted again and relayed back to the user with the right tunnel that has already been established.

VPN Types and Uses

The next thing that we need to take a look at here is the VPN types and uses. They are going to be two main options that we can work with on this server and they are going to be categorized based on their purpose. This includes the site-to-site options and remote access. The remote access VPN is going to be the one that is the most commonly used by home or personal users to either protect their anonymity or to make sure that they can bypass some restrictions such as regional access, corporate access, or ISP access.

Home or corporate users could potentially use this kind of VPN if they would like to reach their own LANs from a location that is outside the office. This arrangement could be the most desirable with a company that has personnel that works remotely or when there are multiple locations, but they still need to have a central access place for their services and databases. Home users have the option of setting up one of these VPN in a manner that is similar here in order to access their files at their own home or to allow them a way to have control over their own computer from a remote location.

Although having that access to a VPN remotely can create a connection that is encrypted, it is going to be done through a process of encapsulating packets that are traveling through the internet in a manner that looks just like the standard traffic. The site-to-site VPNs are going to help us create a more secure connection by employing any protocol that can maintain the communication that happens between the routers. This communication is only something that is possible when the server and the client come together and mutually authenticate the information.

VPN Protocols

The type of protocol that your VPN is going to use depends largely on what the purpose of your server will be, and some of the needs of your user. Many commercial VPN services are going to be helpful in allowing the clients to select the protocol of the server that they would like to work with. This choice is often going to be seen as a type of trade-off that can happen between speed, reliability, and security.

Encryption, by its very nature, is going to slow down the connection speeds a little bit in order to hide the message but since there is often more than one user that us sharing that server access, heavy congestion is going to be a much more likely cause of the slower speeds. The type of content that you want to access can affect the choice is protocol as well. For example, audio streaming and video streaming are going to require the UDP port support and more bandwidth than just what we see with regular HTTP browsing, so we have to consider the speed of that as well.

Now there are a few different protocols that we are able to choose when it comes to the VPN that we want to use and how we want to make sure that it is protected. The first option is going to be an open VPN. This is a very common and popular protocol for VPN that is going to use a lot of different libraries, which are all open-sourced, to help with communication and encryption.

The biggest advantage that we are able to see with this kind of protocol is that it can easily be applied to any port or sub-layer protocol that you want to work with, especially when we are talking about security. One of the drawbacks is that most browsers that are out there right now are not able to support this natively and you will need to rely on some third-party software to make sure that your mobile device or computer is able to connect to this server if you would like to use this protocol.

The next type of VPN protocol that we are able to work with is known as the point-to-point tunneling protocol or PPTP. This is an older protocol, but there are still many programmers who use it. The PPTP is going to offer us some encryption, but it is replete with a lot of security vulnerabilities and because of its age, it is possible that it is going to be exploited more than some of the others.

However, because it is able to support some of the older platforms as well as some of the legacy operating systems, and because it is still easy to use, this is a protocol that, despite the drawbacks, is commonly found. Many of the VPN services are going to provide this PPTP as an option for their clients who like to use it or will need it, but they also take the time to warn the clients about some of the security risks as well.

And the third option that we are able to work with is known as Layer 2 Tunneling Protocol or L2TP. This is one of the protocols that can be chosen because it is easy to use and the native support, but the channel that you are relying on is not going to be all that secure. In fact, this protocol is not going to be able to perform some of its own data encryption, so we will need to combine it together with a few other encryption protocols to get the work done. Another drawback that we may see with this option is that it has to be confined to just one port, which is going to make it easier for an ISP or firewall to block, and not that great for the hacker to work with.

Choosing Our VPN

A home user is going to look to use this kind of VPN, and whatever protocol they decide to go with, for anonymity, security, and freedom when it is time to connect to the internet. And often they are going to come with a few choices, with some trade-offs occurring between the speed, reliability, security, and cost. Although the VPNs provide encryption, and an exit node for clients to hide their identity quite a bit, as a hacker, you want to make sure that you know whether or not someone is able to log or track your activities.

One of the things that we need to take a look at when choosing one of these VPNs is whether user logging is going on. If the VPN activity logs are either being subpoenaed by law enforcement or compromised by hackers, then the relative anonymity that is provided by the exit node is no longer going to be the advantage. If the user would like to add in that layer of anonymity, then they need to make sure that the VPN that they go with is a no-logging service. Though keep in mind that no logging really means minimal logging.

There is going to be a certain amount of internal logging that will occur in order to make sure that the VPN is able to maintain their connection reliability and speed and to make sure that there aren't any attacks on the servers. The best services are going to work with just the minimum amount of logging that is necessary to help keep up a stable operation, and they will not keep records of those logs for any longer than they need.

As a hacker here, we need to make sure that we are skeptical of a VPN, especially one that claims to be free when they state that they do not log any activity, at least until you can read the fine print and find out exactly what the company does and does not log. In addition, these free services are not necessarily going to be that trustworthy on their own. Using your own due diligence is a must before you use any free VPN.

Additional Security Considerations with a VPN
If a user is hesitant to purchase a subscription to some of the reputable VPN services because they are worried that all of the anonymity is going to be lost with that transaction, there are a few commercial

VPNs out there that will allow you to use something like bitcoin to help pay for it. If you are worried about having your identity revealed through the logs of these systems, even if the server is a no logging server, it is possible to combine together a few VPN connections with a process that is known as VPN chaining. This is going to be accomplished when we can connect the VPN over to a host machine, then we will set up a different service for VPN on the virtual machine within the same host. If any of the logs are compromised with the inner VPN, the activity is still going to be logged as it came to form the outer VPN. There is the potential that someone would try to get the logs of the outer one, but it is still an additional obstacle and one that most companies and more are not going to take. Notice here that there are a few VPN services that will provide you with the option of connecting from the VPN server to the destination with the help of the Onion network that we talked about before. Although this is able to provide us with a few extra security advantages, it is also going to come with a reduction in the connection speed so we have to consider that as well.

9. Attacking With Frameworks

Social Engineering

Due to the increase in the use of technology for almost all of our activities, companies and organizations have invested a huge amount of money in ensuring that the technologies they use are properly secured from hackers. These companies have developed and implemented extensive firewalls to protect against any possible security breach. Most internet users are not security conscious despite the ease with which information can be obtained over an internet connection. This is coupled with the fact that most malicious hackers concentrate their efforts on computer servers and client application flaws. Over the years, these hackers have become more creative in how they gather information and structure their attacks on websites and web apps. With the enormous amount of money invested in online security, we would expect that malicious information theft or control would have been eliminated. However, this has not happened.

This is where we use social engineering to achieve our goal. It is a non-technical approach circumvents a company's security measures. No matter how secure a company's online applications are, they are still susceptible to hacking. Hackers have been able to achieve this using social engineering and tools based on social engineering. Social engineering is a hands-on approach to hacking. It involves targeting individuals and manipulating them into giving out vital information that can lead to a breach in the security system. These individuals, who may be employees of the organization or even a close relative of the top person at the target organization, are approached and coerced into trusting the hacker. They begin to gather information that could be of use in the hacking process. This is usually an approach taken when the company's firewalls are effective at thwarting outside penetration. When the hackers have obtained the necessary information (for instance, the login information of the social engineering target), they can hack the company from the inside out.

It is believed that human beings are the weakest link in any information security chain. The physical approach toward social engineering can occur in so many ways that it is impossible to cover all of them in this chapter. However, popular means include approaching and becoming friends with (or even a significant other of) employees at the company. Sometimes the employees are given a flash drive containing movies or other files in which they may be interested. The employees plug in the drive and launch a file that executes scripts in the background, granting the hackers access to the respective machines. The social engineer attack can also occur when a person calls an employee of a firm, impersonates a call center representative and tells the employee that he or she needs information to rectify a service that is important. The hacker would have gathered details about the employee from the employee's social media account or through personal conversations with the person. Once the hacker has received the information (which may include the victim's social security number or login details), the hacker hijacks the account and performs fraudulent transactions on it, or uses it for additional attacks. Social engineering makes it easy to build a username and password list that helps with logging into the target's accounts.

Hackers use the information they have gathered in combination with tools that ensure an easy hack of the company's system. Most of these tools are used in the client-side attack and are enhanced with the information gathered through social engineering. This information is used in conjunction with phishing and spoofing tools to attack a client if a direct social engineering attack fails. Social engineering is the information gathering procedure in this approach when it comes to attacking clients. Hacking has become a business venture. Hackers gain access to information simply to sell it for money, or to use it to transfer money. The motivation now is monetary. Usually, the target is selected, and the hacker uses information available to the public about the client to develop the attack. Typically, information obtained online is sufficient to build an attack. However, with an increase in employee education regarding hackers and social engineering, employees have begun to limit the personal information they share on social media and other public platforms.

The success of a social-engineering-based attack depends solely on the quality of information gathered. The attacker must be sociable and persuasive when interacting with the victim, such that the victim becomes open and begins to trust the hacker. Some hackers outsource this aspect to an individual who is skilled in getting people to tell them secrets.

Social Engineering Toolkit (SET)

The Social Engineering Toolkit is a very important tool used in a computer-aided social engineering attack. It comes pre-installed with the Kali Linux distro. It is written in the Python language and is also an open source toolkit. The Social Engineering Toolkit, or SET, was created by David Kennedy to exploit the human aspect of web security. However, it is important to make sure that the Social Engineering Toolkit is up to date. Once the tool has been updated, the configuration file can be set. The default configuration file is sufficient to make the SET run without any problems. Advanced users may want to edit and tweak certain settings. However, if you are a beginner, it is better to leave it the way it is until you become more familiar with the Social Engineering Toolkit. To access the configuration file, open the terminal and then change the directory to the SET. Open the config folder and you will find the set_config file, which you can open and edit with a text editor to change the parameters.

The Social Engineering Toolkit can be accessed by clicking on the Application icon, then clicking on the Kali Linux desktop. Next, click on BackTrack and then on the Exploitation Tools option. Click on Social Engineering Tools and select the Social Engineering Toolkit by clicking on SET. The SET will open in a terminal window. Alternatively, the SET can be opened directly from the terminal by typing "setoolkit" without the quotes.

The Social Engineering Toolkit opens in the terminal as a menu-based option. The menu contains different options based on the type of social engineering attack you need to use. The option at number 1 is for spear-phishing vectors which enable the user to execute a phishing attack. The phishing attack is an email attack. It is like casting a net by sending emails to random potential victims. Spear-phishing, on the other hand, targets one individual and the email is more personalized.

The second option on the SET menu is the website attack vector, which uses different web-attack methods against its target victim. The website attack vector option is by far the most popular and perhaps most used option in the Social Engineering Toolkit. Clicking on the website attack vector option opens menus containing the Java applet attack vector, the Metasploit browser exploits, the credential harvester attack used in cloning websites, the tabnabbing attack, the man-in-the-middle attack, the web jacking attack and the multi-attack web method.

The third option on the Social Engineering Toolkit menu is the infectious media generator tool. This is a very easy tool to use and is targeted at individuals who can give a hacker access to the organization network, thus enabling the hacker to hack from inside the network. This tool allows the hacker to create a USB disk or DVD containing a malicious script that gives the hacker access to the target shell. Choosing this option opens a menu with a prompt to choose from between a file-format exploit or a standard Metasploit executable. Choosing the file-format option opens a list of payloads from which to select. The default is a PDF file embedded in an executable script. This is then sent to the drive where the autorun.inf is created with the PDF file. When an employee opens the file on the drive, the file is executed in the background and the hacker gains shell access to the victim's computer.

The fourth option is the generate-a-payload-with-listener option. This option allows the hacker to create a malicious script as a payload and therefore generate a listener. This script is a .exe file. The key is getting the intended victim to click and download this script. Once the victim downloads the .exe file and executes it, the listener alerts the hacker, who can access the victim's shell.

The fifth option in the Social Engineering Toolkit is the mass mailer option. Clicking this option brings up a menu with two options: single email address attack and the mass mailer email attack. The single email address attack allows the user to send an email to a single email address while the mass mailer email attack allows the user to send an email to multiple email addresses. Choosing this option prompts the user to select a list containing multiple email addresses to which the email is then sent.

Sixth on the list is the Arduino-based attack. With this option, you are given the means to compromise Arduino-based devices. The seventh option, on the other hand, is the SMS spoofing option, which enables the hacker to send SMS to a person. This SMS spoofing option opens a menu with an option to perform an SMS spoofing form of attack or create a social-engineering template. Selecting the first option will send to a single number or a mass SMS attack. Selecting just a single number prompts the user to enter the recipient's phone number. Then you are asked to either use a predefined template or craft your own message. Typing 1 chooses the first option while typing 2 chooses the second option depending on your preference for the SMS. Then you enter the source number, which is the number you want the recipient to see as the sender of the SMS. Next, you type the message you want the recipient to see. You can embed links to a phishing site or to a page that will cause the user to download a malicious .exe file.

After the message has been crafted, the options for services used in SMS spoofing appear on the screen. Some are paid options and others are free.

Option eight in the SET is the wireless AP attack vector. This option is used to create a fake wireless AP to which unsuspecting users of public Wi-Fi can connect and the hacker can sniff their traffic. This option uses other applications in achieving this goal. AirBase-NG, AirMon-NG, DNSSpoof and dhcpd3 are the required applications that work hand in hand with the wireless AP attack vector.

Option nine in the menu is the QR code attack vector. Today, QR codes are used everywhere, from the identification of items to obtaining more details about products on sale. Now QR codes are even used to make payments. Some websites use QR codes for logins or as web apps. This login method is used because it is perceived as a more secure way of gaining access due to hackers' being able to steal cookies, execute a man-in-the-middle attack and even use a brute-force password to gain unauthorized access. However, this increase in the use of QR codes has given hackers more avenues for exploiting their victims. The QR code attack vector helps the hacker create a malicious QR code. Then the hacker creates or clones a website like Facebook using the credential harvester option and embeds this malicious QR code with the link to the cloned website. The hacker then sends a phishing email or spoofed SMS to a victim, which prompts that person to scan the code with a mobile device. This reveal's the victim's GPS location and other information when the victim visits the website and enters their login details.

The tenth option in the menu is the PowerShell attack vector. This option allows the hacker to deploy payloads in the PowerShell of an operating system. The PowerShell is a more powerful option than the command prompt in the Windows operating system. It allows access to different areas of the operating system. It was developed by Microsoft to ease the automation of tasks and configuration of files and has come with the Windows operating system since the release of Windows Vista. The PowerShell attack vector enables the attacker to create a script that is then executed in the victim's PowerShell. The selection of this option brings out four menu options:

PowerShell alphanumeric injector, PowerShell SAM database, PowerShell reverse and PowerShell bind shells. Any of these options creates a targeted PowerShell program and is exported to the PowerShell folder. Tricking the target to access, download and execute this program creates access for the attacker.

By now, you should realize how powerful the SET is in executing computer-aided social engineering attacks. This tool is very valuable for a penetration tester, as it provides a robust and diverse means of checking the various vulnerabilities that may exist in an organization's network.

BeEF

BeEF stands for Browser Exploitation Framework. This tool comes with most of the security-based Linux distro, like the Parrot OS and Kali Linux. BeEF started as a server that was accessed through the attacker's browser. It was created to target vulnerabilities in web browsers that would give access to the target systems for executing commands. BeEF was written in the Ruby language on the Rails platform by a team headed by Wade

Alcorn. As stated before, passwords, cookies, login credentials and browsing history are all typically stored on the browser, so a BeEF attack on a client can be very nasty.

On Kali Linux, however, BeEF has been included in the distro. The BeEF framework can be started by going into applications, clicking on exploitation tools and then clicking on the BeEF XSS framework. This brings up a terminal that shows the BeEF framework server has been started. Once the server has been started, we open our browser of choice and visit the localhost at port 3000. This is written in the URL space of the browser as localhost:3000/ui/authentication or 127.0.0.1:3000/ui/authentication. This would bring us to the authentication page of the BeEF framework, requiring a login username and password. By default, the username is beef ; the password is also beef.

Once you are in the BeEF framework, it will open a "Get Started" tab. Here you are introduced to the framework and learn how to use it. Of particular importance is hooking a browser. Hooking a browser involves clicking a JavaScript payload that gives the

BeEF framework access to the client's browser. There are various ways by which we can deploy this payload, but the simplest way is to create a page with the payload, prompt the target to visit that page and execute the JavaScript payload. You can be very creative about this aspect. On the other hand, there is a link on the Get Started page that redirects you to The Butcher page. Below this page are buttons containing the JavaScript payload. Clicking on this button will execute the script and, in turn, hook your browser. When your browser is hooked, you will see a hook icon beside your browser icon on the left side of the BeEF control panel with the title "Hooked browser" along with folders for online and offline browsers.

Once a browser is hooked, whether it's online or offline, we can control it from our BeEF control panel. Clicking on the details menu in the control panel will provide information like the victim's browser version and the plugins that are installed. The window size of the browser also can be used to determine the victim's screen size, the browser platform (which is also the operating system on the PC), and a lot more information. For executing commands on the browser, we click on the command menu in the control panel. This brings up a different command we can execute on the victim's browser. This command would create a pop-up message on the victim's browser, so it can be renamed creatively before execution to avoid raising any suspicion. Some of the commands that can be executed in this menu include the Get all Cookie command (which starts harvesting the victim's browser cookies), the Screenshot command, the Webcam command for taking pictures of the victim, the Get visited URL command and so on. There are a lot of commands in this menu.

The BeEF framework JavaScript payload can also hook mobile phone browsers. Checking the details tab after hooking will give that particular information if we end up hooking a phone browser. Clicking on the module and searching the PhoneGap command allows us to execute phone targeted commands like geolocating the device and starting an audio recording on the victim's device. Clicking on the Ipec menu also displays a terminal we can use to send shell commands to the victim's system.

Once the BeEF framework hooks a browser, the possibilities are endless. We can do virtually anything. Therefore, it is important to be careful when clicking links and pop-up or flash messages.

METASPLOIT

The Metasploit framework is perhaps the larget, most complete penetration testing and security auditing tool today. This tool is an open source tool that is regularly updated with new modules for monitoring even the most recent vulnerabilities. Metasploit comes with the Kali Linux distro. It is written in Ruby, although when it was created it was written in Perl. This tool was developed by HD Moore in 2003 and was then sold to an IT company called Rapid7 in 2009.

Metasploit is an immensely powerful tool that has great versatility. To fully utilize Metasploit, you must be comfortable using the terminal, which is a console type window. However, there is an option that allows for the use of Metasploit in a GUI window. Armitage, an opensource tool, makes this possible, although it does not have the capacity to fully utilize all aspects of the Metasploit framework in an attack. The meterpreter in the Metasploit framework is a module that is dumped in the victim's system, making it easy for the hacker to control that PC and maintain access for future hacks in that system. Getting started with Metasploit on Kali Linux is as good as opening the terminal and typing "msfconsole" without the quotes.

Metasploit contains modules that can be used during a hack. Some of these modules are written by developers or contributors from the open source community. An important set of modules includes the payloads. The payloads are very important when it comes to performing attacks within the Metasploit framework. These payloads are codes that have been written so that the hacker can gain a foothold in the victim's computer. Perhaps the most popular among these payloads is the meterpreter. This particular payload is very powerful, as it leaves no trace of a hack on the system's drive. It exists solely on the victim's system memory.

Then there is the Exploits module. These exploits are codes that have been written and packed for specific flaws in a victim's operating system. Different exploits exist for different operating system flaws, so flaws that are targeted for one vulnerability would fail when used for another.

The encoders are modules that encode the different payloads deployed into the target system to avoid detection by the victim's antivirus, anti-spyware or other security tools.

Other modules available on the Metasploit framework are the Post modules (which allow the hacker to gather passwords, tokens and hashes), the Nops modules (most of which allow for 100 percent execution of the payload or exploit) and the Auxiliary modules (which do not fit into other categories).

This framework is quite robust, as many kinds of hacking procedures can be carried out. Several procedures are executed by combining the modules and making them work in different ways. A good way for a beginner to learn more about the Metasploit framework is to type "help" without the quotes in the Metasploit framework console.

10. Real Examples Of How To Hack With Kali Linux

Kali Linux has more than 600 tools. Each one of these tools performs different functions. Since there are different types of hackers, each hacker will always try to look into the vulnerabilities that are present within the system. The white hat hackers ensure that they have patched all the present vulnerabilities. The black hat hackers usually take advantage of these vulnerabilities so that they can gain access to different pieces of information that they will use for their own personal gain. We will now look into some of the examples on how a person can hack when using Kali Linux.

When carrying out an attack, you must make sure that you have carried out a pilot study. It helps you to gather information that you will use hen launching an attack. After identifying some vulnerabilities, you can exploit a network or even the web applications. During the exploitation process, some of the factors that you should consider include:

- The attacker should make sure that the target has been characterized fully. If the attacker has not gained an in-depth understanding of the network, there is a high likelihood that the attack will fully fail. Also, the attacker can be easily detected.

- The attacker should first look into whether the exploit is well known. Are there some actions that have already been defined in the system? If an exploit has not been fully characterized, there might be some consequences that are unintended. It is good to make sure that all exploits have been validated first.

- First look into the manner in which the exploit is being carried out. For instance, the attack may be conducted from a remote location and that means that you cannot be caught easily. The main issue is that you will not have a lot of control over the exploits.

- Consider some of the post-exploit activities. If you need to gather some data first, you must make sure that you have established some interactive actions.

Consider whether you should maintain access or whether you will be compromised. Such factors will help to ensure that you have come up with a stealthy approach to avoid detection.

There are many vulnerabilities that can be easily identified. Some of these exploits are based on different techniques and that is why the system can be compromised easily. We will now provide some real examples on how to hack using Kali Linux.

Threat Modelling

The pilot study comes in handy and it makes sure that you can learn more about the present vulnerabilities. Always make sure that the attack has been coordinated in a planned manner. If not, you may fail to achieve your objectives. Also, you can be caught easily. When carrying out an attack, there is a process commonly referred to as threat modelling. It is good to note that the attackers and testers are using the same tools. The main difference is the motive of each party.

Threat modelling comes in handy when trying to improve the success rate of an attack. There is the offensive threat modelling and it involves the use of the research and the results of the pilot study. As an attacker, you must first consider the availability of targets. The types of targets are as shown in the list below:

Primary targets- when such a target is compromised, they will support the objective.

Secondary targets- this is a target who can provide some information such as passwords and security controls. The information will come in handy when launching an attack.

Tertiary targets- these are targets that can be compromised easily and they can also be distracted easily and that means that they can also provide some information that can be used to launch an attack.

For every target, the attacker should always determine the approach that they want to use. If there are some vulnerabilities, the attacker will go ahead and launch the attack. If there is a large-scale attack, some issues may occur. Some attackers make use of the attack tree methodology. The following diagram will provide some overview about the attack tree methodology:

The approach is used when trying to visualize some attack options that will ensure that the attack has gone accordingly. After generating an attack tree, you can visualize the attack options that are available. The vulnerabilities will ensure that you have learned more about the most suitable attack options.

How to Use the Vulnerability Resources

The pilot study helps you to learn more about the target's attack surface and that means it is the total number of points that you will assess to find the vulnerabilities. If a server has an operating system, it means that the server can only be exploited if the operating system has some vulnerabilities. If many applications have been installed into the system, there will be many vulnerabilities.

As an attacker, you will be tasked with finding some of the vulnerabilities that are present within the system. For starters, you should make sure that you have looked into some of the vendor sites. You will gain access to some information about different vulnerabilities and the period when some patches and upgrades have been released. There are some exploits for different weaknesses and they are commonly known. There are many vendors who will provide some of this information to their clients. When attackers gain access to such information, they will use it to their own advantage. You can gain access to this information from numerous sources.

Kali Linux has an exploit database. It is situated in the /usr/share/exploitdb directory. Before you can use it, you should update it using the following command:

Start by opening a terminal window by searching for the exploitdb local copy. You will then keyin the searchsploit in the command prompt. A script will then search the database that possesses the list of all the exploits. You can then extract the exploits, compile, and run them depending on the present vulnerabilities. The following screenshot showcases some vulnerabilities.

Open a terminal window so that you can search the exploitdb. After opening a terminal window, you can key in the searchsploit command. You will then key in the search term that you want to look up. A script will be invoked and a database will all the exploits will appear. The files will be in the .csv format. The search allows you to learn about different vulnerabilities. You can also extract the exploits, and later compile and run them against various vulnerabilities. The screenshot below showcases a list if various vulnerabilities:

When searching the local database, you will realize that there are many exploits that are present within the system. The path listing will also list some descriptions. You must also make sure that the environment has been customized before you can launch an attack. There are some exploits that are presented in the form of scripts and they include PHP, Perl, and Ruby. Some of these exploits can be implemented easily. If you want to hack into a server such as the Microsoft II 6.0, such an exploit is easy since the server can be accessed remotely using the WebDAV. To exploit the server, you should by copying the exploit and then copying it into the root directory. You will then execute the exploit using a Perl script as shown below:

Some of these exploits are in the form of source codes that should be compiled before you can use them. For instance, if you are searching for the RPC vulnerabilities, you will realize that there are many vulnerabilities. An example is shown in the screenshot below:

There are many vulnerabilities including RPC DCOM. It is normally identified as a 76.c When compiling this exploit, you will start by copying it from the storage directory into the /tmp directory. Within the specified location, you will then compile everything using the command that is shown below:

The 76.c will then be compiled using the GNU compiler. The screenshot below will offer some guidance:

After invoking the application depending on your target, you should make sure that you have called the executable using the following command:

As for this exploit, the source code has been well documented and you should also adhere to some parameters that are quite clear during the execution process. The screenshot below has offered some guidance:

Although there are many exploits, not all of these exploits will exploit the public resources or the database that has been compiled as a 76.c. There are numerous issues that are present and that is why using some of these exploits becomes a problematic affair. Some of the issues include:

The source code may be incomplete and some deliberate errors may also be present as some of the developers try to make sure that some of these exploits cannot be utilized by some users that are not experienced. Some of these beginners may be trying to compromise the system and they may not be conversant with some of the involved risks depending on their specific actions.

Some of these exploits have not been documented in a comprehensive manner and that means that the way in which the use of the source code is used may bring about some issues. If an attacker or a tester encounters some issues, they will not be able to make good use of these exploits.

The changing environments will bring about some inconsistent behavior and that means that the source code will be changed significantly. Only as skilled developer should handle such a task.

Some of the source codes may contain some malicious functionalities and the attacker may use this to their own advantage when trying to penetrate a system. The malicious functionalities come in handy when trying to create a backdoor that will allow them to enter into the system as they wish.

As an attacker, you will want to make sure that your results are consistent and that is why some coders have come together to form a community. They are able to come up with different practices that are also consistent. Some of the suitable exploitation frameworks include the Metasploit framework.

The Metasploit Framework

The Metasploit framework is in the form of an open source tool that has been designed to facilitate the penetration into a network. The framework was created using the Ruby programming language. A modular approach was used during the creation process and that is why people can easily code and develop different exploits. Some complex tasks can be easily be implemented using the Metasploit framework.

The Metasploit framework will always present numerous interfaces to each of the backend modules and it will be easy to control the entire exploitation process. As for this case, we will make use of the console interface since it guarantees high speeds. Also, the interface will present some attack commands and people can also easily understand the interface. You should start by opening the command prompt and after that you will key in the msfconsole.

The Metasploit framework has many modules that have been combined together to affect an exploit. The modules include:

Exploits: the fragments of the code that are normally used to target different vulnerabilities. Some of these active exploits will focus on a specific target. They will run and after that they will exit. As for the passive explots, they only act when a user has connected to a network.

Payloads: the payloads are in the form of malicous codes that normally implement some commands after an exploit has been carried out successfully.

- Post modules- after an attack has been perforemed successfully, the modules will run on some of the targets that have been compromised. Some important data will then be collected and the atacker will gain some deeper access into the network.
- Auxiliary modules- some of these modules do not allow some access between the attacker and the target system. The modules perform some activities such as fuzzing, scanning, or sniffing.
- Encoders- some of the exploits can bypass some of the antivirus defenses. The modules can be used to encode the payload

and it will not be able to detect the techniques that are used to match signatures.

- No operations- these modules are used to facilitate the overflow of buffers during an attack.

When performing a pilot study, you may make use of some of these modules. If you want to use the Metasploit framework when performing an attack, you can follow some of these steps:

1. You will choose an exploit and comfigure it. The configired code will be used to compromise the system depending on the present vulnerabilities.
2. You will then check the target system so that you may determine whether it is vulnerable to an attack.
3. Choosing and configuring the payload.
4. You will choose an encoding technique so that you may bypass th detection controls.
5. Execute an exploit.

Exploiting Vulnerable Applications

The Metasploit framework has come in handy when exploiting some of the vulnerabilities that are present in some of the third-party applications. In this instance, we will look into how the buffer overflow can be exploited. For starters, the vulnerabilities woll be present in the ReadFile function and it is used to store the user data that has not been stored securely. When initiating the attack, the tester will have to generate the BMP file that has been specially crafted. The target will then open the file when using the Chasys application. When such an acitivity occuers, the base operating system will be compromised. The attack is effective on operating systems such as XP service pack 3 and Windows 7 service pack 1.

To initiate the attack, open the msfconsole. The Metasploit will then be used to perform the exploit as shown below:

The exploit is quite simple; however, the attacker should set a reverse shell to the target system. They should also make sure that the system has been compromised. After the exploit is complete, a BMP file will then be created and it will be stored with the name msf.bmp by default. The attacker should make sure that they have enticed the target so that they may open the file. To do so, the attacker should make sure that the file has not been stored using the default name since it may also be detected by different devices. The name should be changed to something that may be relevant to the target. After that, the attacker should then launch a new instance of the msfconsole. A listener will also be set up to keep track of the reverse TCP shell since it will originate from the target's end after they have been compromised. The following screenshot shows a simple listener.

After the target has opened the BMP image file that is present in the vulnerable application. , there will be a meterpreter session that will be established in both systems. The meterpreter prompt will then replace the msf prompt. The attacker will not be able to access the system remotely using the command shell. The first step after ensuring that the system has been compromised is to verify that the system is accessible. The screenshot below showcases the operating system and the computer name after the attacker keys in the sysinfo command into the terminal window:

How to Exploit Numerous Targets When Using Armitage

Armitage's functionality can be likened to the Metasploit console. When using Armitage, you have access to numerous options that come in handy when attacking some targets that have various complexities. The main advantage of using Armitage is that you can exploit multiple targets at once. The maximum number of targets that you can exploit in one instance is 512.

Before starting Armitage, you must make sure that the Metasploit services and the database are up and running. You should use the following command:

You will then type ARMITAGE in the command prompt so that you can execute the command. There are some steps that you should follow when launching Armitage so that it can function accordingly. So that you can discover the targets that are available, you will have to provide an IP address so that you can add a host. You can also enumerate targets when using Armitage since it will use DNS enumeration.

When using Armitage, you can also import some data that is present in files such as amap, Acunetix, Burp proxy, AppScan, Nessus NBE, Foundstine, and XML files.You can also set a host label when using Armitage. You will start by right-clicking so that you may select a host. You will then go to the host menu where you will set the host label. You can then flag a particular IP address. The following screenshot can offer some guidance:

Armitage has also been supporting dynamic workspaces. You may start by testing a network while also trying to identify some of the servers that have not been patched. You can highlight all these servers by issuing a label and then placing all of them in a workspace that has been prioritized. After identifying some targets, you can then select some modules that can be implemented during the exploitation phase. There is also an attack option in the menu bar.

When exploiting a host, you can right-click and navigate to the attack item while also choosing an exploit. Always make sure that you have chosen the right operating system to ensure that the exploit is successful. There is the Hail Mary option. It is present in the Attacks option. When you select this function, you will view all the systems that have been identified and they can be subjected automatically to some of the exploits that can enable an attacker to learn more about a huge number of compromises. Such an attack is quite noisy.

If a system has been compromised, it will appear as an icon and it will have a red border. Some electrical sparks will also be present. In the screenshot that will be displayed here, there will be two compromised systems. There will also be a total of four active sessions.

As an attacker, you must make sure that you have looked into all the present vulnerabilities. In the screenshot above, the Hail Mary Option has showcased that there are two vulnerabilities and there are two active sessions. When carrying out manual testing using a similar target, more vulnerabilities will appear. When carrying out real-world tests, you will realize that there are some advantages and disadvantages of using automated tools.

Network Exploitation

When hacking with Kali Linux, you can easily exploit a network. You can use some of the tools present within the operating system to find some of the vulnerabilities that are present in a network. In this section, we will focus more on the ways through which you can carry out a penetration test on a network while also exploiting different services.

Man, in the Middle Attack Using Ferret and Hamster

The hamster tool comes in handy when carrying out side jacking. The tools usually acts as a proxy server. Ferret is used to sniff for cookies in a network. In this context, we will learn more about how to hack into a network.

Getting Ready

The Kali Linux operating system has many tools that are already pre-installed. Since we are looking into network exploitation, we will now look into how you can use some of these tools.

The Hamster tool is easy to use and it also has its own user interface. To learn more about hamster, you should follow the following steps.

1. You will start by keying in the following command in the terminal window;

```
hamster
```

The output of the 'hamster' command is as shown below:

2. You will then start the browser and try to navigate http://localhost:1234:

Now we just need to fire up our browser and navigate to

3. *We will then click on one of the adapters and then choose the specific interface that we will monitor:*

4. *After some few minutes, the sessions will appear on the left-hand side of the browser tab.*

In some instances, the sessions may fail to appear. In such an instance, you should exercise some patience since the ferret and hamster tools are not located in the same folder. Hamster usually runs while also executing ferret in the background. The main issue with ferret is that it is not suited to being used with the 64-bit architecture. If you are using the 64-but Kali Linux version, you must make sure that you have added the 32-bit repository first. After that, you can install ferret. You should use the following command:

How to explore the msfconsole

It is good to learn about the basics of the Metasploit; however, in this case, we will just learn more about how you can use Metasploit when carrying out an attack.

If you want to learn about Metasploit, the following tips will come in handy:

1. *You should type msfconsole so that you can start the Metasploit console.*

2. There are many exploits available and you can view them using the following command

The output of the command is as shown below:

3. If you want to see the current payloads, you should use the following command:

The output of the command is as shown below:

4. Metasploit has many modules and they contain fuzzers, scanners, sniffers, and many more modules. You can see the auxiliary modules using the following command:

The output of the above command is shown below:

5. If you want to use the FTP fuzzer command, you should use the following command:

6. To see the available options, use the following command:

7. You can use the following command to set the RHOSTS:

596

8. There is the auxiliary that notifies you that a crash has taken place and you should always run it.

The Railgun in Metasploit

In this section, the main focus will be on the Railgun. It is a meterpreter and it is the only feature that can be used to exploit Windows. You can use it to communicate directly with the Windows API.

When using Railgun, you can perform various tasks that the Metasploit cannot including pressing keyboard keys. The Windows API will enable you to perform the exploitation in a better manner.

1. To run the Railgun, you should key in the irb command in the terminal window.

2. If you want to access the Railgyun, you should key in the session.railgun command in the terminal window.

As per the screenshot above, there is a lot of data that has been printed. There are many functions and DLL's that we can utilize.

1. If you want to see the DLL names, you should key in the following command:

The output is as shown below:

1. To view a function of a .dll, we use the following command:

```
session.railgun.<dllname>.functions
```

The following screenshot shows the output for the preceding command:

```
>> session.railgun.kernel32.functions
=> {"GetConsoleWindow"=>#<Rex::Post::Meterpreter::Extensions::Stdapi::Railgun::[
LLFunction:0x000000054088c8 @return_type="LPVOID", @params=[], @windows_name="Ge
tConsoleWindow", @calling_conv="stdcall">, "ActivateActCtx"=>#<Rex::Post::Meterp
reter::Extensions::Stdapi::Railgun::DLLFunction:0x00000005543288 @return_type="B
OOL", @params=[["HANDLE", "hActCtx", "inout"], ["PBLOB", "lpCookie", "out"]], @w
indows_name="ActivateActCtx", @calling_conv="stdcall">, "AddAtomA"=>#<Rex::Post:
:Meterpreter::Extensions::Stdapi::Railgun::DLLFunction:0x00000005542b30 @return
```

2. We can then call an API that will be used to lock the target's screen. We will use the following command:

We were able to lock the screen of the target using the API as shown below:

3. When exploiting a network, we can also gain access to the login passwords of the target user. First, we must have the hash.

We will then crack it. Also, note that we are running Kali Linux on the "Live mode" and we can also access Windows using an API so that it may be easy to perform a penetration test. Depending on the results of the test, you can go ahead and exploit the present vulnerabilities. The Windows API can come in handy when you want to run a keylogger. When the user keys in the logins, you will have access to the passwords. The main advantage is that Metasploit also has a module and it also uses Railgun when trying to retrieve the target's passwords.

4. We will start by exiting irb and the meterpreter session will then start to run in the background. We will use the following command:

The command will give us the following output:

5. To add a session, you will make use of the set session command.

6. We will then set the PID using the following command:

7. After running the command, it is possible to see the password that the user has keyed in:

We have just issued an example. Railgun can be used to perform any more actions including creating DLLs and also deleting different users.

How to Use the Paranoid Meterpreter

Apparently, you can also hack into someone's meterpreter session. The attacker should just play around with the DNS of the target and they will connect after launching their own handler. To ensure that an attack could take place swiftly, the meterpreter paranoid mode was developed and released. An API was also introduced and it could be used to verify the SHA1 hash of any of the certificates that had been presented by the msf. We will now learn more about how to use the meterpreter paranoid mode.

For starters, we will need an SSL certificate.

1. You can generate some SSL certificates using the commands shown below:

The output of the command is as shown below:

```
root@kali:~/Desktop# openssl req -new -newkey rsa:4096 -days 365 -nodes -x509
eyout meterpreter.key -out meterpreter.crt
Generating a 4096 bit RSA private key
............................++
..................................................................................
.......++
writing new private key to 'meterpreter.key'
.....
You are about to be asked to enter information that will be incorporated
into your certificate request.
What you are about to enter is what is called a Distinguished Name or a DN.
There are quite a few fields but you can leave some blank
For some fields there will be a default value,
If you enter '.', the field will be left blank.
.....
Country Name (2 letter code) [AU]:IN
```

You will have to fill in some information such as the country code after keying in the command shown below:

> 2. The first command in this section is used to open two files and then it writes both of them into a single file. To generate a payload using the certificate that has been generated, we will use the following command:

The output of the command is shown in the screenshot below:

3. If you want to set the options, you will use this command:

The preceding command is shown in the screenshot below:

4. We will then run the handler. In this stage, the connection will have been verified by the stager and a connection will have been established.

The tale of the bleeding heart

This is a vulnerability that is present in the OpenSSL cryptography. It had been introduced in 2012; however, the public came to learn about it in 2012. This is a vulnerability where an attacker can gain access to more data than is allowed. In this section, we will look into how to use the Metasploit to exploit the bleeding heart

The following steps will make sure that you have learned more about the bleeding heart.

1. To start the msfconsole, we will use the following command:

The output that you should expect is as shown in the screenshot below:

2. You will then use the following command to search for the HeartBleed auxiliary:

The output to expect is as shown in the screenshot below:

3. To use the auxiliary, you should use the following command:

4. The following command will allow us to see the available options:

The output will be as shown in the screenshot below:

5. The following command will allow us to set the RHOSTS to a specific IP address:

6. To set the verbosity, we will use the following command and it should be set to true:

```
set verbose true
```

7. We will type run so that we may see the data and it normally contains some

sensitive information including email IDs
and passwords.

11. Cryptography And Network Security

With a rapid increase in the rate of cyber attacks, it is of utter importance to protect all forms of confidential data as much as possible. Data leakage can lead to serious loss for various businesses and can also turn out to be a threat for an individual person where the credit card, as well as bank details, are breached. The term cryptography is linked with the technique used for converting plain and ordinary text into unintelligible form. With this method, transmission and storage of sensitive data become a lot easier. Only those to whom the message is intended can process the text and read it. It is not only helpful in protecting data from breaching or theft but it is also useful for data authentication.

In the world of computer science, cryptography is associated with securing all forms of information along with the techniques of communication which are derived from the concepts of mathematics. It uses a definite set of ruled calculations which are known as algorithms. The algorithms are used for transforming the messages in such a way that it becomes very hard to decipher the same. Such algorithms of deterministic character are used in the generation of cryptographic keys along with digital signing for protecting the privacy of data, browsing various websites on the internet and for sensitive communications like email and credit card or bank transaction details.

Techniques of cryptography

The technique of cryptography is often linked with the characteristics of cryptanalysis and cryptology. The technique of cryptography includes the usage of various techniques like merging of words with various images, microdots and several other techniques which are used for hiding that information which is in transit or in storage. However, in the world of computer today, the technique of cryptography is often linked with the process of scrambling ordinary text or cleartext. Such form of ordinary text is known as plaintext. The plaintext is converted into ciphertext with the process of encryption and then back to the original form with the help of decryption.

The people who specialize in the field of cryptography are called cryptographers.

Objectives of cryptography

The modern-day objectives of cryptography are as follows:

- Confidentiality: Confidentiality is the act of keeping all forms of personal and sensitive data protected for the concerned people. The information which is being transmitted or stored cannot be analyzed or understood by any third party for whom it was not at all intended.
- Integrity: The data or information which is being transmitted or stored cannot be changed or altered between the sender and the receiver who is intended to receive the data. In case any form of alteration is made, the sender and receiver will both be notified.
- Non-repudiation: The sender, as well as the creator of the data or information, will not be allowed to deny his/her intentions at a

later stage during the creation or transportation of the data or information.

- Authentication: Both the parties in communication who are the sender and the receiver will have the capability of confirming the identity of each other along with the origin and final destination of the data.

The protocols and the procedures that meet all of the mentioned objectives and criteria are called cryptosystems. The cryptosystems are often taken as only referring to the procedure of mathematics and programs of computer only. However, in actual, they also comprise of human behavior regulation like logging off from the systems which are not used, choosing strong and difficult to guess passwords while logging in and not discussing any form of sensitive data and procedure with the outside world.

Algorithms of cryptography

The cryptosystems work along with a bunch of procedures called ciphers or cryptographic algorithms. It is being used for the purpose of encrypting as well as for decrypting the messages for securing up the communications among smartphones, applications and other computer systems. A suite of cipher uses up one single algorithm for the purpose of encryption, one more algorithm for authentication of messages and another algorithm for exchange of keys. This whole process is embedded within the protocols and is written within the programming of software which runs on the OS along with the computer systems which are based on the network. It also involves generation of public as well as private key for the process of encryption as well as decryption of data, verification for the purpose of message authentication, digital signing along with the exchange of keys.

Cryptography and its types

There are various types of cryptography which are being used today.

- Encryption using single key or symmetric key: The algorithms of this form of cryptography create block cipher which are actually particular length of bits. The block

610

cipher comes along with one secret key that the sender uses for encrypting the data. The same key can be used by the receiver for deciphering the information. AES or Advanced Encryption Standard is a type of symmetric key encryption which was launched by the NIST as Federal Information Processing Standard or FIPS 197 in the year 2001. It is being used for the protection of confidential and sensitive data. In the year 2003, the U.S. government approved of AES for the purpose of classified information. AES is a form of specification which is free from royalty and is used in all forms of hardware and software in the whole world. AES succeeded DES and DES3. AES uses up longer lengths of keys for preventing attacks.

- Encryption using public key or asymmetric key: The algorithms for this form of cryptography uses two keys at a time in pair. One public key which is associated along with the sender and the receiver for the purpose of encrypting the information. Another private key is used for the purpose of decryption of the message. The private key is only known to the originator. There are various forms of cryptography using public key like RSA which is used all over the internet, ECDSA which is being used by Bitcoin and DSA which has been adopted as FIPS for all forms of digital signatures by the NIST.

- Hash functions: For the purpose of maintaining the integrity of data, hash functions are used that returns an accepted value from the value which is used as input. It is being used for mapping the data into a fixed size of data. SHA-1, SHA-2 and SHA-3 are the types of hash functions.

Conclusion

Thank you for reading the Kali Linux guide to the end. I do hope the book was informative and also amusing. I also hope that you were also able to gain access to the information and tools that you needed to achieve all your goals. Although you have read the entire Hacking with Kali Linux handbook, we have not exhausted all the information that there is on Hacking with Kali Linux. You may expound on the knowledge that you possess by conducting some comprehensive research on hacking with Kali Linux.

The next step is to make sure that you can use the information in the handbook practically. You can also formulate a schedule whereby you can get to learn more about Kali Linux.

Studies have showcased that web applications, servers, and networks have vulnerabilities. As an external attacker and a penetration tester, you can make use of these vulnerabilities when launching an attack. You must also make sure that you have goals so that you may be motivated as you perform the tests and attacks.

HACKING WITH KALI LINUX

STEP BY STEP GUIDE TO LEARN KALI LINUX FOR HACKERS, CYBERSECURITY, WIRELESS NETWORK SECURITY AND PENETRATION TESTING. YOUR FIRST HACK AND COMPUTER HACKING BEGINNERS GUIDE.

Introduction

Hackers work with the computer or program code, which is a set of instructions that work in the background and make up the software. While a lot of hackers do know how to program code, many downloads and use codes programmed by other people. The main requirement to know is how to work this code and adjust it to their advantage. For malicious hackers, that can be using it to steal passwords, secrets, identities, financial information, or create so much traffic that the targeted website needs to shut down.

Stealing passwords

Passwords are easy to hack because humans are very predictable. We think we are unique until it comes to passwords, but we are very easy to guess. For example, women will often use personal names for passwords—think kids, relatives, old flings—while men will stick to hobbies. The numbers we use most frequently are 1 and 2, and they are most often placed at the end of our password. More often than not, we use one word followed by some number, and if the website insists on including a capital letter, we place it at the beginning of the word and then whine about how this website is so annoying for making us go through all of this.

But how do hackers access our passwords? Well, there are several useful techniques.

The trial and error technique is called the brute force attack, and it is when you try possible combinations of letters and words to try and guess the right password. This can work because, as previously mentioned, we are very predictable when it comes to the type of passwords we use.

Another similar technique is called the dictionary attack; hackers use a file containing all the words that can be found in the dictionary, and the program tries them all. This is why it is often suggested to add numbers to your passwords as words, but this doesn't mean your "sunshine22" password is hackerproof.

A third technique is the rainbow table attack. The passwords in your computer system are hashed (generated into a value or values from a string of text using a mathematical function) in encryption.

Whenever a user enters a password, it is compared to an already stored value, and if those match, you are able to enter into the website or application. Since more text can produce the same value, it doesn't matter what letters we input as long as the encryption is the same. Think of it as a door and a key. You enter the doors with the key made for that lock, but if you're skilled at lock picking or a locksmith, you don't need that exact key to enter.

How to protect yourself from password attacks
Use the salt technique. This refers to adding simple random data to the input of a hash function. The process of combining a password with a salt which we then hash is called salting. For example, a password can be "sunshine22" but adding the salt is e34f8 (combining sunshine22 with e34f8) makes your hash-stored, new salted password "sunshine22e34f8." The new salted password is thus hashed into the system and saved into the database. Adding the salt just lowered the probability that the hash value will be found in any pre-calculated table. If you are a website owner, adding salt to each user's

password creates a much more complicated and costly operation for hackers. They need to generate a pre-calculated table for each salted password individually, making the process tedious and slow.

Even with the salt technique, determined hackers can pass through the "password salting." Another useful technique is the peppering technique. Just like the salt, pepper is a unique value. Pepper is different than salt because salt is unique for each user, but pepper is for everyone in the database. Pepper is not stored in the database; it's a secret value. Pepper means adding another extra value for storing passwords.

For example, let's say the pepper is the letter R. If the stored password is "sunshine22," the hash stored will be the hashed product of "sunshine22" with the added letter R. When the user logs, in the password they are giving is still "sunshine22," but the added pepper is storing "sunshine22" with the added R. The user has no knowledge that pepper is being used. The website will then cycle through every possible combination of peppers, and by taking upper and lowercase letters, there will be over 50 new combinations. The website will try hashing "sunshine22A," "sunshine22B," and so on until it reaches "sunshine22R." If one of the hashes matches the stored hash, then the user is allowed to log in. The whole point of this is that the pepper is not stored, so if the hacker wants to crack the password with a rainbow table or dictionary attack, it would take them over 50 times longer to crack a single password.

Phishing attacks

The easiest way to get someone's password is to ask them. After all, why bother with all the algorithms and cracking codes when you can just politely ask?

Phishing is often a promise of a prize if you click on a certain link that then takes you to a fake login page where you simply put in your password. The easiest way to defend from this is smart clicking, or not clicking on scammy pop-up ads.

Vacations and iPods are not just given away with a click and "you won't believe what happened next" is a sure sign of a clickbait leading to phishing.

Miracle weight loss pills, enlargement tools, singles waiting to meet you in the area and other promises of luxurious life with just one click are all phishing. Unfortunately, we have to work for money and workout for weight loss.

1. Hacking with Kali Linux

Kali Linux is an operating system that has many tools that are supposed to be utilized by security experts. There are more than 600 tools that have been pre-installed in the operating system. In this chapter, the main discussion will be about the Kali Linux for beginners. There are many people who may not be conversant with Kali Linux; however, in this chapter, it will be possible to learn how you can easily maneuver Kali Linux.

Kali Linux

The BackTrack platform was mainly formed for the security professionals and there are many tools that had been pre-installed in the Operating System. Since Kali Linux is the predecessor of the platform, the operating system also has many tools that can be utilized by the security professionals. The tools are mainly to be used by professionals such as network administrators and the security auditors. When using these tools, it is possible to assess the network and also ensure that it is secure. There are different types of hackers and they all have access to these tools.

BackTrack was useful to the security professionals, however, the main issue was that the architecture was quite complex and the tools that have been pre-installed could also not be used easily. The tools were present in the pentest directory and they were very effective when carrying out a penetration test. Many subfolders were also present and most of the tools could also be detected easily. The tools that were available in the platform include sqlninja- the tool comes in handy when carrying out SQL injection. Many more tools are also available and they can also be used to perform web exploitation when you are assessing the vulnerabilities that are present in the web applications.

Kali Linux replaced BackTrack and the architecture of the operating system is based on the Debian GNU, and it adheres to the Filesystem Hierarchy System (FHS) which also has many advantages as compared to the BackTrack platform. When you use the Kali Linux operating system, you can access the available tools easily since some of the applications can be located in the system path.

Kali Linux offers the following features:

- The operating system supports many desktop environments such as XFCE, Gnome, KDE, and LXDE. The operating system also offers some multilingual support.
- The tools offered by the operating system are Debian-compliant and they can also be synchronized at least four times daily using the Debian repositories. The packages can also be updated easily while also ensuring that some security fixes have also been applied.
- Kali Linux allows ISO customization and that means as a user, you can come up with different versions of Kali Linux that suit your needs.
- The operating system has both ARMEL and ARMFH support and that means that the

users can also be able to install the Kali Linux operating system in different devices.

- The tools that have been pre-installed also have some diverse uses.
- Kali Linux is open source and that means it is free.

In this chapter, the main focus will be on the Kali Linux operating system as a virtual machine. For starters, the main focus will be on the Kali Linux for beginners to ensure that as a reader, you can get an overview of the operating system. To use an operating system as a virtual machine, you should utilize the VMware and that means that the Kali Linux operating system will be running on the "Live Mode."

There is a reason why the VMware is used and it is because it is easy to use and it comes in handy, especially when you execute different applications that are located in the primary operating system. For example, when you install the "Live Mode" on any operating system, you can use the applications that are present in the operating system. Additionally, you can retrieve the results that you have obtained when you carry out penetration testing using the virtual machine. The test results will allow you to learn about the vulnerabilities that are present in the system.

When you launch the Kali Linux operating system, the default desktop will appear and you will also notice that there is a menu bar as well as different icons. After selecting the menu item, you will be able to gain access to numerous security tools that have been pre-installed in the operating system.

How to Configure Secure Communications

When you use Kali Linux, you must ensure that there is connectivity to a wired or wireless network. After ensuring there is connectivity, the operating system will be able to handle various updates. Also, you can customize the operating system as long as there is connectivity. First, make sure there is an IP address. After that, confirm the IP address using the ifconfig command. You can confirm it using the terminal window and an example of the command being executed is as shown below:

In this case, the IP address is 192.168.204.132. At times, you may not be able to obtain the IP address and that means that you should use the dhclient eth0 command. The DHCP protocols will issue the IP address. Other interfaces can also be used to obtain the IP address and it will depend on the configurations that are present within the system.

When using a static IP address, you can also provide some additional information. For example, you can use the following IP address in such a manner:

After opening the terminal window, make sure that you have keyed in the following command:

Make sure that you have noted the changes that have been made to the IP settings. The changes will also not be persistent and they will not reappear after you have rebooted the operating system. In some instances, you may want to make sure that such changes are permanent. To do so, ensure that you have edited the /etc/network/interfaces file. The screenshot below can offer some subtle guidance:

When you start the Kali Linux operating system, the DHCP service will not be enabled. You are supposed to enable the DHCP service automatically. After

630

enabling the service, the new IP addresses within the network will also be announced and the administrators will also receive an alert that there is an individual carrying out some tests.

Such an issue is not major; nonetheless, it is advantageous for some of the services start automatically in the process. Key in the following commands so that you may be able to achieve all this.

When using Kali Linux, you can also install varying network services including DHCP, HTTP, SSH, TFTP, and the VNC servers. The users can invoke these services straight from the command-line. Also, users can access these services from the Kali Linux menu.

Adjusting the Network Proxy Settings

Users can use proxies that are authenticated or unauthenticated and they can modify the proxy settings of the network using the bash.bashrc and apt.conf commands. The files will be present in this folder- /root/etc/directory.

1) Edit the bash.bashrc file first. A screenshot will be provided below since it will come in handy when offering some guidance. The text is also useful in such instances, especially if you want to add lines to the bash.bashrc file:

2) The proxy IP address will then be replaced with the Proxy IP address that you're using. Also, you will have administrator privileges and that means that you can also change the usernames and the passwords. In some instances, you may also have to perform some authentication and you must key in the '@'symbol.

3) Create an apt.conf file in the same directory while also entering the commands that are showcased in the following screenshot:

4) Save the file and then close it. You can log in later so that you can activate the new settings.

Using Secure Shell to Secure Communications

As a security expert, you must ensure that the risk of being detected is minimized. With Kali Linux, you will not be able to use the external listening network devices. Some of the services that you can use are such as Secure Shell. First, install Secure Shell and then enable it so that you can use it.

The Kali Linux has some default SSH keys. Before starting the SSH service, disable the default keys first and also generate a keyset that is also unique since you may need it at some point. The default SSH keys will then be moved to the backup folder. To generate the SSH keyset.

To move the original keys, you should use the following command. Also, you can generate some new keysets using the same command.

Make sure that each of the keys has been verified. You can verify each key by calculating the md5sum hash values of every keyset. You can then compare the results that you have with the original keys.

When you start the SSH service, start with the menu and then select the Applications- Kali Linux- System Services-SSHD- SSHD start.

It is also possible to start the SSH when you are using the command line and this screenshot will guide you:

To verify that the SSH is running, execute the netstat query. The following screenshot will also guide you:

To stop the SSH, use this command:

Updating Kali Linux

For starters, the users must patch the Kali Linux operating system. The operating system must also be updated regularly so that it may also be up to date.

Looking into the Debian Package Management System

The package management system relies on the packages. The users can install and also remove packages as they wish when they are customizing the operating system. The packages support different tasks such as penetration testing. Users can also extend the functionality of the Kali Linux such that the operating system can support communications and documentation. As for the documentation process, run the wine application so that you can run applications such as the Microsoft Office. Some of the packages will also be stored in the repositories.

Packages and Repositories

With Kali Linux, you can only use the repositories provided by the operating system. If the installation process has not been completed, you may not be able to add the repositories. Different tools are also present on the operating system, although they may not be present in the official tool repositories. The tools may be updated manually and you should overwrite the packaged files that are present and the dependencies should also be present. The Bleeding Edge repository can also maintain various tools including Aircrack-ng, dnsrecon, sqlmap, and beef-xss. You should also note that it is impossible to move some of these tools from their respective repositories to the Debian repositories. The Bleeding Edge repository can be added to the sources. List using this command: *Dpkg*

This is a package management system that is also based on Debian. It is possible to remove, query, and also installs different packages when you are using the command-line application. After triggering the dpkg-1, some data will be returned in the process. In the process, you can also view all the applications that have been pre-installed into the Kali Linux operating system. To access some of the applications, you should make use of the command line.

Using Advanced Packaging Tools

The Advanced Packing Tools (APT) is essential when you are extending the dpkg functionally when searching and installing the repositories. Some of the packages may also be upgraded. The APT comes in handy when a user wants to upgrade the whole distribution.

The common APT (Advanced Packaging Tools) is as follows:

- *Apt-Get Upgrade* - This is a command that is used to install the latest versions of various packages that have been installed on Kali Linux. Some of these packages have also been installed on Kali Linux and it is also possible to upgrade them. If there are no packages present, you cannot upgrade anything. Only installed packages can be upgraded.

- *Apt-Get Update* - This is a command that is used when resynchronizing the local packages with each of their sources. Ensure that you are using the update command when performing the upgrade.
- *Apt-Get Dist-Upgrade* - The command upgrades all the packages that are already installed in the system. The packages that are obsolete should also be removed.

To view all the full descriptions of some of the packages, you should use the apt-get command. It is also possible to identify the dependencies of each package. You may also remove the packages using various commands. Also, it is good to note that some packages may also not be removed using the apt-get command. You should update some packages manually using the update.sh script and you should also use the commands that are shown below:

Customizing and Configuring Kali Linux

The Kali Linux operating system framework is quite useful when performing penetration tests. As a security expert, you will not be limited to using the tools that have been pre-installed in Kali Linux. It is also possible to adjust the default desktop on Kali Linux. After customizing Kali Linux, you can also make sure that the system is more secure. After collecting some data, it will also be safe and the penetration test can also be carried out easily.

The common customizations include:

- You can reset the root password.
- You can add a non-root user.
- Share some folders with other operating systems such as Microsoft Windows.
- Creating folders that are encrypted.
- Speeding up the operations at Kali Linux.

Resetting the Root Password

Use the following command so that you can change the root password:

Key in the new password. The following screenshot will guide you:

How to Add a Non-Root User

There are many applications that are provided by Kali Linux and they usually run as long as the user has the root-level privileges. The only issue is that the root-level privileges have some risks and they may include damaging some applications when you use the wrong commands when testing different systems. When testing a system, it is advisable to use user-level privileges. You may create a non-root user when using the adduser command. Start by keying in the following command in the terminal window. This screenshot will guide you:

How to Speed Up the Operations on Kali Linux

You can use different tools to speed up the processes in Kali Linux:

- When creating the virtual machine, ensure that the disk size is fixed and that way it will be faster as compared to a disk that is allocated in a dynamic manner. As for the fixed disk, it will be easy to add files fast and the fragmentation will be less.
- When using the virtual machine, make sure that you have installed the VMware tools.
- To delete the cookies and free up some space on the hard disk, use the BleachBit application. To ensure that there is more privacy, ensure that the cache has been

cleared as well as the browsing history. There are some advanced features such as shredding files and also wiping the disk space that is free. There are some traces that cannot also be fully deleted since they are hidden.

- Preload applications exist and they can also be used to identify different programs that are also used commonly by various users. Using these applications, you can preload the binaries and the dependencies onto the memory and that will ensure that there is faster access. Such an application will also work automatically after ensuring that the installation process is complete.

- Although Kali Linux has many tools, they are not all present on the start-up menu. The system data will also slow down when an application has been installed during the start-up process and the memory use shall also be impacted. The unnecessary services and applications should also be disabled; to do so, make sure you have installed the

Boot up Manager (BUM). This screenshot will guide you:

- You can also launch a variety of applications directly from the keyboard and make sure that you have added gnome-do so that you can access different applications from the accessories menu. After that, you will launch gnome-do and select the preferences menu and also activate the Quite Launch function afterward. Select the launch command and then clear all existing commands and enter the command line so that you can execute different commands after you have launched the selected keys.

Some of the applications can also be launched using various scripts.

Sharing the Folders with Another OS

Kali Linux has numerous tools. The operating system is also suitable since it offers some flexibility with regard to the applications that have already been pre-installed. To access the data that is present in Kali Linux and the host operating system, make sure that you are using the "Live Mode." You will then create a folder that you can also access easily.

The important data will be saved in that folder and you will then access it from either of the operating systems. The following steps will guide you on how to create a folder:

1) Create the folder on the operating system. For example, will be issued in the form of a screenshot, the folder, in this case, is named "Kali."

2) Right-click the "Kali" folder. You will then click 'share.'

3) Ensure that the file is shared with 'everyone'. People can also read and write an

4) My content is present in the "Kali" folder.

5) You can also install some VMware tools of you have not yet shared and created the folder.

6) After the installation process is complete, select the virtual machine setting. It will be present in the VMware menu. You will then share the folders and make sure that you have selected enabled. You will then create a path that allows

you to select shared folders that are located in the primary operating system.

7) Open the browser that is present on the Kali Linux default desktop. The shared folder will be present in the mint folder.

8) Ensure that the folder has been dragged to the Kali Linux desktop.

9) Make sure that all the information that has been placed into the folder is also accessible from the main operating system and Kali Linux.

When undertaking a pen test, make sure that you have stored all the findings in the shared folder. The information that you have gathered may be sensitive and you must ensure that it is encrypted. You can encrypt the information in different ways. For example, you can use LVM encryption. You can encrypt a folder or even an entire partition on the hard disk. Make sure that you can remember the password since you will not be able to reset it in case your memory fails you. If you fail to remember the password, the data will be lost in the process. It is good to encrypt the folders so that the data may not be accessed by unauthorized individuals.

Managing Third-Party Applications

Kali Linux has many applications and they are normally pre-installed. You may also install other applications on the platform but you need to make sure that they are from verifiable sources. Since Kali Linux is meant for penetration testing, some of the tools that are present on the platform are quite advanced. Before using these applications, make sure that you understand them fully so that you can use them effectively. You can also locate different applications easily.

Installing Third-Party Applications

There are many techniques that you can use when installing third-party applications. The commonly used techniques are such as the use of apt-get command and it is useful when accessing different repositories including GitHub and also installing different applications directly.

When you install different applications, make sure that they are all present in the Kali Linux repository. Use the apt-get install command during the installation process. The commands should be executed in the terminal window. During the installation process, you will also realize that the graphical package management tools will come in handy.

You can install different third-party applications and some of them include:

- *Gnome-Tweak-Tool* - This is a tool that normally allows the users to configure some desktop options and the user can also change the themes easily. The desktop screen recorder will also allow you to record different activities that may be taking place on the desktop.
- *Apt-File* - This is a command that is used to search for different packages that may be present within the APT packaging system. When using this command, you can list the contents of different packages prior to installing them.
- *Scrub* - The tool is used to delete data securely and it also complies with various government standards.

- *Open office* - This application offers users the productivity suite that will be useful during the documentation.
- *Team Viewer* - This tool ensures that people can have remote access. The penetration testers can use the tool to carry out the penetration test from a remote location.
- *Shutter* - Using this tool, you can take screenshots on the Kali Linux platform.
- *Terminator* - The tool allows users to scroll horizontally.

There are numerous tools that are not available in the Debian repository and they can also be accessed using various commands such as apt-get install command which can also be installed on the Kali Linux platform. Users should first learn that the manual installation techniques involve the use of repositories and it is also possible to break down the dependencies which means that some of the applications may also fail in the process.

The GitHub repository has many tools and they are used mainly by the software developers when handling different projects. Some of the developers will prefer to utilize open repositories since they will gain a lot of flexibility. Different applications should also be installed manually. Make sure that you have also perused through the README file since it provides some guidance on how to use some of these tools.

Running the Third-Party Applications Using Non-Root Privileges

Kali Linux supports different activities such as penetration testing. There are some tools that can only run when a user has root-level access. Some of the data and tools may also be [protected using password and different encryption techniques. There are some tools that you can also run using the non-root privileges. Some of these tools are such as web browsers.

After compromising tools such as web browsers, the attackers will have some root privileges. To run applications as a non-root user, you should log in to Kali Linux first while using the root account. Ensure that the Kali Linux has been configured using a non-root account after that. An example will be provided whereby a non-root user account was formulated using the add user command.

The steps that you should follow are outlined below. In this instance, we will run the Iceweasel browser and we will use the non-root Kali Linux user account.

1. Create a non-root user account.
2. We will use the sux application. The application is used when transferring different credentials from the root user account to the non-root user. When installing the application, use the apt-get install command.
3. You can launch the web browser and you should minimize it after that.
4. Use this command: ps aux | grep Iceweasel. In this case, you will be running the browser using the root privileges.
5. Close the browser and then start it all over again. Use the sux- noroot Iceweasel command to relaunch the application. The screenshot below will offer some subtle guidance.

Examine the browser title bar and you will realize that the browser was run as a non-root user and no administrator privileges are present.

Observe all the open processes after ensuring that the browser is running under the noroot account.

Effectively Managing the Penetration Tests

When you perform the penetration tests, you will come across a series of challenges and every test will also be carried out to unveil different vulnerabilities that may be present within the network or server. In some instances, you may not remember that you had conducted some tests and you may also be unable to keep track of the tests that you had already completed.

Some of the penetration tests are quite complex and the methodology used must adapt to that of the target. There are many applications that may be used when performing the tests and they include keyloggers and also Wireshark, just to mention a few. Each application is used when performing specific tests. The data that is gathered using these applications comes in handy. After the packets have been analyzed, it is easy to identify the packet tools that may have been affected.

There are many tools that are present in Kali Linux and some of them can also be used to make some rapid notes while serving as repositories using the KeepNote desktop wiki and Zim. Testers will also be able to carry out a variety of tests. In the process, they will collect some data that will also be used to facilitate the tests. The tests help to identify some of the changes that have taken place in the system. Some vulnerabilities may emerge and they should be sealed immediately to ensure that external attackers will not be able to access the system and gain access to sensitive pieces of information. As a tester, make sure that you have collected some evidence in the form of screenshots and you can present your findings to the clients while explaining to them about some of the vulnerabilities that are present in the network. Use tools such as shutter to take screenshots. You can also use CutyCapt and it will save the images in a variety of formats.

2. Back Door Attacks

Imagine you're going to a concert, but you don't have a ticket. You see the line of people all with their purchased tickets waiting to get through security. You see cameras pointing at the front door and a few extra security guards guarding the sides. You don't have a ticket or the money to buy one. Then, you see a little unguarded, dark, hidden alley with no cameras and the back door. The doors that lead to the venue. They are unlocked, and there are no security or cameras around. Would you go through the door? That's the concept behind a back-door attack.

How do backdoors even end up on our computers? Well, they can end up there intentionally by the manufacturer; this is built in so they can easily test out the bugs and quickly move in the applications as they are being tested.

The back door can also be built by malware. The classic backdoor malware is the infamous Trojan. Trojan subtly sneaks up on our computer and opens the back door for the people using the malware. The malware can be hidden into anything—a free file converter, a PDF file, a torrent, or anything you are downloading into your computer. Of course, the chances are higher when what you're downloading is a free copy of an otherwise paid product (lesson to be learned here). Trojans have an ability to replicate, and before you know it, your computer is infected with malware that is opening a backdoor for the whole line up to come in to see the show for free.

The back door can be used to infiltrate your system not only for passwords but also for spying, ransomware, and all kinds of other malicious hacking.

How to protect yourself from back door attacks
Choose applications, downloads and plugins carefully; free apps and plugins are a fantastic thing, but YouTube to MP3 converters, torrents of the latest Game of Thrones season, and a copy of Photoshop might not be the best option if you're interested in keeping your passwords safe. Android users should stick to Google Play apps, and Mac users should stick with the Apple store. Track app permissions too and

be sure to read, at least a little, before you sign your life away to a third-grade flashlight application.

You can also try:

Monitoring network activity - Use firewalls and track your data usage. Any data usage spike is a sure sign of backdoor activity.

Changing your default passwords - When a website assigns a default password, we may find that we are just too lazy to take the 30 seconds necessary to change it. Just do it. You might not be locking the back door with the latest state-of-the-art security system, but at least you are not keeping them wide open with a neon sign pointing to your password. Freckles might be your puppy, but he can't be a password for everything. A common complaint is, "I will forget it." Write it down. Contrary to popular belief, hackers won't go into your house and search for that piece of paper, but they will go into your computer. Which option seems safer?

Zombie Computers for Distributed Denial of Service (DDoS) attacks

Sounds extremely cool, right? Well, it's not. Basically, a computer becomes a zombie computer when a hacker infiltrates it and controls it to do illegal activities. The best part (for the hacker, not for you) is that you are completely unaware that all this is happening. You will still use it normally, though it might significantly slow down. And then all of a sudden, your computer will begin to send out massive spam emails or social media posts that you have nothing to do with. DDoS attacks are lovely (for the hacker, not for you) because they work on multiple computers at once, and the numbers can go into millions. A million zombie computers are mindlessly wandering around the internet spamming everything in sight, infecting other computers. The version where your computer is infected only to send out spam is the light version. DDoS attacks can also be used for criminal activity, and this is why it is important to prevent them.

How to protect from DDoS attacks

Larger scale businesses require more substantial protection against DDoS attacks, and we will go over that in detail, but even for individuals, half of the protection is prevention.

Understand the warning signs—slowed down computers, spotty connection, or website shutdowns are all signs of a DDoS attack taking place.

What can you do?

Have more bandwidth - This ensures you have enough bandwidth to deal with massive spikes in traffic that can be caused by malicious activity

Use anti-DDoS hardware and software modules - Protect your servers with network and web application firewalls. Hardware vendors can add software protection by monitoring how incomplete connections and specific software modules can be added to the webserver software to provide DDoS protection.

Smart clicking - This should go without saying, but for those in need of hearing it—pop-up ads with a "No, thanks" button are hateful little things. Just exit the website, don't click anything on that ad, especially not the "No, thanks," button or you will instantly activate an annoying download, and now your computer is a zombie.

Man in The Middle

When you're online, your computer does little back-and-forth transactions. You click a link, and your computer lets the servers around the world know you are requesting access to this website. The servers then receive the message and grant you access to the requested website. This all happens in nanoseconds, and we don't think much about it. That nanosecond moment between your computer and the web server is given a session ID that is unique and private to your computer and the webserver. However, a hacker can hijack this session and pretend to be the computer and as such, gain access to usernames and passwords. He becomes the man in the middle hijacking your sessions for information.

How to protect yourself from the man in the middle

Efficient antivirus and up-to-date software go a long way in preventing hijacking, but there are a couple of other tips that can help you prevent becoming a victim.

Use a virtual private network - A VPN is a private, encrypted network that acts as a private tunnel and severely limits the hacker's access to your information. Express VPN can also mask your location, allowing you to surf the web anonymously wherever you are.

Firewalls and penetration testing tools - Secure your network with active firewalls and penetration testing tools.

Plugins - Use only trusted plugins from credible sources and with good ratings.

Secure your communications - Use two-step verification programs and alerts when someone signs in to your account from a different computer.

Root Access

Root access is an authorization to access any command specific to Unix, Linux, and Linux-like systems. This gives the hacker complete control over the system. Root access is granted with a well-designed rootkit software. A quality designed rootkit software will access everything and hide traces of any presence. This is possible in all Unix-like systems because they are designed with a tree-like structure in which all the units branch off into one root.

The original Unix operating system was designed in a time before the personal computer existed when all the computers were connected to one mainframe computer through very simple terminals. It was necessary to have one large, strong mainframe for separating and protecting files while the users simultaneously used the system.

Hackers obtain root access by gaining privileged access with a rootkit. Access can be granted through passwords; password protection is a significant component in restricting unwanted root access. The rootkit can also be installed automatically through a malicious download. Dealing with rootkit can be difficult and expensive, so it's better to stay protected and keep the possibility of root access attacks to the minimum.

How to protect yourself from root access attacks

Quality antivirus software is one of the standard things recommended in all computers, be it for individuals or businesses. Quality antivirus helps the system hardening making it harder for installation of rootkits.

Principle of least privilege - PoLP gives only the bare minimum privilege that a program needs to perform allows for better protection from possible attacks. For example, in a business, a user whose only job is to answer emails should only be given access to the emails. If there is an attack on the user's computer, it can't spread far because the person only has access to email. If a said employee has root access privilege, the attack will spread system-wide.

Disable root login - Servers on most Unix and Linux operating systems come with an option for the root login. Using root login allows for much easier root access, and if you pair it with a weak password, you are walking on a thin line. Disabling the option for root access keeps all the users away from the root login temptation.

Block brute forces - Some programs will block suspicious IP addresses for you. They will detect malicious IP and prevent attacks. While manually detecting is the safest way, it can be a long process; programs that are designed to block malicious IPs can drastically save time and help prevent root access attacks.

The best way to protect yourself from hack attacks is through prevention because the alternative can be lengthy, exhausting, and costly.

3. Cybersecurity

The internet is a vast place, and most people are not experts on protecting the information about them that is available. It's no surprise that there are people out there who take advantage of others' ignorance. But there are ways to protect yourself from those kinds of attacks, and that's where cybersecurity comes in.

What is Cybersecurity?

By the time you finish reading this sentence, over 300 million people will have clicked on a single link. You are part of a universe that generates information every millisecond. We do everything from home— buy, sell, eat, drink, fight, tweet, click, and share. We don't need to go to the movies to see a movie or go to the stores to shop. Information exchanges happen online every time you connect to Wi-Fi, publish content, buy something online, like a post on social media, click a link, send an email...you get the gist. We produce much more information than we can grasp, so we underestimate the quantity and value of protecting it.

Cybersecurity is the protection of hardware, software, and data from cyberattacks. Cybersecurity ensures data confidentiality, availability, and integrity. A successful and secure system has multiple layers of protection spread across the networks, computers, data, and programs. For cybersecurity to be effective, all the people involved in different components must complement each other. It is always better to prevent cyberattacks then deal with the consequences of one.

Cyberattacks hit businesses every day. The latest statistics show that hackers now focus more on quieter attacks, but they are increased by over 50%.

During 2018, 1% of websites were considered victims of cyberattacks. Thinking about 1% of all websites that exist, that adds up to over 17 million websites that are always under attack. Cyberattacks cost an average of $11 million per year, so cybersecurity is a crucial aspect of saving your business much money.

That's where the most prominent problem occurs. Small business owners and individuals don't grasp the potential threat to their data because they don't see the value they bring to a hacker attacking. The value is in the lack of security.

Many small businesses with no security are more accessible to penetrate than one large corporation. Corporations invest in cybersecurity; small business owners and individuals do not. They use things like the cloud. Their data migrate with them to the cloud allowing criminals to shift and adapt. The lack of security on their part is crucial to these statistics. The most definite form of on-going attacks remains ransomware; it is so common-place that it is barely even mentioned in the media. Ransomware infects a website by blocking access to their data until a business or an individual transfer a certain amount of money. Hackers hold your data hostage, and it's always about the money.

Cybersecurity is not complicated, it is complex. However, it is also very important to understand. Implementing just the top four cybersecurity strategies diminishes attacks by over 70%. Here are some of the techniques:

Application whitelisting - allowing only approved programs to run

Applications security patching - enforcing security patches (fixes) promptly for applications

Operating systems security patching - enforcing security patches (fixes) promptly for the whole system

Limiting administrative privileges - allowing only trusted individuals to manage and monitor computer systems

Cybersecurity Benefits

There's a variety of benefits cybersecurity can bring to you or your business, and some aren't as obvious as you may think.

Prevents ransomware - Every 10 seconds, someone becomes a victim of ransomware. If you don't know what is happening in your network, an attacker probably found a way to get into it.

Prevents adware - Adware fills your computer with ads and allows the attacker to get into your network.

Prevents spyware - The attacker can spy on your activity and use that information to learn about your computer and network vulnerabilities

Improves your search engine rankings - SEO is the key in the modern digital market. Small businesses looking to rank up on search engines have to be educated in SEO if they want to advance financially. HTTPS (HyperText Transfer Protocol Secure), or the encryption of username, passwords, and information, is one of the critical SEO ranking factors.

Prevents financial loss and saves your startup - More than half of small business go down after a cyberattack. The downtime required to fix the damage prevents any new business, and the data breach causes you to lose the trust of your current customers. Stable businesses can find a way to recover from this, but startups rarely make it out alive.

4. Wireless Networking

While talking about networking, one of the most trending topics is wireless networking. It has allowed people to reach new heights of reliability along with benefits which allow them to use the internet with their devices without any form of cable or wire in between. All of these have been possible only because of wireless networking. In wireless networking, all the devices connect with a network switch or router which helps in establishing connection between the devices and the Web via radio waves. All the information and connection are established through the air. Thus, it can be regarded as a mobile form of network where you are no longer required to be seated in one single place for surfing the internet. Wireless networking comes with various components along with some very interesting features which will be discussed further in this chapter. So, let's start with wireless networking and its various features.

Hacking and Penetration Testing with Kali Linux

Each and every organization and companies come with certain weak points which might turn out to be malicious for the organization. Such weak points can also lead to some serious form of attack which can be later used for manipulation of organizational data. The only thing that you are left with in such a situation which can ultimately help you in preventing all forms of hackers from getting into your systems is regular checking of infrastructure security. You will also need to ensure that no form of vulnerability is present within the infrastructure. For serving all of these functions, penetration testing is something which can ultimately help you. It helps in detecting the vulnerabilities within a system and forwards the same information to the organization administrators for mending up the gaps. Penetration testing is always performed within a highly secure and real form of environment which helps in finding out the real form of vulnerabilities and then mends the following along with securing the system.

Details about penetration testing

It is a process which is used for testing of the systems for finding out or ensuring that whether any third party can penetrate within the system or not. Ethical hacking is often being mixed up with penetration testing as both of them somewhat serves the similar purpose and also functions more or less in the same way. In penetration testing, the pen tester scans the systems for any form of system vulnerability, flaws, risks and malicious content. You can perform penetration testing either in an online form of environment or server or even in a computer system. Penetration testing comes with some ultimate form of agendas: strengthening the system of security and defending the structure of an organization from potential attacks and threats.

Penetration testing is absolutely of legal nature and is done along with the other official workings. When used in the proper and perfect way, penetration testing has the ability of doing wonders. If you want you can also consider penetration testing as a potential part of ethical hacking. You will need to perform the penetration tests at a regular form of intervals as it has the ability of improving the system capabilities. It also helps in improving the cyber security strategies. In order to fish out all the weak points within a program, system or application, various forms of malicious content are constructed or created by the pen testers. For an effective form of testing, the harmful form of content is spread across the overall network for the testing of vulnerability.

The technique used by penetration testing might not be successful in handling all the security concerns but it can help to minimize the chances of probable attacks on the system. Penetration testing ensures that an organization or company is absolutely safe from all forms of threats and vulnerabilities and it ultimately helps in providing security from the cyber form of attacks. It also makes sure that the system of defense of an organization is working properly and is also enough for the company or organization to prevent the probable attacks and threats. Not only that but it also indicates the measures of security which are required to be changed by the organization for the only motive of defending the system from attacks and vulnerabilities. All the reports regarding penetration testing are handed over to the system administrators.

Metasploit

Metasploit is nothing but a framework meant for penetration testing which actually makes the concept of hacking much simpler and easier. It is regarded as an important form of tool for majority of the attackers along with the security defenders. All you need to do is to just point out Metasploit at the target, pick any exploit of your choice, choose the payload which you want to drop and just hit enter. However, it is not that casual in nature and so you will need to start from the beginning. Back in the golden days, the concept of penetration testing came with lots of repetitive form of labor which is now being automated by the use of Metasploit.

What are the things that you need? Gathering of information or gaining of access or maintaining the levels of persistence or evading all forms f detection? Metasploit can be regarded as the Swiss knife for the hackers and if you want to opt for information security as your future career then you are required to know this framework in detail. The core of the Metasploit framework is free in nature and also comes pre-installed with the software Kali Linux.

How to use Metasploit?

Metasploit can seamlessly integrate itself with SNMP scanning, Nmap and enumeration of Windows patch along with others. It also comes with a bridge to the Tenable's scanner of vulnerability along with Nessus. Most of the reconnaissance tools which you can think of can integrate along with Metasploit and thus it makes it possible to find the strongest possible point in the shield of security. After you have identified the weakness in a system, you can start hunting across the huge and extensible form of database for the need of the exploit which will help in cracking the strongest armor and will let you in the system. Just like the combination of cheese and wine, you can also pair an exploit with the payload for suiting any task at the hand.

Most of the hackers are looking out for a shell, a proper payload at the time of attacking a system based on Windows acts as the Meterpreter and also as an in-memory form of interactive shell. Linux comes with its own set of shellcodes which depends on the exploit which is being used. Once within a target machine, the quiver of Metasploit comes with a complete suite of post-exploitation tools which also includes escalation of privileges, pass the hash, screen capture, packet sniffing, pivoting and keylogger tools. If you want you can also easily set up a proper form of backdoor if the target machine gets rebooted somehow.

Metasploit is being loaded up with more and more features each year along with a fuzzer for identifying the potential flaws of security in the binaries as well as a too long list of the modules which are of auxiliary nature. What we have discussed till now is only a high-level vision of what can be done with Metasploit. The overall framework is modular in nature and can be extended easily and it also enjoys an active form of community. In case it is not doing what you want, you can easily tweak the same for meeting your needs.

How can you learn Metasploit?

You can find out various cheap as well as free forms of resources for the purpose of learning Metasploit. The best way of starting with Metasploit is by downloading Kali Linux followed by the installation of the same along with a virtual machine for practicing of the target. The organization which maintains Kali Linux and also runs the OSCP certification, Offensive Security, offers a free course that includes training of Metasploit and is known as Metasploit Unleashed.

Where can you download Metasploit?

Metasploit can be found along with the hacking software Kali Linux. But, if you want you can also download it separately from the official website of Metasploit. Metasploit can be used on the systems which are based on Windows and *nix. You can find out the source code of Metasploit Framework on GitHub. Metasploit is also available in various forms which you can easily find over the internet.

Datastore

The datastore can be regarded as a core element of the Metasploit Framework. It is nothing but a table of several named values which allows the users to easily configure the component behavior within

Metasploit. The datastore allows the interfaces to configure any of the settings, exploits for defining the parameters and also payloads for the purpose of patching the opcodes. It also allows Metasploit Framework to pass internally between the options of modules. You can find two types of datastores, the Global datstore which can be defined by using 'setg' and the Module datastore which can be defined at the modular level of datastore by using 'set'.

SQL Injection and Wi-Fi Hacking

When it comes to cyber-attacks one of the most widely used forms of attack is the SQL Injection attack. In this, an attacker performs the attack by executing threat or invalid form of SQL statements which is used for database server control for an application of web. It is also being used for modifying, deleting or adding up records within the database without even the user knowing anything about the same. This ultimately compromises the integrity of the data. The most important step which can be taken for avoiding or preventing SQL injection is by input validation.

SQL Injection and its types

There are various types of SQL injection which you can find today. Let's have a look at them.

- Classic or In-band SQL injection: 1. Error based: Attackers employ the generated error by the database to attack the database server.

2. Union based: In this UNION SQL operator is employed for combining a response for returning to the HTTP response.

- Inferential or Blind SQL injection: 1. Based on Boolean: It is based on return of true or false.

2. Time based: It sends out SQL injection which forces the database just before responding.

- Out of band SQL injection: This takes place when an attacker is unable to use the similar form of channel for attacking and gathering the results.

Tools used for SQL injection

There are various tools which are being used for carrying out SQL injection.

- SQLMap: This tool is used for an automatic form of SQL injection and it is a tool which helps in taking over the database.

- jSQL Injection: It is a Java based tool which is being used for SQL injection.

- Blind-SQL-BitShifting: It is a tool which is used for blind SQL injection by the use of BitShifting.

- BBQSQL: It is a blind form of SQL injection exploitation tool.

- explo: It is a format of machine and human readable web vulnerability testing.

- Whitewidow: It is a scanning tool which is used for checking out the vulnerabilities of the SQL database.

- Leviathan: It acts as an audio toolkit.

- Blisqy: It is used for the purpose of exploiting time-based SQL injection within the headers of HTTP.

Detection tools for SQL injection

A tool named Spider testing tool is widely being used for the purpose of identifying the holes of SQL injection manually by the use of POST or GET requests. If you can resolve the vulnerabilities within the code then you can easily prevent the SQL injections. You can also take help of a web vulnerability scanner for identifying all the defects within the code and for fixing the same f0r preventing SQL injection. The firewalls present in the web application or within the application layer can also be used extensively for preventing any form of intrusion.

Hacking of Wi-Fi

Wi-Fi or wireless networking can be regarded as the most preferred medium which is being used for the purpose of network connectivity in today's world. However, because of so much popularity of the same, the wireless networks are also subjected to various attacks and also comes with several issues of security. In case the attacker gains complete access of the network connection then it is possible for the attacker to sniff off the data packets from any nearby location. The attackers employ sniffing tools for finding out the SSIDs and then hacks the Wi-Fi or wireless networks. After successful hacking, the attackers can monitor all the devices which are connected with the same SSID of the network. In case you use authentication of WEP then it might be subject to dictionary attack. The attackers employ RC4 form of encryption algorithm for the purpose of creating stream ciphers which is very easy to be cracked. In case you are using authentication of WPA then it might subject to DOS along with dictionary attack.

Tools for hacking of Wi-Fi

For the purpose of cracking WEP, the attackers use various tools such as WEPcrack, Aircrack, Kismet,

WEPDecrypt and many others. For cracking WPA, tools such as Cain, Abel and CowPatty are being used by the hackers. There are also various types of tools which are used in general for hacking of wireless network system like wireshark, Airsnort, Wifiphisher, Netstumbler and many others. Even the attackers are now able to hack the mobile phone platform via the wireless network system. Android can be regarded as the most found mobile phone-based platform but it is also very much susceptible to some specific types of vulnerabilities which ultimately makes it easier for the attackers to exploit the device security and then steal data from the same. The most dangerous threats for the mobile devices are third party applications, email Trojans, wireless hacking and SMS.

How are Wi-Fi attacks carried out?

Most of the wireless network attacks are carries out by setting up rogue Access Point.

- *Evil Twin attack:* In this, the hacker sets up a false access point with the same name as that of the corporate AP which is close to the premises of the company. When any employee of the company connects to that access point by regarding that access point to be genuine in nature, that employee unknowingly gives out all the details of authentication of the actual access point. Thus, the hacker can easily compromise the overall connection.

- *Signal jamming:* The hackers can easily disrupt the network connection which can be done by jamming the network signals. This is done by various forms of tools which are used for creating noise.

- *Misconfiguration attack:* When the router of a network is set up by using a default form of configuration, weak form of encryption, weak credentials and algorithms, an attacker can easily crack the network.

- *Honey spot attack:* The attackers set up false hotspots or access points with the same name of the SSID similar to any public Wi-Fi access point. When any user connects with that access point unknowingly, the hackers can easily get access to the actual network.

How To Carry Out An Effective Attack

When it comes to the term 'hacking' it doesn't mean that it has to be negative all the time. You will be able to have a proper idea about the overall process of hacking only when you will have a clear perception about the process behind it. Not only that you will be able to gather knowledge about the process of hacking but you will also be able to make your system much more protected from external attacks. Most of the times, when an attacker tries to gain access to a server of an organization or a company, it is generally done by using 5 proper steps. Let's have a look at those steps.

• Reconnaissance: This can be regarded as the very first step that comes in the hacking process. During this phase, the attacker uses all the available means for the purpose of collecting all forms of relevant information about the primary target system. The relevant set of information might include the proper identification of the target, DNS records of the server, range of the IP address which is in target, the network and various other aspects. In simple terms, the attacker tries to collect all sorts of information along with the contacts of a website or server. This can be done by the attacker by the use of several forms of search engines like maltego or by researching about the system which is in target or by using the various tools like HTTPTrack for the purpose of downloading a complete website for enumeration at a later stage.

By performing all these steps, the attacker will be able to determine the names of all the staffs within an organization very easily, find out the designated posts along with the email addresses of the employees.

• Scanning: After collecting all the relevant information about the target, the attacker will now start with the process of scanning. During this phase, the attacker employs various forms of tools like dialers, port scanners, vulnerability scanners, sweepers and network mappers for the sole purpose of scanning the target website or server data. During this step, the attackers try to seek out all that information which can actually help in the execution of a successful attack such as the IP address of the system, the user accounts and the computer names within that server. Right after the hackers are done with scanning of basic information, they start to test the network which is in target for finding out the possible avenues of attack. They might also employ several methods for network mapping just like Kali Linux.

The hackers also search out for any automatic email system by which they can mail out the staffs of the target company about some false form of query like mailing the company HR about a job query.

• Access gaining: This is the most important of all the steps. In this phase, the attacker designs out the blueprint of the target network along with the help of all relevant information which is also collected in the first and second step of hacking. As the hackers are done with enumeration of data followed by scanning of the system, they will now move to the step of gaining access to the system which will be based on the collected information.

For instance, the attacker might decide to use a phishing attack. The attackers will always try to play safe and might employ a very simple attack of phishing for gaining overall access to the system. The attacker might also penetrate into the system from the IT department shell. The hackers use phishing email by employing the actual email address of the company. By using this phishing email ID, the attacker will send out various emails to the techs that will also contain some form of specialized program along with a phishing website for gathering information about the login passwords and IDs. For this, the attackers can use various methods such as phone app, website mail or something else and then asking the employees to login with their credentials into a new website.

As the hackers use this method, they already have a special type of program running in the background which is also called as Social Engineering Toolkit which is used for sending out emails with the address of the server to the users.

• Maintaining access to the server: After the attackers have gained access to the target server, they will try out every possible means for keeping their access to the server safe for future attacks and for the purpose of exploitation. As the attacker now has overall access to the server, he might also use the server as his very own base for launching out several other forms of attacks. When an attacker gains access to an overall system and also owns the system, such a system is called as zombie system. The hacker might also try to hide himself within the server by creating a new administrator account with which he can easily mingle with the system without anyone knowing about it. For keeping safe access to the system, the hacker traces out all those accounts which are not being used for a long time and then elevates the privileges of all those accounts to himself.

As the hacker makes sure that no one has sensed his presence within the system, he starts to make copies of all the data on that server along with the contacts, messages, confidential files and many more for future use.

• Clearance of tracks: Right before starting with the attack, the hackers chalk out their entire track regarding the identity so that it is not possible for anyone to track them. The attackers begin by altering the system MAC address and then run their entire system via a VPN so that no one can trace their actual identity.

5. How to Initiate A Hack Using Kali Linux?

When planning an attack, the most important factor to consider is the pilot study. It should come first before you carry out an attack or a penetration test on a target. As an attacker, you will have to dedicate a lot of time to the reconnaissance. In this stage, the attacker will be able to define, map, and also explore some of the vulnerabilities that are present and they will be able to successfully perform an exploit. There are two types of pilot studies; passive and active.

The passive pilot study involves the analysis of the information that is available. For instance, some information can be obtained online through search engines. The information can be analyzed first. Although an attacker can use this information to their advantage, it is not possible to trace the information back to them. As for passive reconnaissance, it is mainly carried out to ensure that the target cannot easily notice that there is a looming attack.

The major practices and principles of the passive reconnaissance include:

OSINT (Open-source intelligence).

How to obtain user information.

The basics of the pilot study.

The Basic Principles of the Pilot Study

The pilot study is the first step when a person wants to launch an attack. The study is carried out after identifying a target. The information that is gained during this stage will come in handy when performing the actual attack. A reconnaissance will ensure that they have provided a sense of direction which will be required when trying to look into some of the vulnerabilities that are present in the network or target's server.

The passive pilot study does not involve physically interacting with the target and that means that the IP address of the attacker is not logged. For instance, the attacker may search for the IP address of the target. It may be difficult to gain access to such information; however, it is also possible. The target will also not be able to notice that an attacker is

690

trying to harvest some information as they plan an attack.

The passive reconnaissance will focus more on the business activities as well as the employees within the organization. The information that is readily available on the internet is known as OSINT (Open source Intelligence).

As for the passive reconnaissance, the attacker will interact with the target in a manner that is expected. For instance, the attacker will visit the website of the attacker. They will then view the available pages and they will then download some of the available documents. Some of these interactions are always expected and they are not detected easily and the target may not know that there is a looming attack.

The active reconnaissance involves interacting through port scanning in the specific network as well as sending direct queries that will then trigger the system alarms and that means that the target can easily capture the IP address of the attacker and their activities. The information that the target has gained can also be used to arrest the attacker. Additionally, the information can also be presented before a court of law as evidence that the attacker was planning something malicious. As for the active pilot study, there are various activities that the attacker should consider so that they can conceal their identity.

As an attacker, you should also follow some steps during the process of gathering information. The main focus is on the user account data. For the pilot study to be effective, as an attacker, you should always know what you are looking for. Also, make sure that you have gathered all the data that you need. Although the passive reconnaissance is less risky, it minimizes the amount of data that you can collect.

OSINT (Open-Source Intelligence)

This is the first step when planning an attack. In this case, the attacker should make use of the present search engines preferably Google. There is a lot of information that could come in handy when facilitating an attack. The process of collecting the information is quite complex.

In this book, we will just issue an overview since the main focus is on how to hack with Kali Linux. The essential highlights will offer some suitable guidance. The information collected by an attacker will always depend on their initial motives and their major goals when they plan an attack. For instance, the attacker may want to access the financial data within a specific organization. Other types of information that they may need is the names of the employees. Most of the attackers will focus more on the senior employees who are working as executives. Some of these employees include the CFO among other seniors. The attacker will focus on obtaining their usernames and their respective passwords. In some instances, an attacker may try to carry out social engineering. In this case, they will have to supplement the information that they possess so that they may appear as credible individuals. After that, they can easily request for the information that they need.

As for the Open source Intelligence, the attacker will start by reviewing the online presence of the target. They will start by observing their social media pages, blogs, and websites. The public financial records also come in handy in some cases. The most important information is:

- The geographical location of the offices. For instance, there can be some satellite offices that also share some corporate information but they have not set up any measures that will ensure that the information is safe as it is being transmitted from one office to another.

- The overview of the parent and subsidiary firms matters especially when dealing with a new company that has also been acquired through M&A transactions. The acquired companies will not be as safe as compared to the parent company.

- The contact information and the names of the employees. The phone numbers and email addresses should also be obtained.

- Looking for clues about the target company's corporate culture so that it may be possible to facilitate the social engineering attack.

- The business partners are also eligible to access to network of the target.

- The technology being used. For instance, the target may issue a press release about how to adopt software and the attacker will go ahead and review the website of the vendor as they try to look for bug reports. After finding some vulnerabilities, they will be able to launch an attack.

Some of the online information sources that can also be used by an attacker when they are planning an attack include:

- Search engines including Google. There are also other search engines such as Bing. It's only that we have gotten used to Google. During the search process, you will realize that the process is highly manual. You may have to type the name of the company as well as other relevant details. Since technology has also advanced, there are some APIs that can be used to automate the searches of the search engines. Some of the effective APIs include Maltego.

There are other sources and they include:

- The financial and government sites since they provide some information about the key individuals within the company as well as some supporting data.

- The Usenet newsgroups. The man focus should be on the posts by the employees that you are targeting as a tester or an attacker. You may also seek some help with different forms of technology.

- Jigsaw and LinkedIn; these companies come in handy since they provide some information about the employees within a company.

- The cached content. It can be retrieved easily by search engines including Google.

- The country as well as the specific language being used.

- Employee and corporate blogs.

- Social media platforms such as Facebook.

- The sites whereby you can look up the server information and the DNS as well as routes. Some of these sites include myIPneighbors.com.

The main issue arises when you have to manage the information that you have found. The main advantage is that kali Linux has an application known as Keep Note. It supports the rapid importation and management of different data types.

Route Mapping DNS reconnaissance

As a tester or an attacker, you will have to make sure that you have identified the targets that have an online presence. Make sure that you have also gained access to some of the items that may pose some interest. You will then go ahead and identify the IP addresses of the targets. The DNS reconnaissance will come in handy when identifying the domains as well as the DNS information that will help to define some of the IP addresses as well as actual domain names. The route between the attacker and the target will also be identified.

The information is easily available in some of the open sources. Some information is mainly present in some of the DNS registrars and they are referred to as third parties. The registrar may collect an IP address as well as some of the data requests that have been brought forth by an attacker. Such information is rarely provided to the specific target who will be a victim of an attack. As for the target, they can easily monitor the DNS server logs. The information needed can also be obtained using an approach that is systematic.

WHOIS

The first step entails researching the IP address so as to identify the addresses that have also been assigned to the sites of the target. You will then make use of the whois command and it will allow you to query the databases that have also stored the information about certain users. The information that you will obtain includes the IP address and domain name.

The whois request will then come in handyu when providing physical addresses, names, e-mail addresses, as well as phone numbers. Such information is very important when it comes to performing a social engineering attack.

As an attacker or tester, you can use the whois command to carry out the following activities:

Supporting a social engineering attack against a target that has been identified using the whois query.

Identifying the location whereby you can launch a physical attack.

Conducting some research that will allow you to learn more about the domain names that are present on the server. You can also learn more about the number of users operating it. As an attacker, you will also gain an interest in learning whether the domains are insecure and whether you can exploit the present vulnerabilities to gain access while also compromising the target server.

Identifying the phone numbers since you may also have to launch a dialing attack while conducting the social engineering attack.

The attack will then use the DNS servers to carry out the DNS reconnaissance.

In some cases, the domain may be due to expire and
the attacker may go ahead and try to seize the
domain while also creating look-a-like website
that will be used to lure unsuspecting visitors who
think that they are entering into the original
website.

To make sure that the data has been shielded
accordingly, there has been an increase in the use of
third parties. Also, when using public domains, you
cannot access domains such as .gov and .mil. The
mentioned domains belong to the military and the
government and that is why they have been secured
so that they cannot be accessed by other parties.
When you send a request to such a domain, it will be
logged. There are many online lists that can also be
used to describe the IP addresses as well as
domains. If you want to use the whois query, the
following screenshot will offer some guidance when
running the query against some of the Digital
Defense domains:

There is a whois command record that will be
returned and it will contain some names and
geographical information as well as contact
information that will come in handy when facilitating

700

a social engineering attack. There are also many websites that are also used to automate the whois lookup. Some of the attackers use some of these sites to insert a step that will be between them and the attackers. The site that is doing the lookup may then log the IP address of the requester.

Mapping the Route to the Target

The route mapping was once used as a diagnostic tool. The tool would allow the attacker to view the route that is followed by the IP packet as it moves from one host to another. When using the TTL (time to live) field in the IP packer, an ICMP TIME_EXCEEDED message will then be elicited from one point to another. The message will be sent from the receiving router and it will also help to determine the value that is in the TTL field. The packets will also count the number of routes and hops that have been taken.

From the perspective of the attacker or penetration tester, the traceroute data will help to yield the following pieces of data:

The hints about the topology of the network.

The path that is present between the target and the attacker.

Identifying the firewalls and other devices that are used to control access to the network.

Identifying whether the network has been misconfigured.

In Kali Linux, you can map the route using the tracerouteis command. If you are using Windows, you can use the tracert command. If you happen to launch an attack when using Kali Linux, you will notice that most of the hops have been filtered. For instance, when using Google to trace the location of a certain target, the results will be as shown below:

If you were to run the same request when using the tracert on the Windows platform, you will see the following:

We will get the complete path and we have also noticed that Google is showcasing an IP address that is slightly different. The load balancers have also been indicated. The main reason why the path data is different is because the traceroute used the UDP datagrams whereas the Windows tracert will use the ICMP request (specifically the ICMP type 8). When you complete the traceroute when using the tools that have been provided by Kali Linux, you should also make sure that you have used multiple protocols so that you may obtain the complete path while also bypassing some of the devices that carry out packet-filtering.

Obtaining User Information

When an attacker or a penetration tester manages to gather the usernames and the e-mail addresses of the targets, they can then manage to gather into the systems. The most common tool that is deployed is the web browser and you have to perform a manual search. You have to search some of the third-party sites including Jigsaw and LinkedIn. You can also use some of the tools provided by Kali Linux to automate the search.

6. Your First Hack

As for the first hack, we can use a simple example detailing how to hack the WPA2 Wi-Fi networks using Kali Linux. Using such an example, the reader can get an overview of how to hack different systems before they try to hack into other systems that may be more complex.

Hacking the WPA2 Wi-Fi using Kali Linux

After learning about how to hack using Kali Linux as well as the tools that you may need to facilitate the attack, it is good to provide an example of how you can actually hack wireless networks. In this case, the example will entail hacking the WPA2 Wi-Fi network using Kali Linux.

When hacking a WPA2 network, make sure that you are conversant with some of the tools that Kali Linux has to offer. The operating system has some pre-installed tools and they are about 600 in total. You can also go ahead and install some other tools from the Kali Linux and GitHub repositories. Before installing other applications, you should ensure that each of the applications is verified. If you want to hack the WPA2 Wi-Fi, first make sure that you are conversant with various tools including the Aircrack-ng tool. There are some people who have been propagating rumors that it is possible to hack a WPA2 network using other operating systems such as Microsoft Windows. Such rumors are far-fetched and you should also note that only Kali Linux has the necessary tools that you can use to launch an attack on the WPA2 networks.

If you want to crack the network, make sure that you have installed the Kali Linux on your PC. If you want to successfully launch an attack on the WPA2 networks, ensure that you are conversant with the authentication processes of the WPA2 networks. Also, ensure that you also know your way around the Kali Linux operating system. If you are knowledgeable about how to launch such an attack, we will now discuss more about the steps that are involved when hacking into a WPA2 network successfully.

To successfully launch the attack, you need the following:

- Make sure that you have installed Kali Linux into your PC.
- Ensure you have a wireless adapter and it should also have capabilities such as monitor mode. There are some PCs that also have network cards and they are preferred in such a case. If the PC you are using does not have the network card, make sure that you have purchased it.
- Come up with a wordlist since it will be used when cracking the WPA2 network.
- You must be patient and spare enough time to handle the process.

After ensuring that you have heeded to all the requirements that have been outlined, you can follow these steps and you will be able to hack into the WPA2 network successfully.

The tutorial may come in handy; nevertheless, you should not hack into WPA2 networks without the necessary authorization. The tutorial will come in handy for the professionals who carry out security audits and penetration tests. After carrying out some tests, the ethical hackers are able to issue a detailed report indicating whether the network is safe or not. If there are some loopholes, some recommendations will be issued.

Step One:

Powering the computer and logging into Kali Linux.

Step Two:

Ensure that you have plugged in the wireless adapter. When you run Kali Linux in the "Live Mode," ensure that you have also plugged in the wireless adapter and there is an icon that will also appear on the device menu and it is as shown below:

Step Three

Make sure that you are not connected to any wireless network. Also, open a terminal where you will key in the airmon-ng command.

```
root@kali:~# airmon-ng

Interface       Chipset         Driver

wlan0           Realtek RTL8187L        rtl8187 - [phy0]
```

The airmon-ng command lists all the wireless cards that will support the monitor mode. In an instance whereby there are no cards, make sure that you reconnected the network adapter and also inquire whether the monitor mode is supported by the card.

Step Four:

Open the terminal window and type the airmon-ng start command. After that, type the interface name of your wireless card. In this case, the interface name for our wireless card is wlan0; as a result, our command should be airmon-ng start wlan0.

```
root@kali:~# airmon-ng start wlan0


Found 2 processes that could cause trouble.
If airodump-ng, aireplay-ng or airtun-ng stops working after
a short period of time, you may want to kill (some of) them!
-e
PID     Name
3115    NetworkManager
3464    wpa_supplicant


Interface       Chipset         Driver

wlan0           Realtek RTL8187L        rtl8187 - [phy0]
                                (monitor mode enabled on mon0)
```

As per the screenshot above, the monitor mode has also been enabled. The new interface has been named mon0.

Step Five:

Key in the airodump-ng command in the monitor interface. A new monitor interface will be added and it is named mon0.

```
root@kali:~# airodump-ng mon0
```

Step Six:

The airodump command ensures that you can gain access to a list that contains all the wireless networks within your locality. You can also gain access to important information about the networks that have been listed. First, ensure that you have located the network that you will crack. After identifying one network that you are interested in, you should click Ctrl + C and the entire process will stop. Ensure that you have noted the channel of the network target.

Step Seven:

Copy the BSSID of the target network.

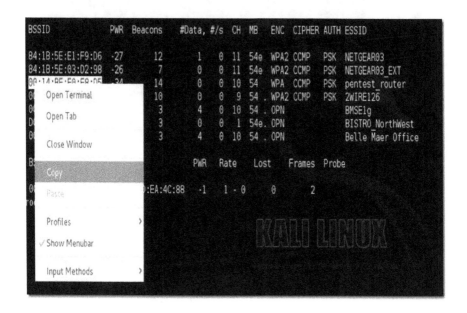

```
BSSID              PWR Beacons    #Data, #/s CH  MB   ENC  CIPHER AUTH ESSID

84:1B:5E:E1:F9:D6  -27     12        1    0  11  54e  WPA2 CCMP   PSK  NETGEAR03
84:1B:5E:03:D2:98  -26      7        0    0  11  54e  WPA2 CCMP   PSK  NETGEAR03_EXT
00:14:BF:F0:F9:D5  -24     14        0    0  10  54   WPA  CCMP   PSK  pentest_router
  [Open Terminal]         10        0    0   9  54 . WPA2 CCMP   PSK  2WIRE126
                           3        4    0  10  54 . OPN            BMSE1g
  [Open Tab]               3        0    0   1  54e. OPN            BISTRO_NorthWest
                           3        4    0  10  54 . OPN            Belle Maer Office
  Close Window

B                                  PWR  Rate  Lost   Frames Probe
  Copy

0                     :EA:4C:88    -1    1 - 0    0       2
  Paste
0

  Profiles          >

 ✓Show Menubar

  Input Methods     >
```

Open the terminal window and key in this command-
airodump-ng -c [channel] --bssid [bssid] -w
/root/Desktop/ [monitor interface]
Ensure that you have replaced the target's channel
with yours in the network. Go ahead and copy-paste
the BSSID of the target network and replace the
name of the monitor interface with mon0 since it is
the name of your monitor interface. The "-w" and the
file path will go ahead and specify where the
intercepted handshakes will be saved by the
airodump so that you can hack the Wi-Fi network at
ease. In this instance, the handshakes will be saved
on the desktop.

The entire command is as shown below:

airodump-ng -c 10 --bssid 00:14:BF:E0:E8:D5 -w /root/Desktop/ mon0

```
airodump-ng -c 10 --bssid 00:14:BF:E0:E8:D5 -w /root/Desktop/ mon0
```

Press enter to launch the command.

Step Eight:

Use the airodump command so that you can monitor the network. The command will also allow you to capture specific pieces of information about the target network. In this instance, we have to wait for the device to connect to the network. The router usually sends four-way handshakes and the attacker can capture them and they will eventually crack the Wi-Fi password. Four files will also be present on the desktop. The handshake is present in one of the folders on the desktop and you should make sure that none of the desktop folders is deleted.

Some people are usually impatient and it means that they may not be willing to wait for the device to connect. If you do not want to wait, you should use one of the tools belonging to the Aircrack suite. Some of the tools that you can use include the aireplay-ng;

the tool comes in handy if you want to speed up the entire process. The tool ensures that the device has reconnected; first, some deauthentication packets are usually sent and they will trigger the reconnection. The packets will ensure that the network device thinks that it must reconnect and that means that as an attacker, you will not have to wait for a prolonged period.

When using this tool, you must ensure that there is someone who is connected to the target network. Also, keep track of the airodump-ng tool while waiting for the specific client to show up. The process might take longer.

In the screenshot below, the client has already connected to the network and that means that the Wi-Fi hacking process can proceed.

Step Nine:

Ensure that the airodump-ng is running. The hacker should open another terminal window and key in this command:

If you are using the default mode, you will notice that there is a shortcut named -0. There will be a number 2 and it will be representing the number of packets that you can send by default. −Indicates the router's BSSID and it will also be replaced by 00:14:BF:E0:E8:D5. −c indicates the client's BSSID and it will be replaced eventually. The complete command is as shown below:

Step Ten:

When you press Enter, the aireplay-ng command will send the packets. If you are close enough to the target, you can facilitate the deauthentication process accordingly. Some messages will also appear on the airodump screen.

```
WPA handshake: 00:14:BF:E0:E8:D5
```

The screenshot above showcases that the handshake has been captured. After the password has been acquired, the aireplay-ng terminal should be closed. You should then click Ctrl + C and make sure that the airodump-ng is still running. The tools will stop and monitor the network. In an instance whereby you need more information, you should not close the terminal window.

There are various instances, you may not receive the "handshake message." It means that some issues were present when the packets were being sent. Some challenges may arise in the process. Ensure that you have moved closer. There are some devices that may also not be able to reconnect automatically and it means the deauthentication process may fail when you try to reconnect. Make sure that you have tried new devices or also leave the airodump running while waiting for someone to reconnect to the target network. There are some instances when you might be close to the network, and you should make use of the spoofing tools. Some of the widely used spoofing tools include Wi-Fi Honey. When using such a tool, the devices may be tricked into thinking that you are the router. To successfully launch the attack, make sure that you are very close to the target. If you are not close to the target, do not attempt to hack the network since your attempts will prove to be futile. You can use some of these tools to hack WPA2 networks. There are some networks that may also be cracked when you are using some of these tools. The networks that cannot be cracked easily are the ones that have long passwords that have many characters.

Step 11:

All the steps during the hacking process are external and this is the last process whereby the attacker cracks the WPA2 networks. There are four files situated in the desktop and they were generated during the retrieval of the handshake messages. The most important file, in this case, is the one with the .cap command. Open a new terminal and key in this command:

The Aircrack tool will then use the –a method. The tool comes in handy when you want to crack the handshake. There is a –b and it stands for the BSSID and it will also replace the BSSID of the router with the BSSID of the target of the router. The BSSID, in this case, is 00:14:BF:E0:E8:D5. There is a –w and it represents the wordlist. It shall be replaced with a path to the wordlist and you will have to download it. There is a wordlist located in the root folder and it is named "wpa.txt." The .cap file is located in the /root/Desktop/*cap. The password is also contained in that folder.

This is the complete command:

aircrack-ng –a2 –b 00:14:BF:E0:E8:D5 –w /root/wpa.txt /root/Desktop/*.cap

```
aircrack-ng -a2 -b 00:14:BF:E0:E8:D5 -w /root/wpa.txt /root/Desktop/*.cap
```

Press enter.

Step 12:

Launch the Aircrack-ng will also be launched and it will crack the password used to access the WPA2 network. You can only crack the password if it is present in the wordlist that you had compiled. There are instances whereby you may be unable to crack the network if the exact password is not present in the wordlist. The wordlist comprises of numerous passwords that are supposedly used to access the WPA2 target network. After a failed attempt, compile a new wordlist. If you are unable to crack the network, that is an indicator that the network is safe from external attackers. Even when an attacker launches a brute-force attack, they cannot attack a WPA2 network that is secure. In some instances, the WPA2 hacking process may take longer. Make sure that you have considered the length if the wordlist. If the correct password is present in the wordlist, the Aircrack-ng should look like this:

```
Opening /root/Desktop/-01.cap
Reading packets, please wait...

                      Aircrack-ng 1.2 beta3


         [00:00:00] 192 keys tested (1409.45 k/s)


                  KEY FOUND! [ notsecure ]


     Master Key    : 42 28 5E 5A 73 33 90 E9 34 CC A6 C3 B1 CE 97 CA
                     06 10 96 05 CC 13 FC 53 B0 61 5C 19 45 9A CE 63

     Transient Key : 86 D0 43 C9 AA 47 F8 03 2F 71 3F 53 D6 65 F3 F3
                     86 36 52 0F 48 1E 57 4A 10 F8 B6 A0 78 30 22 1E
                     4E 77 F0 5E 1F FC 73 69 CA 35 5B 54 4D B0 EC 1A
                     90 FE D0 B9 33 06 60 F9 33 4B CF 30 B4 A8 AE 3A

     EAPOL HMAC     : 8E 52 1B 51 E8 F2 7E ED 95 F4 CF D2 C6 D0 F0 68
root@kali:~#
```

In this case, the password to the network is "notsecure." You can note that the password is present in the wordlist that was used during the hacking process. In some instances, you can gain access to the password without struggling a lot. As the attacker, you can also change the password to the network and that way you can gauge whether the network is indeed secure. When you change the password, it will all work out to your advantage. After accessing the network, you will also be able to gain access to some sensitive pieces of information.

7. Ethical Hacking and Penetration Testing

There is a misconception among most people which is that they think ethical hacking and penetration testing is both the same thing. However, in reality, it is not so in actual. Not only normal human beings who are not acquainted with the world of cyber security but the cyber security experts also get confused at times between the two. Although both of them fall under the same section of offensive security, there is a thin line that differentiates both. Offensive security is composed of various objects such as penetration testing, reverse engineering of software, social engineering, ethical hacking and many more.

In the world of cyber security, both the items ethical hacking and penetration testing are of utter importance. Let's have a look at some of the aspects of both the components.

Penetration Testing

Penetration testing, as the name goes by, can be understood that it is a process of testing whether penetration is possible or not. It looks out for all sorts of vulnerabilities, risks, malicious content and flaws within a system. By system, it can either be a computer system or an online server or network. This process is done for the purpose of strengthening the system of security in an organization for the sole purpose of defending the infrastructure of IT. It is a procedure which is official in nature and can be regarded as very helpful and not at all a harmful attempt if used wisely. Penetration testing is an essential part of ethical hacking where it is focused on the attempt of penetrating a system of information.

As it is very helpful in readily improving the overall strategies of cyber security, the process of penetration testing needs to be performed at regular intervals. Several forms of malicious content are built up for finding out the weak points within an application, program or system. The malware is spread throughout the network for testing the vulnerabilities. Pentest might not be able to sort out all forms of concerns regarding security, but it can actually minimize the chances of any attack. Penetration testing helps in determining whether an organization or company is vulnerable to any form of cyber attack or not, whether the measures of defense are on point and which of the security measures needs to be changed for decreasing system vulnerability.

Penetration testing can easily show the strengths and weaknesses of the structure of an IT system at one point of time. The pentesting process is not at all a casual process. It comes with lots of planning, granting of permission for pentesting from the management and then starting the process without preventing the normal flow of work in an organization.

Ethical Hacking

The role of an ethical hacker is somewhat similar to that of a penetration tester. But, the process of ethical hacking comes with various forms of diversified duties. Ethical hacking encompasses all the methodologies of hacking along with all forms of methods related to cyber attack. The process of ethical hacking is targeted to the identification of vulnerabilities and also fixes all of them just before any attacker can exploit the information for the purpose of executing cyber attack. Ethical hacking is being called as ethical as all the required functions are performed only after the granting of required permissions from the authority for intruding the system of security. The ethical hackers perform their role on the ground of ethics whereas the attackers hack without any prior alarm.

The role of a professional ethical hacker is very critical as well as complex as the person who is intruding the system of security needs to perform everything without even affecting the overall functioning of the system and then locate the available vulnerabilities as well. The ethical hacker traces out the possible vulnerabilities and reports the authority about the required measures. An ethical hacker not only works with the methodologies of security but also suggests the implementation of the same. The safety of an IT infrastructure is in the hands of an ethical hacker.

Penetration testing Vs. Ethical hacking

Although the functioning of both penetration testing and ethical hacking might seem similar but both differ from each other in various aspects. The main goal of penetration testing is to look out for vulnerabilities within a specific environment. In the case of ethical hacking, it uses various types of attacks for finding out the flaws in security. Penetration testing deals with the security of a particular area whereas ethical hacking itself is a comprehensive term and pentesting is a function of the ethical hacker. For being a good pentester, past experience is required in the field of ethical hacking. Ethical hacking is one step towards pentesting. Unless and until someone knows the methodologies properly, they will not be able to carry on with a penetration testing.

Penetration testing does not require very detailed writing of reports. However, in the case of an ethical hacker, an ethical hacker needs to be an expert report writer. Paper work is comparatively less in penetration testing when compared to ethical hacking. In the case of ethical hacking, detailed paper work with legal agreements is required. Penetration testing consumes very less time which is not the case with ethical hacking. It requires a lot more time and effort. For penetration testing, accessibility of the overall system is not required. In the case of ethical hacking, a hacker requires complete accessibility of the target system.

Bottom line

As penetration testing techniques are being used for protecting the systems from all forms of threats, the attackers are also coping up with the same and are coming up with new vulnerability points in the target applications. So, it can be said that some sort of penetration testing is not at all sufficient for protecting the system of security. This is not the case with ethical hacking as it effectively finds out the loopholes and reports about the same for further improvement. There are many cases where it has been found that when a new vulnerability has been found in a system, the attackers hacked the system immediately after the testing. However, it does not imply that penetration testing is not useful at all. It cannot prevent an attack from taking place but can help in the improvement of a system.

8. Solving Level Problems

Since it is extremely simple, it is just meant to make you understand some of the concepts you will need to move on to the next levels. I will take this space to explain. Our main objective at level0, as in all others, is to get the password to the next level. This can be done by running the vo pass, which is in the bin directory. Try connecting to HackersLab and typing pass. A screen appears that will wax and show you the level0 password. So, to get the password for thelevel1, do I have to login as this user? How is this possible?

There is another way. At every level, there is a file that has the UID (user identification number) higher than yours and the GID (Identical group identification number). The task is: how to explore this file so that through it you can execute the pass command and get the next password? Now if we do this through it and it has a higher user privilege (UID), our system will "think" that we are the other user. Difficult? Let's see an example.

Suppose we connect to HackersLab. Let's create one imaginary level0, just as a test: 8 Login: level08 Password: [level0 @ level0] $ whoamilevel0 [level0 @ level0] $ idUID = 2000 GID = 2000 OTHER ANY = 9999 So far, what have we achieved? We have successfully logged in to level0, we have entered the whoami command, which informed us that the username is level0, and the id command, which provided us with user IDs (UID), group IDs (GID), and other things that will not be needed for us.

Now I will have the system search for files that have a UIDsuperior to ours. For example, if our UID is 2000, then I want to search for files that have UID 2001 (level1). [level0 @ level0] $ find / -uid 2001 – gid 2000/ tmp / suzuki: Permission Denied/ bin / joy: Permission Denied/ etc / test/ usr / local / yu: Permission Denied/ var / shenmue: Permission Denied.

I asked the system to show me all the files that they allowed and are user level1 (which has UID 2001) and group level0 (from GID 2000). Why look for the GID? Simple. The file needs to be from our group so that we can manipulate it. This will become clearer in a moment. We only found the / etc / test file. Everything else with Permission Denied is rubbish.

How to list, then, only the files we want? [level0 @ level0] $ find / -uid 2001 –gid 2000 2> / dev / null/ etc / test Redoing the command, I included the string 2> / dev / null , which I told the system" anything not necessary (2) send to (>) the trash (/ dev / null)". Thus, we only got the result we expected. So, let's list the in-file formations. [level0 @ level0] $ ls – la / etc / test-rwx — x— 1 level1 level0 10876 Mar 8 06:24 test.

From the information, we confirmed what we wanted. It is a file created by user level1 and that belongs to group level0. The user who created it has the permission of total users, group users are allowed to execute only, and others not even that. Just out of curiosity, I could browse the file using the username instead of UID? Of course!

Let's check: Let's try the id command. Oh! A surprise! A new ID has appeared with EUID number 2001 (level1). This EUID didn't exist before ... it was given to us by the program. We will then try the whoami command, just to take the doubts. That!!

The command informed us that we are level1 (or at least that we have permission from level1). How could .hi do this? Simple, he was a backdoor.funds or trojan horse). The moment we ran it, he ran the/ bin / sh command and created another shell (command session) within the first one, but with your permissions. This means that if we try to type thepass command (which returns the level password), now we get ...The password for the next level !!! The password for level1, then, is the newworld.

Level 1 Problem

Login: level18 Password: newworld Study: External Execution of Commands and Pipes.

The necessary knowledge to have at this level is to know how to take advantage of a program that executes external commands. If the program has an EUID (ID) higher than yours, this can be a serious issue. For a demonstration, let's follow the example of level0. I will create an imaginary level1, with dummy files, as a test. Login: level18 Password:

[level1 @ level1] $ find / -user level2 -group level1 2> /dev / null/ usr / bin / list[level1 @ level1] $ cd / usr / bin[level1 @ level1 bin] $ ./ listEnter a file: / usr / bin / list-rwx — x— level2 level1 876 Jun 23 13:12 / usr / bin / list.

Let's take a slow look at what we did. We are supposed to log in to the HackersLab system, we look for the file (s) that have level2 UID and Level1 GID (if you still don't understand why the search is done this way, re-read level0). We found the file / usr / bin / list .I tried to run it and got it. He asked me for any file and informed me the same as we were using, just to see what would happen (could be any other). The list program then returned me information about the file I provided. The problem is there. The list executed from within it the command is -lato show file information. He performed the following on the system: [level1 @ level1] $ ls -la / usr / bin / list-rwx — x— level2 level1 876 Jun 23 13:12 / usr / bin / list But he executes with privileges superior to ours (forgot that your creative user and IDs are level2???). So what can we do to add another command since it executes ls externally? The easier way is using the pipe (|), which we saw in the command section. He will allow you to enter another command to be executed. But where will we do it? Let's run the list again: level1 @ level1 bin] $ ./ list. Enter a file: / usr / bin / list Here is the secret. Instead of just putting the PATH of the file, how about we add the pipe and some command in front? Would be like this: Enter a file: / usr / bin / list | pass That! If our theory is right, it will run ls, listing ourprogram / usr / bin / list and then immediately run the program in the for-provides the passwords. Complete now: level1 @ level1 bin] $ ./ list. Enter a file: / usr / bin / list | pass-rwx — x— level2 level1 876 Jun 23 13:12 / usr / bin / list The password for level2 is ...Ready! We get a new password. Let's get to the real walkthrough now.

Step by step Log in to HackersLab and log in with the level1 password. The first thing to do (already classic) is type the command find / -userlevel2 - group level1 2> / dev / null to find our target file. We found two, / proc / 20840 and / usr / bin / amos . But wait a minute ... Amos is the name of a prophet (dim, dim, dim ... we found why this tip level). Let's check the amos file, then: Seeing the information from the masters, we find that again we have group permission to execute it (x). We managed to rotate it without needing " ./ " (slash) before it means that it is in the PATH. How did it happen in our study session simulation? The program asks us the PATH of any file. We put the file we are currently running (such as said before, can be anyone). He informed us that it is executable.

Getting back to the problem at this level, we saw that Matthew had to use the file command to make the amos program. So, is the program running externally file archives? You? Let's try it out! Yes!! The sample runs the file externally. Let's try to run it and make a pipe to try to get your privilege. So let's do it the same way we study: we put the information for / usr / bin / amos, the | (pipe) and the pass command. Thus, the program will have the file / usr /bin / mas | pass. Result? The password for level2. One more stage won.

Level 2 Problem

Kevin, a BBS programmer, wants to add an alert on your homepage so your members can see your posts every time they log in. Unfortunately, the message has more than one page and its members cannot read it. As a result, he has been warming his brain night and day, trying to find a solution. Finally, he considered using the more command to solve your problem. However, this method is risky because of security issues. TIP: Nuff said!

Login: level28 Password: DoItYourself Study: Shells and Subshells

The shell of a system is nothing but the execution of a shell interpreter commands entered. It is a text-mode screen in which you can interact through system commands. In the DOS system, for example, the command interpreter is the command.com file. At the Windows NT and compatible, it is cmd.exe. You can prove it on NT by going to Start / Run and typing cmd. A command screen will open.

Level 3 Problem

Login: level38 Password: hackerproof Study: PATH
and IFS HackersLab

Levels 3 and 4 are pretty much the same, in the two;
you will need to understand the concept of PATH,
IFS, and export. These levels at the beginning of the
challenge are really interesting and difficult ones (you
will see later level5 and 6 are much easier). Although
the book focuses on how to break a Linux system, I
will explain the PATH in brief. Learning this term
makes it easier to understand others. First, let's go
to the concept:

PATH is the absolute path of directories, where the
system always looks for a file to run. For example,
typing in the root of a system the commands ls, dir,
date or any other, the OS will search directoriesPATH
by these commands and execute them. If not, it will
return an error. Complicated? Not so much.

Let's look at a simple example. In the above DOS
example, I listed the data that was in the directory
called test director. I found that there was a program
called app.exe. I then tried to run the app from the
root. I received an error saying that the command is

not recognized (not found). So, I modified the PATH and pointed it to the test director where was the app. Just use PATH = C: \ directoriotest. I tried to run the app again and voila! It rolled right. Of course, now the command was inside the system search PATH. Okay, but how does this relate to a hacking challenge? All. Imagine that a Windows application externally calls the send NET.EXE (the command that controls the NetBIOS protocol, and may be connected to shares, sends messages, enables users, etc.). What would happen to this program if I had created another with the same name (NET.EXE), put it in the test director and set the PATH? NET would be run normally by the individual program, but my NET, which could be an intrusion program like a backdoor (or horsebackTrojan).

Going back to Linux, then imagine that Steven's program simply writes the date. That's easy, just create a fake version in a directory (whichever one you want to choose), move the PATH there and export it (send it back to the system).

But we have a problem ... What if his program runs directly / bin / date instead of just date? Even if we modified PATH, the program would be running directly in the directory ... Now what? Who can help us? The fearless IFS. The IFS or Internal Field Separator has an interesting feature – you can give it an ASCII character and whenever a command is typed in the system, this character will be separated. This process has some very interesting uses: In our problem, the Steven program runs directly / bin / date on the system. If we configure IFS as follows: export IFS = / (configuring and exporting to the system in only one line, saves time) What will this entail? Instead of the program running /bin/date, it will run bin date (as two separate commands) because IFS has removed the slash. Well, if it will run date, it will fall on our nasty PATH and we'll be able to break the system ...If you still have questions, they will be taken now in the practical part.

Repeating the (already starting to get boring) process of connecting to HackersLabas level3 and look for the file made by steven, we found the file today (which is curiously in the / usr / man / en / man8 / directory which is the Brazilian Portuguese version of the manual that comes with Linux). We listed the file (only usual) and we saw that it has permission to execute.

Enter the file directory and type the pwd command just to confirm (to show the current directory). Try rotating the file by typing ./today, this way, it returns me the date. Everything is now following what was specified in the initial problem.

Enter the date command as a test and it returns the results in the common format. This is not necessary to be done, it is just curiosity. Entering the set command (shows, changes, and creates system variables, we saw the PATH. The executable file date, which is used externally, is inside the bin directory. Let us then take the necessary steps – those explained in the study.

Level 4 Problem

Login: level4 Password: AreUReady? Study: More Deduction and More PATH.

Level 4 is very similar to the third. Everything I showed in that level study in the past applies here. But there is a big difference. How did I know that?

According to the problem, Kevin added just one line of code in your game. This line of code could be anything ... a message on the screen, a comment, or an external command being executed. There is only one way you know: running the game and trying to identify some command it is running (Does it list directories? Show date? Time?). There are commands like strace and others you can use to try to figure out external references. But the easiest way is by trying to run the game and find out. The big difference I was referring to is this: at level3, you knew which should impersonate the date command, but at this level, besides you knowing which command is used, you are not sure if this is the right procedure. Only by analyzing it will you know. Let's go to step by step and check how the procedure should be.

We connect to HackersLab as level4 and look for files with a per-level5 user mission. We found our game, the trojan file, which is inside the / usr / games directory. Let's run it to see what happens. The game prompts you to select the speed with which you want to play. That game is a kind of Tetris. An interesting thing that we saw here is that the game cleared the screen when it started. And it also cleans the screen many times while you play. Is it then the clear command, which clears the screen, running externally? Let's follow this deduction and try to proceed as at level3.

Again, we export PATH to the / home / level4 / tmp directory (the only one we can record). We also exported IFS to the system. We have a file called clear inside our recording directory and we use the / bin / pass command inside it. If that's right then, when we run trojka, it would have the same effect as the past level, but now with the program executed, we have cleared the bad one. So...Silent night, holy night! And onwards to level5 !

Level 5 Problem

Login: level5 Password: Silent night, holy night!
Study: Strings in Binaries.

First, what is a string? It's a char grouping, as taught in college. In common language, it is a word, a sentence or a text. Whenever we program, we need to use strings to communicate with each other and with the user. Two examples in different languages of strings for the user. Pascal writeln ('Enter a number'); 8 C ++ cout >> "Enter a number \ n"; Strings are also used to make simple comparisons of words and phrases.

I know all programmers are tired of seeing this, but a basic explanation is important for non-programmers not to get so lost. A comparison example: Test Program; varx : string; beginwriteln (' Enter your password: '); readln (x); if x = ' binladen ' then beginwriteln (' Correct Password '); endelse beginwriteln (' Incorrect password '); end; end;

In this little program in Pascal, I first send the user a text requesting your password. I read the variable that contains the password and then the comparison: if the string (password) is the same as binladen, I write in that the password is correct, otherwise, type Incorrect password. This is nothing new to anyone. Here, what is interesting to us will be the compiled program and not the source. When we do not use an encryption feature or executables in our compiled program, it leaves most of our strings on display. You can see this using a hexadecimal edit. But there is an easier way, the strings command, which scans any binary file (not just executables) and shows you the strings found. I will compile the code shown earlier in DOS and show the problem step by step. I did the program and tested it.

I typed saddamhussein as a password. It returned incorrect password, so I tested with the default password, binladen. The program returned the correct password. Soon after, I'll type the strings command progteste.exe to try and find the string binladen.

Oops ... Quickly, looking at the result generated by the strings command, we found four interesting lines: Type your password: bin Laden. Correct password and so we can figure out simple passwords without using neither the encryption features nor some compression on any executable. We saw it in DOS, but what about Linux? So, let's go step by step.

We connect to HackersLab as level5. We are looking for the target file, the new modified backdoor location cited in the problem. We found / lib / security /pam_auth.so (file pam_auth.so within the directory / lib / security). I listed your information and again we are allowed to execute. Let's do it then.

We ran pam_auth.so and he asked for the password, we put any string of words and it returned Password incorrect. Let's first check your directory for more interesting files. There are many files. We would waste a lot of time trying the command strings in each and every one. So, we will try the main one, pam_auth.so. Will we find something interesting? We found several possible passwords: abcd1234, loveyou!, flr1234 and we will have to try all of these ones by one as a level6 password. There are also two phrases that could be passwords: what the hell are you thinking? And Best of The Best Hackerslab. Hmmm, this Best of TheBest Hackerslab is very suspicious. Let's try it first.

Best of The Best Hackerslab was the correct password. Direct to the top level. If you want, instead of going straight to logging in as level6 and entering the password, use the right password on the backdoor to make John angry again!

Level 6 Problem

Login: level6 Password: Best of The Best Hackerslab
Study: Port Scan.

This is one of the easiest levels of HackersLab. It's for a really relaxed time. It focuses on the following fact: there is a second open door for access to the system. What are these doors? Whenever you connect to a system, a "Socket" is created. A socket is nothing more than the IP + address combination service door. This allows the same internet address to have multiple services running as Web Server, FTP, SMTP, POP, and others.Some common port numbers:21 - FTP22 - SSH23 - TELNET25 - SMTP79 - FINGER80 - WWW3128 - PROXY6000 – XWINDOWSSERVER, common ports using TCP and UDP protocols.

For example: when I connect to any web page like http://www.visualbooks.com.br, I'm actually connecting to HTTP: //www.visualbooks.com.br:80 (visualbooks.com.br, on port 80, which is the web standard). So far it seems easy. But we fall into the following problem - there are 65535 ports for both TCP and UDP protocols. There are doors that never end anymore. How can we find out which ones are open and which aren't? By using door scanners. Port scanners are applications that try to find out in a certain IP address or host, which ports are open.

They can usually use a list of most known ports, or a range (example: from 1000 to 8000). They are usually extremely fast and results quickly return to us. Common port scanners perform a TCP connect () on the most targeted machine. This means that it performs the three TCP authentication paths (syn-syn / ack-ack). Using this system, it is easy for the scanner to discover the scanning attempt. A firewall or IDS, for example, quickly captures the hacker's IP. To end this, there are now more sophisticated scanners, like NMAP.NMAP, which can scan in many ways besides TCP connect (), has half syn () scanning (only sent syn), fin, Xmas and others. Each type uses different flags to make it difficult to detect the scanned host. At this step-by-step level, I will use two different scanners: NMAP, for Linux, and VALHALLA for Windows and we'll try to find the port.

Level 7 Problem

Login: level7 Password: Can't help falling in love
Study: Breaking Unix / Linux Passwords.

Many older hackers are already used to the words DES, shadow, Cracker Jack, John the Ripper ...

shame the new generation doesn't have such intimacy with these terms. Unix / Linux uses a password encryption system called DES. This system creates an encrypted string and places it in the security file.system names which are usually / etc / passwd. Used to use now / etc /shadow. They moved to the shadow archive hoping to increase the security, leaving the original password with only the usernames. Those who take control of the system can get any file, even the shadow. A typical shadow entry: mflavio: yFdrXa1EwNYng: 12126: 0: 99999: 7 ::: According to the previous information, we have the username asmflavio. Encrypted Password: yFdrXa1EwNYng. The rest of the numbers are System IDs (UID, GID, etc.).

Great, I have a user's password on Linux, but it's encrypted! No problem, I'll get a program that decrypts. That sounds feasible, but that's impossible. As I said before, DES creates a hash, which is a one-way encryption system. It cannot be decrypted. But then ... how do we find out the password? Just use your imagination. Think: if the password in shadow cannot be decrypted, how does the system compare this password with the password that the user types

748

when logging in? Easy. The system encrypts the new password and compares the two encrypted values. If they are equal, that is the password CrackerJack and John The Ripper are programs that allow you to use a wordlist or brute force to "crack" Unix /Linux. They will encrypt each word using DES and compare it with the password that is in the password file. If the result hits ... that's the right password. Of course, for this, you need to have a good wordlist. A wordlist contains passwords commonly used and divided into categories like movie names, German words, etc ...Let's see again, in practice, how this process is done.

We log into HackersLab and look for the file with UID level8 and GIDlevel7. We found / dev / audio2 . We enter the / dev directory and run ./audio. The program shows some trash on the screen. But is it really rubbish? It shows three strings (which could probably also be obtained using this string) command: level8, shadow, and VoE4HoQCFfMW2. Well, I deduced a little bit, by the hash face of the last string and the other two, I think we found the password ... encrypted.

We will have to try to find out the password using John the Ripper (which can be obtained at http://www.blackcode.com). But first, we need to stop the wordlist and adapt the encrypted password. Is there a way you can try to figure out the password just by typing the hash as John the Ripper's command line? For this, you could use a single option. But for study questions, we took a shadow file and replaced the root password with our obtained hash. Thus, we simulated and cracked a shadow file. The JTR (John The Ripper) will try all the words in this list as passwords. The list has been saved as passwords.txt. Now, let's use JTR. JTR was executed as john –wordfile: passwords.txt shadow (sig-Nice: Dear John, please use the wordlist passwords.txt to remove passwords which will be tested in shadow). It quickly returned the password to me.

It is wonderfu. What a strange word is that? Pen-a little while later we find out: wonderfu actually is wonderful only from English), one of the words on our list. But why did he only show eight characters (the last one is the missing "l")? This is the same problem that occurs when the Program File directory becomes a file. The program is DOS-based, and it can show only eight characters. Of course, you can change that in the rules. To learn more, take a look at the JTR manual. What matters is that the password for level8 is wonderful!

Level 8 Problem

Login: level8 Password: wonderful Study: Race Conditions.

At this point, a lot of changes in the HackersLab challenge. Levels below these were pretty simple so there wasn't much to talk about studying, this change now from race conditions. They are conceived a little more complicated than we dealt with till now and these require a greater knowledge (including code examples) to be properly understood. If you don't know C, it would be better if you had a notion before, but for now, it doesn't matter. Understanding the general concept behind the problem is already a step forward.

This much theoretical introduction of the race condition problem is necessary to understand how it occurs, how problems occur between two reads and write functions and get a sense of which functions can be used to correct a certain problem. If you have no notion of C and were "floating" in the explanation, I suggest you try to learn a little, because all levels after this will use programming. This level was much higher than the previous ones and it will be easy to understand step by step.

We connect to HackersLab as level8, we find the file for level9 UID and level8 GID. We found what was mentioned in the problem, /usr / bin /ps2. After entering the / usr / bin directory , I tried to run ./ps2 . Nothing happens ... but really? We know that it creates a temporary file, but suppose that we were not told about it. So we can "check" our actions using the strace command. Typing strace / usr / bin / ps2 (without the quotation marks). Let's take a look at what the command generated: Sounds like a joke ... there is everything we saw in the study ... the open () function opening a temporary file without any descriptor checks, attempting to write the string hahahahahahaha using the write () function without reading any of the permissions, and worse, giving us the filename instead of creating a random file.

Let's try to create some "little scripts" to link the temporary file /var/tmp2/ps2.tmp created by the ps2 program to some content of our interest. You will have to use the VI text editor to create two small little programs or scripts. One will be running the ps2 file so we can enjoy our race condition before it "closes" the /var/tmp2/ps2.tmp file. Just type vi <file name> . In the first script, for example, create a file named race1 (or other filename) inside the var / directorytmp2 (or other temporary directory) using the vi / var / tmp2 / race1 command. The same goes for the second script. When starting the VI, type " a " to enter edit mode and press Esc to return to program mode. race1 while trueof/ usr / bin / ps2donerace2while trueof/ usr / bin / ps2 &rm -rf /var/tmp2/ps2.tmpln -sf / var / tmp2 / race1 /var/tmp2/ps2.tmpdone. A little tip about VI: When you're done typing, press the Esc key; to save (after pressing Esc), type: w (colon+ w); and to exit: q (colon + q), as in the following example: Let's take a look. Both scripts will loop. The first (race1) normally runs the ps2 file but keeps repeating, giving us a long time to change the temporary file. Already the second script (race2), runs the ps2 program again, but as background (using do &), thus giving us even more time to win the race. In the loop, race2 tries to remove the temporary file and replace it with a link to the race1 file.

Let's go line by line to not complicate: / usr / bin / ps2 & (run the program again);rm -rf /var/tmp2/ps2.tmp (delete temporary file);ln -sf / var / tmp2 / race1 /var/tmp2/ps2.tmp (overrides the temp- a link to the first script, so the program will try to record the string in our script instead of the temporary file). Having created both scripts, we will have to give them execute permission. IS just type the commands: chmod + x race1 and chmod + x race2, as shown in the permissions before chmod and after? Now we can execute. Now we have to do something unheard of in HackersLab: We connect it twice. That is, you will have to open two telnet windows and log in as level8 twice at the same time. In one of the windows, you will rotate race1 by typing ./race1, and in the other, race2 by typing ./race2. You will get some "junk" on the screen when you run both, something like "existing file".

But after running race2, if race1 is already running, your "trash" will become this:

"Congratulations!!! Your race attack was a success ... the level9 password is! Secu! "

Note: At this level, there was no need to worry about/bin/pass file, since ps2 itself contained the password.

Level 9 Problem

Login: level9 Password:! Secu! Study: Overflow Buffers

We are looking for a file that has level10 UID and level9 GID. We found the file / etc / bof (what a suggestive name ... bof = bufferoverflow). We list your permissions and see something interesting. Besides our permission to execute, there is a bit there. It is a level10 SUID bit. Continuing to check, we ran the program. He asks you to put a nickname (nick_name). I wrote my name and he showed us on the screen "hello~ macros_flavio ". Just as a test, what would happen if I put a string too long? Would the program do "bound checking"? Or will I flood the buffer? Just testing to know ...I put a lot of "x" on the screen. An error occurred: Segmentation fault. Bingo!

Level 10 Problem

Until we finish the connection, We will have to keep spoofing and sniffing at the Target, really thinking that is talking to the victim. Of course, doing it "by hand" is horrible, so there are various applications to

756

accomplish the process. We have dozens of them for Linux, like spoofit, lcrzoex (which is multiplatform) and others. We also have programs for Windows 2000 that spoof IP and MAC addresses. One is sterm, where it is super easy to configure IP spoofing, as shown in the following figure. Look at Appendix B where to get these programs. UDP Spoof Now that we've seen how spoofing is done on IP, it's easy to understand how we'll do a UDP spoof to get the next level HackersLab password. The principle is the same but much easier. UDP, unlike TCP, has no three-way authentication. It is considered an "unreliable" communication protocol because if a packet is lost it doesn't matter. UDP is widely used for broadcasting (when streaming some video or music on the Internet, for example). Consequently, we need not have to try to find out some type of sequence number to send a spoofed UDP packet to. Just get the header of this package (still on the root machine that allows usRAW packets) and include the new "spoofed" address. We have two options to do this: use the excellent hping tool(www.hping.org), which performs various types of spoofing, including UDP, with the exception of result lenses. Or we will write our own code in C to do so. As per a didactic question, we will have the second option.

Exchange my code email for yours, and you will receive the password. Remember in the beginning I said that few people can get through even at this level? Well, the problem is this: too many firewalls and routers block spoofed packets. That means there is a very good chance great that on the route between your computer and HackersLab, a router "Prevent" the spoiled package. How to do then? Try multiple routes ... I tried to run the program several free shells I could get on the Internet until from a shell of a friend of mine from Fortaleza worked and I received the password by email. Let's run it step by step to see then. Step by step So let's try our spoofing. In the figure below, we compile the udpspoofbr (or whatever name you want), which we saw the code in the sectionstudy, and we perform. He asked us for source IP, source port, destination IP and destination port. In the problem, it asked us to send a message as if it were from www.hackerslab.org, from any door, todrill.hackerslab.org on port 5555. So I typed the command like this: ./udpspoofbr www.hackerslab.org

1234 drill.hackerslab.org5555 Note that the source port makes no difference, so much so that we put1234. But I got a "socket failed" error. Of course, I have to be root to do it, or the system won't allow you to manipulate RAW packets to spoof. Let's try again as root.

Level 11 Problem

Just as stack overflow is a danger, so is heap overflow. Whenever we use the dangerous combination of non-limiting functions' buffer size with programs that have SUID bit and file rights .root, we created a big problem. Understanding this concept well, the walkthrough will be quite simple. Find the problem files, choose the exploit and change the values PROGVULN and ARQVULN. Step by step We connected to HackersLab and found the file / usr / local /bin/hof, quoted in the problem description. Let's take a look and see if it really causes a segmentation error. Let's execute it.

And there it is. He asked us for the level 11 password, and shortly thereafter a failed segmentation fault has occurred. It's our gateway, as in the stack. Only now there's a different thing. The program acts as follows: If we provide the correct password, it will access the passwd.success file (or access if the error did not occur), and if we make a mistake, it accesses passwd.fail. We will try to exploit passwd.success, using the segmentation error to access the contents of this file with the hof program's SUID permissions. I do our exploit in VI and set the PROGVULN constants to /usr / local / bin / hof and ARQVULN as /usr/local/bin / passwd.success. SavedWe compiled it (cc exploit.c -o exploit) and that's it! Let's test and perform a little brute force with hexadecimal addresses until we can.

Ready! After a few attempts with different addresses, (note something: to find the right address, we were trying to address until PATH / usr / local /bin/hof appears full on the screen.). And voila! I want to love forever is the password for level 13.

Level 12 Problem

Login: level128 Password: I want to love forever
Study: Simple Encryption

We have already discussed encryption, and from that level, HackersLab started repeat techniques already seen (read on other levels). At level 7, I had said we must use the John the Ripper program to try to find out the password encrypted.

Of course, the chances are slim when encryption involves Lots of numbers. In this case, you can make a script that automates the process. Is it with this value that we come to the password to the next level? Let's test it step by step. Step by step We connected to HackersLab and found the encrypted program. Let's guess it now with the string chl1296rh which we got in the study where We tested encrypt thoroughly.We then run ./encrypt chl1296rh | more (to go to screen byscreen).Encryption will be applied a few dozen times and we will reach the encrypted result:

It's really the password we try to match the encrypted password that we were given. But does it work? Just testing to know ...That!!! The password works yes. This means that the password for level13 ischl1296rh.

9. Exploitation of Computer Systems

With the increase in the use of computer systems day by day, the percentage of attacks by third parties on the systems is also increasing gradually. There were days when people used to store all their data and confidential information in the form of physical copies. But, today most of the people prefer their confidential information in the computer systems and that is what gave birth to the attacks on computer systems. Exploitation is nothing but a programmed script or software which allows hackers to gain control over the entire system and then exploit the same for the benefit of the hackers.

The exploitation attacks try to take advantage of any form of weakness in an OS of the user, in the application or in any other form of software code that also includes plug-ins of the applications or of the libraries of software. The owners of such codes issue a patch or fix in response. The system users or the users of the applications are completely responsible behind obtaining the patch. It can be downloaded from the developer of software which is readily available on the web or it can also be downloaded by the OS automatically or by the application that needs the same. In case the user fails to install the required patch for a specific problem, it will expose the user to the exploitation of the computer system and might also lead to breaching of security.

Computer exploits and its types

Computer exploits can be categorized into two different types:

- *Remote exploits:* Remote exploits are those exploits types where it is not possible to access a network or remote system. Such exploits are generally used for gaining access to the systems which are remote in nature.

- *Local exploits:* Local exploits are used for those systems which are having local system access. The attackers use this for over-passing the rights of the users of the local systems.

The security exploits can come in all forms of size and shape. However, there are certain techniques among the lot which are more often used than the others. The most common vulnerabilities which are web-based are XSS or cross-site scripting, SQL injection along with cross-site request forgery. It also includes abuse of authentication codes which are broken in nature or other misconfigurations of system security.

Zero-day exploit

The exploits of computer systems can be differentiated in various ways that will depend on the process of working of the exploits along with the attack type that it can accomplish. The most common form of exploit is zero-day exploit. This form of exploit takes ultimate advantage of the zero-day susceptibility. Zero-day susceptibility takes place when a software that might also be an application or an OS, consists of some critical form of vulnerability in the security measures that the vendor is also unaware of. The system vulnerability can only be detected when any hacker is detected with exploiting the susceptibility of the system. That is why it is known as zero-day exploit. After such an exploit takes place, the system which is running the software is also left vulnerable to all forms of attacks until and unless the software vendor releases the required patch for the correction of the system vulnerability.

The computer exploits can also be characterized according to the expected form of an attack like the execution of remote code, delivery of malware, escalation of privilege, denial of service and various other harmful goals. The exploits can be characterized according to the vulnerability type which is being exploited that also includes code injection, exploits of buffer overflow and various other attacks of side channel and vulnerabilities of input validation.

How does exploit take place?

It is a fact that exploits can take place in various ways. However, one of the most common methods of all is exploits being launched from the websites which are malicious in nature. The victim of such exploits generally visits the malicious websites by mistake. The victim might also be tricked into surfing or clicking on a malicious site link that can come attached with a phishing mail or in the form of advertisement of malicious nature.

The malicious websites which are being used for the computer exploits come equipped with various toolkits of software and exploit packs which can be used easily for unleashing the attacks against the various vulnerabilities of the browser right from a harmful website. It might also be from a hacked website. Such form of attack generally attacks the software which is coded in JAVA, browser plug-ins and the browsers which are unpatched. It is used for planting malware into the computer system of the targeted victim.

The automated form of exploits which are generally launched by various malicious websites are designed with two components: exploit code and shell code. Exploit code is a software which tries to exploit a known form of vulnerability. The payload of the exploiting software is the shell code which has been designed for running one single time when the breaching of the system is complete. The name of shell code comes from the very fact that many of the payloads open up command shell which is used for running the commands in opposition to the system of the target. However, all shell codes are not capable of opening a command shell.

Shell code

Shell code acts as a tiny piece of code which is used as the payload in the process of software exploitation. The shell codes are written in the form of machine codes. Download and execute is a form of shell code that performs by downloading and then executing some malware from directly on the targeted system. This form of shell code do not generate shell but instructs the target machine for downloading a form of an executable file which will be off the network, then save the same into the disk and execute the file. This form of shell code is most often used in drive download form of attack in which the victim clicks on a malicious website link and the shell code downloads the malware and installs the same on the system of the targeted victim.

10. How to Spoof Addresses

Macintosh address ridiculing is a system for incidentally changing your Media Access Control (MAC) address on a system gadget. A MAC Address is an interesting and hardcoded address customized into system gadgets which can't be changed forever. The MAC address is in the second OSI layer and ought to be viewed as the physical location of your interface. Macchanger is an instrument that is incorporated with any rendition of Kali Linux including the 2016 moving release and can change the MAC address to any ideal location until the following reboot. In this instructional exercise we will parody the MAC address of our remote connector with an irregular MAC address created by Macchanger on Kali Linux.

➤First we have to bring down the system connector so as to change the MAC address. This should be possible utilizing the accompanying direction: The ifconfig instrument will be supplanted by iproute2. Utilize the accompanying direction to bring down wlan1 with iproute2:

➢   Replace wlan1 with your own system interface.

➢   Now utilize the accompanying direction to change your MAC address to another irregular MAC Address:

➢   As appeared on the screen capture, Macchanger will demonstrate to you the perpetual, current and changed MAC address. The lasting MAC Address will be reestablished to your system connector after a reboot or you can reset your system connectors MAC address physically. Utilize the accompanying direction to reestablish the perpetual MAC address to your system connector physically:

➢   You can likewise parody a specific MAC address utilizing the accompanying direction: ifconfig wlan1 up

➢   Or utilize the accompanying iproute2 direction to bring the wlan1 gadget back up: ip connection set wlan1 up

A developing position of Internet hooligans are currently utilizing new deceives called "phishing" and "ridiculing" to take your personality. Sham messages that endeavor to fool clients into giving out close to home data are the most sizzling new trick on the Internet.

"Parodying" or "phishing" cheats endeavor to cause web clients to accept that they are getting email from a particular, confided in source, or that they are safely associated with a believed site, when that is not the situation by any stretch of the imagination, a long way from it. Mocking is commonly utilized as a way to persuade people to reveal individual or money related data which empowers the culprits to submit charge card/bank extortion or different types of wholesale fraud.

➢   In "email ridiculing" the header of an email seems to start from somebody or some place other than the genuine source. Spam merchants frequently use email mocking trying to get their beneficiaries to open the message and perhaps even react to their sales.

"IP ridiculing" is a system used to increase unapproved access to PCs. In this example the deceitful interloper makes an impression on a PC with an IP address showing that the message is originating from a confided in source.

"Connection change" includes the modifying of an arrival web address of a page that is messaged to a shopper so as to divert the beneficiary to a programmer's website as opposed to the authentic webpage. This is cultivated by including the programmer's IP address before the genuine location in an email which has a solicitation returning to the first site. On the off chance that an individual accidentally gets a satirize email and continues to "click here to refresh" account data, for instance, and is diverted to a site that looks precisely like a business site, for example, eBay or PayPal, there is a decent shot that the individual will finish in submitting individual as well as credit data. Furthermore, that is actually what the programmer is relying on.

The most effective method to Protect Yourself

· If you have to refresh your data on the web, utilize a similar strategy you've utilized previously, or open another program window and type in the site address of the genuine organization's page.

· If a site's location is new, it's likely not real. Just utilize the location that you've utilized previously, or even better, begin at the typical landing page.

· Most organizations expect you to sign in to a protected site. Search for the lock at the base of your program and "https" before the site address.

· If you experience a spontaneous email that demands, either straightforwardly or through a site, for individual budgetary or personality data, for example, Social Security number, passwords, or different identifiers, practice outrageous alert.

· Take note of the header address on the site. Most real locales will have a generally short web address that typically delineates the business name pursued by ".com," or potentially ".organization." Spoof destinations are bound to have an exorbitantly long solid of characters in the header, with the real business name some place in the string, or perhaps not in the least.

· If you have any questions about an email or site, contact the real organization legitimately. Make a duplicate of the flawed site's URL address, send it to the genuine business and inquire as to whether the solicitation is authentic

How computerize undertakings

For the individuals who don't have the foggiest idea how full scale programming computerizes undertakings, or whether they even have large scale programming, the basic answer is that you perused this book and after that you have a total comprehension of how full scale programming robotizing assignments.

Keeping an eye on similar locales, recollecting passwords, submitting to look through architects, just as testing sites again and again are the dreary undertakings for each internet browser ordinary. What's more, filling structures, running projects at a specific time, messing around, just as planning errands consistently are dull redundancy. Your undertaking can be any of those monotonous assignments. On the off chance that at least one of these assignments are happening each day, mechanizing these monotonous undertakings will assist you with saving your valuable time and to improve efficiency.

There are two fundamental approaches to computerize dull assignments - record keystroke and mouse exercises or alter content physically with full scale programming. Both of the ways can be spared as a full scale and later it would be replayed by utilizing any of these strategies - hotkey, scheduler and trigger. Clearly, attempted these errands by chronicle keystroke and mouse exercises is a basic way. Nonetheless, the way can not finish those unpredictable assignments except if the undertakings are finished just by utilizing keystroke and mouse exercises, for example, clicking catches on a window. So for those mind boggling errands, there is an a lot simpler and faster way - alter content physically.

To start utilizing along these lines, you should comprehend what content manager is in large scale programming. Large scale content manager is a device for altering full scale activities. Albeit a large scale can be made by account, in any case, the chronicle just catches the mouse and the console exercises. In this manner, for getting other complex activities, for example, sitting tight for a window centered, you can utilize content editorial manager worked in large scale programming to alter these activities and computerize to execute them later.

By utilizing thusly, you can computerize any arrangement of undertakings on your PC, running from just individual errands, to complex business assignments and significantly more. Simultaneously, you can utilize large scale programming to effectively make the errands: browsing email, moving or support up documents, sending email, and progressively complex computerization, including restrictive IF/ELSE explanations, circles, factors and other propelled alternatives.

Presently, you have realized how large-scale programming robotizes assignments. In the event that you have no one, you have to either download a free or preliminary duplicate from the web, or buy a duplicate of your picked programming.

11. FAQs

How often should penetration testing be done?

The organizations perform according to their own set of regulations and mandates. The standard that they follow will determine whether they need penetration testing or not. The standards of the organizations come with their own methodologies that help in describing what will be the best practice for protecting the security system. The standard will also determine that whether documentation of the tests needs to be done for compliance and purpose of auditing afterwards.

What is the rogue wireless network?

Rogue wireless network acts simply as a point of access just like a router or Wi-Fi station. It is plugged into the network of the organization; however, it does not even adhere to with the organization's standards for the wireless infrastructure which is in existence.

How a rogue wireless network can be installed?

This form of security threat occurs when any device has been adapted in an organization and is connected with the network, either knowingly or unknowingly. There are various types of equipment that come with activated Wi-Fi by default which is not configured at all. This means, that when the device gets turned on for the first time, it will start broadcasting signal for connection.

Can the employees of a business expose the organization to cyber threats?

Yes, they can. Any person who carries a device that has a connection with the Wi-Fi of the company might turn out to be a potential threat for the business. Malware can get into a system unknowingly via a network through laptop, tablet or smartphones. It happens when the segments of Wi-Fi are not properly locked. If the business servers are not separated on a completely different VLAN and all wireless network traffic can access the same, there is a high chance of security breaching and data theft.

Is it required to have wireless networks for businesses in spite of the associated potential risks?

Modern businesses cannot function without wireless technologies. However, the standards of technology and configuration which are applied for the wireless equipment will determine the usefulness of the wireless technologies and also the potential risks of security breach. There are various forms of businesses where the employees are required to work with tablets and scanners, especially in the manufacturing and warehousing sector. It will not be possible for such businesses to operate without the presence of a wireless network within the organization.

What are the most common types of Wi-Fi attacks?

When it comes to Wi-Fi attacks, the list is never-ending. There are several vulnerabilities, exploits and shortfall of security when it is related to wireless attacks. But, the attackers employ certain common methods for the purpose of accessing the wireless networks.

Is MITM a serious security threat?

Also known as man in the middle, it is one of the most commonly found forms of attack and is the most used tactic as well by the attackers. The attacker tricks the victim and transmits data so that the sufferer believes that the communication is coming from a legitimate form of contact only. Using MITM, the attackers can easily target the system of the victim and control it remotely, gain access to several sensitive data such as bank details along with exploits.

What are packet analyzers?

The attackers are capable of analyzing and sniffing the data packets which are being transported through a wireless network. The attackers can also intercept various unencrypted data which is inside the packets of TCP as well. When data is gathered using this method, the attackers can easily gain insight into the internal working system of an organization which is being targeted and can also fish out valuable information that might turn out to be a huge loss for the business.

What is malware?

Malware is a form of cyber attack and is the most common form of attacks. It possesses a serious kind of threat to the networks and servers. It also comes with the power of self-propagating over various networks. It becomes very difficult to detect and stop it once it has gained access to a network segment. It can infect the system when two devices are being connected with the same network which makes the spread of infection very fast.

Can poorly configured Wi-Fi lead to cyber attack?

Yes, it is possible when the Wi-Fi is configured poorly. It is the main reason behind the infiltration of a wireless network. This becomes more serious when there are no available management tools for the IT staffs to gain a perspective of the wireless environment.

Is it okay to share the result of penetration test outside the organization?

No, you should never disclose the test report outside the organization. You can only share it with the company officials and authorities. Sharing test results with the outside world will open up vulnerabilities for the organization and might lead to a serious cyber attack.

Conclusion

Congratulations! You've come a long way since you first opened this book! It might've been difficult but progressing through the cyber-security field can be extremely rewarding and satisfying. You should not be ready to start with penetration testing on your own without the training wheels. You will become a professional ethical hacker in no time if you put the work into it.

The journey is not over yet, however. Don't rely on this content alone, because penetration testing is such a developed topic that you can write entire bookcases on it. This guide should clear up the mystery behind ethical hacking and guide you through all the basic penetration testing methods, however reading a book is not enough. You must take action! Develop your skills further by taking advantage of all the online resources on hacking and join a community with the same interests as you.

With that message in mind, let's go briefly through everything you gained by reading this book:

It's important to understand basic terminology and what a penetration test actually is. We also spent some time exploring the mind of the black hat hacker, because as an ethical hacker you will have to walk in his shoes sometimes in order to create accurate simulations of a real attack. Do not take unnecessary risks, and always perform a test only if you are fully authorized to do so.

www.ingramcontent.com/pod-product-compliance
Lightning Source LLC
LaVergne TN
LVHW051219050326
832903LV00028B/2154

* 9 7 9 8 6 0 6 5 8 0 8 5 9 *